W9-BGP-415

HOLT FRENCH 1A

Bien dit! ™

John DeMado

Séverine Champeny

Marie Ponterio

Robert Ponterio

HOLT, RINEHART AND WINSTON

A Harcourt Education Company

Orlando • **Austin** • New York • San Diego • London

Contributing Authors

John DeMado

John DeMado has been a vocal advocate for second-language acquisition in the United States for many years. He started his career as a middle/high school French and Spanish teacher, before entering the educational publishing profession. Since 1993, Mr. DeMado has directed his own business, John DeMado Language Seminars, Inc., a company devoted exclusively to language acquisition issues. He has authored numerous books in both French and Spanish that span the K–12 curriculum. Mr. DeMado served as the lead consultant for program content at all levels. He created and recorded the **On rappe!** songs for Level 1.

Séverine Champeny

Séverine Champeny, a native of Provence, has been involved in the development of French language educational programs for over 12 years. She has worked on print and media products ranging from introductory middle-school texts to advanced college-level texts. She created activities for the core sections of the chapters. She authored the **Télé-roman** scripts and wrote activities for the DVD Tutor.

Marie Ponterio

Marie Ponterio is a native of France and teaches French language and civilization at the State University of New York College at Cortland. She's the author of the web site **Civilisation française** and the recipient of several awards from Multimedia Educational Resource for Learning and Online Resources. She has co-authored video activities for several high-school textbooks for Harcourt. She has co-authored the culture notes in the program and reviewed all the **Géoculture** sections.

Robert Ponterio

Bob Ponterio is Professor of French at the State University of New York College at Cortland where he teaches all levels of French. He is a moderator of FLTEACH, the Foreign Language Teaching Forum e-mail list. He has published numerous articles and is a recipient of the Anthony Papalia Award for Outstanding Article on Foreign Language Education and the Dorothy S. Ludwig Award for Service to the FL profession. He has co-authored the culture notes in the program and reviewed all the **Géoculture** sections.

Contributing Writers

Dianne Harwood
Austin, TX
Ms. Harwood wrote the grammar presentations, created activities for the review sections and reviewed all core content.

Dana Chicchelly
Missoula, MT
Ms. Chicchelly developed activities for the **Vocabulaire** sections.

Virginia Dosher
Austin, TX
Ms. Dosher researched and wrote material for the **Géoculture** and **Variations littéraires** sections.

Serge Laîné
Austin, TX
Mr. Laîné·wrote the content for the **Comparaisons** feature.

Karine Letellier
Paris, France
Ms. Latellier contributed to the selection and creation of readings in the **Variations littéraires.**

Annick Penant
Austin, TX
Ms. Penant contributed to the selection and creation of the readings in the **Lecture et écriture** sections.

Samuel J. Trees
Christoval, TX
Mr. Trees compiled the content for the grammar summary at the end of the chapter.

Mayanne Wright
Austin, TX
Ms. Wright wrote material for the **Géoculture.** She also created activities for the **Lecture et écriture** sections.

Reviewers

These educators reviewed one or more chapters of the Student Edition.

Todd Bowen
Barrington High School
Barrington, IL

Janet Bowman
Ithaca High School
Ithaca, NY

Marc Cousins
Lewiston-Porter High School
Youngstown, NY

Catherine Davis
Reagan High School
Pfafftown, NC

Douglas Hadley
New Haven High School
New Haven, IN

Todd Losie
Renaissance High School
Detroit, MI

Carolyn Maguire
Marshfield High School
Marshfield, WI

Judith Ugstad
Encina High School
Sacramento, CA

Thomasina I. White
School district of Philadelphia
Philadelphia, PA

Lori Wickert
Wilson High School
West Lawn, PA

Field Test Participants

Geraldine Bender
Callaway High School
Jackson, MS

JoAnne A. Bratkovich
Joliet West High School
Joliet, IL

Bruce Burgess
Culver Academy
Culver, IN

Melanie L. Calhoun
Sullivan South High School
Kingsport, TN

Karen Crystal
Austin High School
Chicago, IL

Magalie Danier-O'Connor
William Allen High School
Allentown, PA

Anita Goodwin
Reading High School
Reading, PA

Sophie Kent
Rye High School
Rye, NY

Nancy Kress
Briarcliff Middle School
Briarcliff Manor, NY

Amy Lutes
Richmond Burton High School
Richmond, IL

Anne L. MacLaren
Harlan Community Academy HS
Chicago, IL

Cynthia Madsen
St. Joseph High School
Lakewood, CA

Ellen Stahr
Waverly High School
Waverly, IL

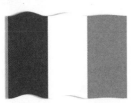   

Sommaire

L'Île-de-France

Chapitres 1 et 2

Chapitre 1 Salut, les copains! 4

Objectifs

In this chapter you will learn to
- greet someone and say goodbye
- ask how someone is
- introduce someone
- ask how old someone is
- ask about things in a classroom
- give classroom commands and ask the teacher something
- ask how words are spelled
- ask for and give e-mail addresses

Options DVD

Géoculture	**Géoculture**
Vocabulaire 1 et 2	**Télé-vocab**
Grammaire 1 et 2	**Grammavision**
Grammaire 2	**On rappe!**
Télé-roman	**Télé-roman**

Online Practice
go.hrw.com
Online Edition

KEYWORD: BD1 CH1

Chapitre 2 Qu'est-ce qui te plaît? 38

Objectifs

In this chapter you will learn to
• ask about likes or dislikes
• agree and disagree
• ask how often you do an activity
• ask how well you do an activity and talk about preferences

Options DVD

Géoculture	**Géoculture**
Vocabulaire 1 et 2	**Télé-vocab**
Grammaire 1 et 2	**Grammavision**
Application 2	**On rappe!**
Télé-roman	**Télé-roman**

Online Practice
go.hrw.com
Online Edition

KEYWORD: BD1 CH2

La province de Québec

Chapitres 3 et 4

Options DVD

Géoculture	**Géoculture**
Vocabulaire 1 et 2	**Télé-vocab**
Grammaire 1 et 2	**Grammavision**
Application 2	**On rappe!**
Télé-roman	**Télé-roman**

Online Practice

go.hrw.com
Online Edition

KEYWORD: BD1 CH3

Géoculture

Chapitre 4 Mon année scolaire

Objectifs

In this chapter you will learn to
• ask about classes
• ask for and give an opinion
• ask others what they need and tell what you need
• inquire about and buy something

Options DVD

Géoculture	Géoculture
Vocabulaire 1 et 2	Télé-vocab
Grammaire 1 et 2	Grammavision
Application 2	On rappe!
Télé-roman	Télé-roman

Online Practice
go.hrw.com
Online Edition

KEYWORD: BD1 CH4

L'Ouest de la France

Chapitre 5 Le temps libre 148

Objectifs

In this chapter you will learn to
- ask about interests
- ask how often someone does an activity
- extend, accept, and refuse an invitation
- make plans

Options DVD

Géoculture	Géoculture
Vocabulaire 1 et 2	Télé-vocab
Grammaire 1 et 2	Grammavision
Application 2	On rappe!
Télé-roman	Télé-roman

Online Practice
go.hrw.com
Online Edition

KEYWORD: BD1 CH5

Références

Why Study French?

French Can Take You around the World!

Margot M. Steinhart, Ph.D.

Chers élèves,

Formidable! You have chosen to learn French, the most frequently studied world language after English, and are becoming a citizen of the world. Your sphere immediately expands to include 175 million French speakers in more than 50 countries and millions of people who have studied French on five continents. And did you know that about 2 million people speak French as a first language in the U.S.?

In addition to learning the language, you will discover the uniqueness of many cultures from around the world. You will have the opportunity to explore Quebec, the Caribbean, West and North Africa, Europe, and the Pacific Ocean islands, to name a few. It is remarkable that through one language, French, the richness of these diverse regions can be learned and experienced. You can connect to the Francophone world through e-mail correspondence or by travel and study experiences.

Did you select French because it is a language associated with renowned artists, literary giants, medical, scientific, and techno-logical break-through discoveries, and an enviable sense of style? French can also improve your English-language skills since French is more like English than is any other Romance language, such as Italian and Spanish. More than 30% of English vocabulary is derived from French. How many French expressions related to government, law, food, art, music, dance, cinema, literature,

Browse the flower market in Rennes. It's a visual delight!

Take the bullet train from Paris to Nice. It can be fun!

Buy souwère paintings by local artisans in markets all over Senegal.

architecture, fashion, or diplomacy do you already know: *coup d'état, bon appétit, faux pas, genre, à la mode, pas de deux, carte blanche,* and *déjà vu*?

As you plan your future, French can lead to fulfilling careers in many fields: manufacturing, finance, law, government, education, the sciences, journalism, advertising, telecommunications, tourism and hospitality. Your language skills will also benefit you in working with international agencies like the International Red Cross, UNESCO, the World Health Organization, and the International Olympic Committee. Did you know that the majority of U.S. exports are to countries having French as a national language? Exports to bilingual Canada alone are greater than the combined exports to all countries south of the United States. Approximately $1 billion in commercial transactions take place between the U.S. and France each day. In terms of emerging markets, French-speaking Africa occupies an area larger than the U.S.

You undoubtedly chose French for very personal reasons. Imagine yourself as a fluent speaker of the language, communicating in French with people all around the globe, being an international student in a French-speaking country, or attending the Cannes Film Festival. How about serving in the Peace Corps in a Sub-Saharan African country, working with **Médecins sans Frontières** *(Doctors Without Borders)*, or negotiating a business deal for a multinational company?

As you continue your journey as a French speaker, and as you open doors to opportunities that become possible just because you have chosen to communicate in French, let me wish you **Bonne chance!** *(Good luck!)*. May you enjoy the adventure that awaits you.

Bonne Continuation,

Margot M. Steinhart

Discover modern art at the MAMAC museum in Nice!

Meet French-speaking teens from around the world.

Ride the funicular in Quebec!

Stop at a crêperie in Paris for a tasty treat!

Le monde francophone

Welcome to the French-speaking World

Did you know that French is spoken not only in France but in many other countries in Europe (Belgium, Switzerland, Andorra and Monaco), North America (New England, Louisiana and Quebec province), Asia (Vietnam, Laos and Cambodia), and over twenty countries in Africa? French is also the official language of France's overseas territories like Martinique, Guadeloupe, French Guiana, and Reunion.

As you look at the map, what other places can you find where French is spoken? Can you imagine how French came to be spoken in these places?

La France

Le Québec

La Louisiane

La Martinique

QUÉBEC

NOUVELLE-ANGLETERRE

ÉTATS-UNIS

LOUISIANE

HAÏTI

GUYANE FRANÇAISE

Saint-Pierre-et-Miquelon

OCÉAN ATLANTIQUE

Antilles françaises

OCÉAN PACIFIQUE

Polynésie française

N
O E
S

OCÉAN ARCTIQUE

Le Maroc

Le Sénégal

Le Mali

Le Viêtnam

BELGIQUE

LUXEMBOURG

SUISSE

FRANCE

ANDORRE   MONACO

TUNISIE

MAROC

ALGÉRIE

MAURITANIE

MALI   NIGER

SÉNÉGAL   TCHAD

GUINÉE   BÉNIN

CÔTE   TOGO
D'IVOIRE   RÉPUBLIQUE
CENTRAFRICAINE

BURKINA   CAMEROUN
FASO

GABON   RÉPUBLIQUE   RUANDA
DÉMOCRATIQUE
DU CONGO   BURUNDI
CONGO

DJIBOUTI

Mayotte

OCÉAN
ATLANTIQUE

OCÉAN INDIEN

MADAGASCAR

Île de la
Réunion

VIÊTNAM

LAOS   OCÉAN

PACIFIQUE

CAMBODGE

Îles Wallis

Île Futuna

Nouvelle-
Calédonie

L'alphabet

a *(a)*
arbre

b *(bé)*
bébé

c *(cé)*
canoë

d *(dé)*
dinosaure

e *(e)*
éléphant

f *(effe)*
fromage

g *(gé)*
girafe

h *(ache)*
hippopotame

i *(i)*
île

j *(ji)*
judo

k *(ka)*
kangourou

l *(elle)*
lampe

m *(emme)*
maïs

n *(enne)*
nez

o *(o)*
olive

p *(pé)*
plante

q *(ku)*
quiche

r *(erre)*
robot

s *(esse)*
stylo

t *(té)*
tigre

u *(u)*
uniforme

v *(vé)*
vélo

w *(double vé)*
western

x *(ixe)*
xylophone

y *(i grec)*
yo-yo

z *(zède)*

zèbre

Quelques prénoms français
Common Names

Here are some common names from French-speaking countries.

Prénoms féminins

Amélie	Delphine	Marie
Aminata	Diama	Marion
Anaïs	Élodie	Mathilde
Anne	Émilie	Noémie
Aurélie	Fatima	Océane
Axelle	Florence	Ophélie
Binetou	Inès	Romane
Camille	Jaineba	Solène
Céline	Juliette	Sophie
Coumba	Léa	Yacine

Prénoms masculins

Amadou	Florian	Maxime
Adrien	Guillaume	Nicolas
Alexandre	Habib	Quentin
Ahmed	Hugo	Romain
Baptiste	Julien	Sébastien
Bernard	Laurent	Théo
Christophe	Lucas	Thierry
Clément	Malick	Tristan
Étienne	Mamadou	Valentin
Florent	Mathieu	Youssou

Instructions

Directions

Throughout the book, many activities will have directions in French. Here are some of the directions you'll see, along with their English translations.

Complète... avec un mot/une expression de la boîte.
Complete . . . with a word/an expression from the box.

Complète le paragraphe avec...
Complete the paragraph with . . .

Complète les phrases avec la forme correcte du verbe (entre parenthèses).
Complete the sentences with the correct form of the verb (in parentheses).

Indique si les phrases suivantes sont vraies ou fausses. Si la phrase est fausse, corrige-la.
Indicate if the following sentences are true or false. If the sentence is false, correct it.

Avec un(e) camarade, jouez...
With a classmate, act out . . .

Réponds aux questions suivantes.
Answer the following questions.

Réponds aux questions en utilisant...
Answer the questions using . . .

Complète les phrases suivantes.
Complete the following sentences.

Fais tous les changements nécessaires.
Make all the necessary changes.

Choisis l'image qui convient.
Choose the most appropriate image.

Écoute les phrases et indique si...
Listen to the sentences and indicate if . . .

Utilise les sujets donnés pour décrire...
Use the subjects provided to describe . . .

Écoute les conversations suivantes. Choisis l'image qui correspond à chaque conversation.
Listen to the following conversations. Match each conversation with the appropriate image.

Choisis un mot ou une expression de chaque boîte pour écrire...
Choose a word or expression from each box to write . . .

En groupe de..., discutez...
In groups of . . ., discuss . . .

Demande à ton/ta camarade...
Ask your classmate . . .

Suis l'exemple.
Follow the model.

Échangez les rôles.
Switch roles.

Remets... en ordre.
Put in . . . order.

Regarde les images et dis ce qui se passe.
Look at the images and tell what is happening.

Suggestions pour apprendre le français
Tips for learning French

Listen

Listen carefully in class and ask questions if you don't understand. You won't be able to understand everything you hear at first, but don't feel frustrated. You are actually absorbing a lot even when you don't realize it.

Visualize

It may help you to visualize the words you are learning. Associate each new word, sentence, or phrase with a mental picture. For example, if you're learning words for 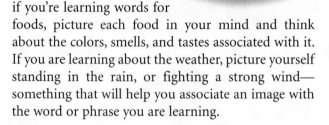 foods, picture each food in your mind and think about the colors, smells, and tastes associated with it. If you are learning about the weather, picture yourself standing in the rain, or fighting a strong wind—something that will help you associate an image with the word or phrase you are learning.

Practice

 Short, daily practice sessions are more effective than long, once-a-week sessions. Also, try to practice with a friend or a classmate. After all, language is about communication, and it takes two to communicate.

Speak

 Practice speaking French aloud every day. Don't be afraid to experiment. Your mistakes will help identify problems, and they will show you important differences in the way English and French work as languages.

Explore

Increase your contact with French outside class in every way you can. Maybe someone living near you speaks French. It's easy to find French-language programs on TV, on the radio, or at the video store, and many magazines and newspapers in French are published or sold in the United States and are on the Internet. Don't be afraid to read, watch, or listen, even if you don't understand every word.

Connect

Making connections between what you learn in other subject areas and what you are learning in your French class will increase your understanding of the new material, help you retain it longer, and enrich your learning experience.

Have fun!

Above all, remember to have fun! Learn as much as you can, because the more you know, the easier it will be for you to relax—and that will make your learning enjoyable and more effective.

Bonne chance! (Good luck!)

Géoculture
L'Île-de-France

DVD
Géoculture

➤ **Notre Dame de Chartres**
Located just outside Île-de-France, Chartres' cathedral is known for its architectural style and its remarkable stained-glass windows.

Versailles
In 1682, Louis XIV moved the royal court from Paris to Versailles.

La galerie des Glaces
This 73-meter room, decorated with mirrors, is one of the main attractions of the palace. ⬇

Almanac

Population
Over 11 million

Cities
Paris, Meaux, Versailles, Melun, Chartres, Giverny

Industries
Tourism, Construction

➤ **Fontainebleau**
This forest is popular for cycling, rock climbing, and horseback riding.

Le jardin du Luxembourg
Kids enjoy sailing boats in the pond of this popular Parisian park.

Savais-tu que...?

With over 11 million people, the Île-de-France region represents 20% of France's population.

L'Île de la Cité
This island, in the middle of the Seine river, is known as the "cradle of Paris."

La tour Eiffel
This Parisian monument was the tallest in the world when it was built in 1889.

Giverny

Oise

Seine

Meaux

Marne

Rueil-Malmaison

PARIS

Versailles   Sèvres

Marne-la-Vallée

ÎLE-DE-FRANCE

Melun

Chartres

Fontainebleau

Seine

La Seine
This river runs through Paris. It is the second longest river in France.

Le château de Vaux-le-Vicomte
This chateau, located near Melun, is known for its beautiful garden in a classic style called **jardin à la française**.

Géo-quiz
What river runs through Paris?

Découvre l'Île-de-France

Gastronomie

Le brie
This cheese, known as the "king of cheese," is a specialty of Meaux.

Les escargots
Originally from Burgundy, snails are popular in restaurants all over the country.

Les pâtisseries
Éclairs, **tartes aux fruits**, and **millefeuilles** are typical French desserts.

Beaux-arts

Claude Monet is one of the most significant painters of the Impressionist movement. Many of his paintings were inspired by the gardens in Giverny situated in the outskirts of Île-de-France.

Le jardin à Giverny   Neue Galerie in der Stallburg, Kunsthistorisches Museum, Vienna, Austria

Le Centre Pompidou, or **Beaubourg,** houses the leading collection of modern and contemporary art in Europe.

La fontaine Stravinsky
This fountain, near the Beaubourg, consists of sixteen separate sculptures set in motion by the force of the water. Niki de Saint Phalle (1930–2002) created the colorful figures of the fountain.

Histoire

➤ **Napoléon Bonaparte**
(1769–1821), emperor of France, died in exile on an island called St. Helena. His remains were returned to France and were buried in the **Invalides**, in Paris.

Online Practice
go.hrw.com
Photo Tour

KEYWORD: BD1 CH1

Savais-tu que...?

To eat snails, you use a special fork and tongs to hold the snail shell.

Interactive
TUTOR

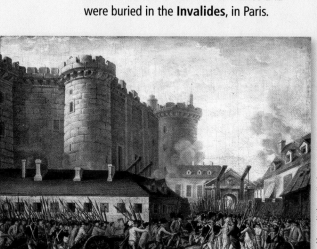

⬆ **La Révolution française**
The fourteenth of July is France's national holiday. It marks the fall of the Bastille prison and is the symbol of the end of the Monarchy.

⬆ **La Bataille de la Marne**
In September 1914, French soldiers were transported to the battlefield outside Paris using a fleet of about 600 taxi cabs. This incident is referred to as **taxis de la Marne**.

Loisirs

➤ **Disneyland® Paris**
opened its doors in Marne-la-Vallée in 1992.

➤ **Le Parc Astérix®**
In this theme park, you can meet the French comic strip character Astérix and his friends.

Activité

1. **Gastronomie:** What is Meaux's specialty?
2. **Beaux-arts:** To what artistic movement does Monet belong?
3. **Histoire:** When is the French national holiday celebrated?
4. **Loisirs:** Where is Disneyland Paris located?

1

Salut, les copains!

Objectifs

In this chapter, you will learn to
- greet someone and say goodbye
- exchange names
- ask and say how someone is
- introduce someone
- ask and tell how old someone is
- talk about things in a classroom
- ask and tell how words are spelled
- exchange e-mail addresses

And you will use
- subjects and verbs
- subject pronouns
- indefinite articles and plural of nouns
- the verb **avoir** and negation

▶ *Que vois-tu sur la photo?*

Where are these teenagers?

What are they doing?

How do you usually greet your friends?

Le musée du Louvre et la pyramide de I.M. Pei, à Paris

Objectifs
- to greet someone and say goodbye
- to ask how someone is
- to introduce someone

Vocabulaire
à l'œuvre 1

Télé-vocab

À Paris!

Comment tu t'appelles?

Je m'appelle Émilie. Et toi?

Bonjour, monsieur Mercier.

Salut, Marine!

À tout à l'heure.

À plus tard.

Exprimons-nous!

To greet someone	To say goodbye
Salut! *Hi!*	**À bientôt./À demain.** *See you soon./See you tomorrow.*
Bonjour, monsieur/madame/mademoiselle... *Hello Mr./Mrs./Miss . . .*	**À plus tard./À tout à l'heure.** *See you later.*
Bonsoir. *Good evening.*	**Au revoir.** *Goodbye.*
To ask someone's name	**To respond**
Comment tu t'appelles? *What is your name?*	**Je m'appelle...** *My name is . . .*
Comment il/elle s'appelle? *What is his/her name?*	**Il/Elle s'appelle...** *His/Her name is . . .*

Interactive
TUTOR

Vocabulaire et grammaire, pp. 1–4

Online workbooks

1 La bonne réponse

Lisons It's the first day of school! Choose the most logical response you might hear for each phrase in the left column.

1. Bonjour, madame Fayot.
2. À tout à l'heure.
3. Comment il s'appelle?
4. Comment tu t'appelles?
5. Bonsoir, monsieur.

a. Je m'appelle Anne.
b. Il s'appelle Maxime.
c. Bonsoir, Mélanie.
d. Bonjour, Ludovic.
e. À plus tard.

2 Écoutons

Listen to the following people and decide if they are **a) greeting someone** or **b) saying goodbye.**

3 Qu'est-ce qu'on dit?

Écrivons What do you think these people are saying? Write a short conversation for each situation.

1.

2.

3.

Communication

HOLT **SoundBooth**
ONLINE RECORDING

4 Scénario

Parlons Say hello and exchange names with another classmate. Then say hello and introduce yourself and your partner to a third classmate. Continue circulating around the classroom and try to meet as many classmates as possible.

MODÈLE —Bonjour. Je m'appelle Lauren. Comment tu t'appelles?
—Salut. Je m'appelle Mike.
(to a third student)
—Bonjour. Je m'appelle Lauren. Il s'appelle Mike...

Comment ça va?

Exprimons-nous!

To ask how someone is	To respond
Ça va?/Comment ça va? (informal) *Are you doing OK?/How's it going?*	**Oui, ça va (bien).** *Yes, fine.*
Comment allez-vous? (formal) *How are you doing?*	**Bien/Très bien, merci.** *Fine/ Very good, thank you.*
Et toi? (informal) *And you?*	**Pas mal./Plus ou moins.** *Not bad./So-so.*
Et vous? (formal) *And you?*	**Non, pas très bien.** *No, not too good.*

Interactive TUTOR

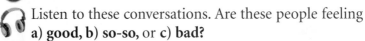
Vocabulaire et grammaire, pp. 1–4   Online workbooks

5 Écoutons

Listen to these conversations. Are these people feeling
a) **good,** b) **so-so,** or c) **bad?**

6 Faisons des phrases

Écrivons Unscramble the sentence fragments to create logical
sentences and questions. Don't forget the punctuation!

1. allez / comment / -vous

2. je / bonsoir / m'appelle / Richard

3. pas / toi / mal / et

4. très / merci / bien / et / vous

5. elle / comment / s'appelle

6. bien / très / et / pas / vous

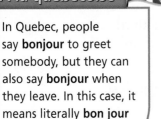

À la québécoise

In Quebec, people
say **bonjour** to greet
somebody, but they can
also say **bonjour** when
they leave. In this case, it
means literally **bon jour**
as in *Have a good day.*

7 Jérémy et Julia

Lisons/Écrivons Jérémy is introducing himself to Julia, a new student at his school. Complete Julia's part of the conversation.

JÉRÉMY	Bonjour.
JULIA	___1___
JÉRÉMY	Comment tu t'appelles?
JULIA	___2___
JÉRÉMY	Jérémy. Comment ça va?
JULIA	___3___
JÉRÉMY	Très bien, merci. Au revoir.
JULIA	___4___

Entre copains

Here are some fun expressions that teens use in everyday conversations.

À plus.	*See you later.*
Ça roule!	*It's going great!*
Pas terrible./ Pas génial.	*Not great.*
un/une prof	*teacher*
un copain	*(male) pal*
une copine	*(female) pal*

8 Bien ou mal?

Parlons Look at the images and tell how each person would most likely answer the question **Comment ça va?**

1. 2. 3.

9 Et vous?

Écrivons On your way home, you run into your friend Lise and then, your neighbor Mme Renaud. Write two conversations where you greet each of these people, ask how they are and say goodbye.

Communication

10 Sondage

Parlons Conduct a survey among 8–10 classmates to find out how they're doing today. Say hello and ask the name of each classmate. Then ask how they're feeling today. Write down their responses in a table. Look at the results and report the overall mood of the class.

Nom	Bien	Pas très bien
John		
Melissa		

MODÈLE —Salut. Comment tu t'appelles?...

Les nombres de 0 à 30

0	1	2	3	4	5
zéro	un/une	deux	trois	quatre	cinq

6	7	8	9	10
six	sept	huit	neuf	dix

D'autres mots utiles

11 onze	16 seize	21 vingt et un	26 vingt-six
12 douze	17 dix-sept	22 vingt-deux	27 vingt-sept
13 treize	18 dix-huit	23 vingt-trois	28 vingt-huit
14 quatorze	19 dix-neuf	24 vingt-quatre	29 vingt-neuf
15 quinze	20 vingt	25 vingt-cinq	30 trente

11 Écoutons

Amélie is calling out the winning numbers in the school raffle. Write down the winning numbers in the order they're called out.

12 Et la suite...?

Lisons Select the number that would logically come next for each series on the left.

1. un, deux, trois,...   **a.** trente
2. dix, vingt,...   **b.** huit
3. quinze, dix,...   **c.** quatorze
4. dix-huit, seize...   **d.** quatre
5. un, deux, quatre,...   **e.** douze
6. six, huit, dix,...   **f.** cinq

13 Des numéros de téléphone importants

Parlons In France, phone numbers are given two digits at a time. Can you say each telephone number below?

MODÈLE 02.12.30.21.24
zéro deux, douze, trente, vingt et un, vingt-quatre

1. 04.10.14.22.28   4. 02.12.15.18.26
2. 01.08.11.27.21   5. 06.24.13.19.05
3. 03.30.29.25.14   6. 01.17.16.21.23

Exprimons-nous!

To introduce someone	To respond to an introduction
Je te/vous présente... *I'd like to introduce you to . . .*	**Bonjour./Salut!** *(informal)* *Hello./Hi!*
Ça, c'est Youssef/Marine. **C'est un ami/une amie.** *This is . . . He/She's a friend.*	**Enchanté(e).** *(formal)* *Very nice to meet you.*
To ask how old someone is	**To respond**
Tu as quel âge? *How old are you?*	**J'ai... ans.** *I am . . . years old.*
Il/Elle a quel âge? *How old is he/she?*	**Il/Elle a... ans.** *He/She is . . . years old.*

> *Vocabulaire et grammaire,*
> *pp. 1–4*

Interactive TUTOR

Online workbooks

14 **Un nouveau au lycée**

Lisons/Parlons Mathieu is a new French student at your school.
You meet him and two of his friends. Respond to him in
complete sentences.

1. Bonjour. Tu t'appelles comment?
2. Comment ça va?
3. Tu as quel âge?
4. Je te présente Martin.
5. Et ça, c'est Caroline. C'est une amie.
6. Salut. À plus!

15 **Correspondance**

Écrivons The e-pal program you signed up for just found you
a francophone e-pal. Write a short e-mail message introducing
yourself and telling your age. Be sure to ask how your e-pal is,
his or her age, and finally say goodbye.

MODÈLE **Salut! Je m'appelle...**

Communication

HOLT SoundBooth ONLINE RECORDING

16 **Scénario**

Parlons One of your classmates introduces you to his French
friend who is visiting from Paris. In groups of three, create and
act out your first meeting.

MODÈLE —Salut. Je te présente...
—Bonjour, ... Enchanté(e)...

Vocabulaire 1

Grammaire
à l'œuvre 1

DVD

Grammavision

Interactive

TUTOR

Subjects and verbs

1 In English, sentences have a subject and a verb. The subject is the person or thing that is doing the action or that is being described. The verb is the action word, like jump or sing, or a linking word, like are or is, that links the subject to a description.

subject   verb

Denise sings well.

subject   verb

Simon is blond.

2 French sentences also have a subject and verb.

subject   verb

Denise chante bien.

subject   verb

Simon est blond.

3 Both English and French use nouns as subjects. Nouns can be replaced by pronouns. Some of the French pronouns you've already seen are je, tu, il, elle, and vous.

Denise is a friend. She is fifteen years old.

Denise est une amie. Elle a quinze ans.

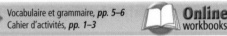

Vocabulaire et grammaire, *pp. 5–6*
Cahier d'activités, *pp. 1–3*

Online workbooks

🗙 Mon amie Michèle

Lisons Identify the subject and verb in each sentence of the following conversations.

1. What is her name?
   Her name is Michèle.
   How old is Michèle?
   She is 15 years old.

2. Elle s'appelle comment?
   Elle s'appelle Michèle.
   Michèle a quel âge?
   Elle a 15 ans.

Grammaire 1

18 Qu'est-ce que c'est?

Lisons List the subject and verb in each of the following sentences.

1. Comment tu t'appelles?
2. Comment allez-vous?
3. Tu as quel âge?
4. J'ai seize ans.
5. Je te présente mon ami Georges.
6. Je m'appelle Stéphanie.

19 Faisons des phrases

Lisons/Parlons Create complete sentences by matching each phrase in the first column with its logical completion in the second column.

1. Comment il
2. Tu
3. Comment allez-
4. Je te
5. Ça
6. Il

a. va?
b. a quinze ans.
c. s'appelle?
d. vous?
e. as quel âge?
f. présente Nina.

Communication

HOLT **SoundBooth**
ONLINE RECORDING

20 Devine!

Parlons Take turns describing the people in these photos. Use the expressions from the box for your description. Your classmate will guess which person you've just described. Then, switch roles.

Elle a quatorze ans.	Il a quinze ans.
C'est un ami.	Il s'appelle Omar.
Elle s'appelle Frida.	Elle a trente ans.
C'est une amie.	Il s'appelle M. Guérin.
Il a vingt-huit ans.	Elle s'appelle Mme Durand.

1.

2.

3.

4.

Subject pronouns

1 These are the **subject pronouns** in French.

je (j')	*I*	nous	*we*
tu	*you*	vous	*you* (plural or formal)
il	*he*	ils	*they* (all male or mixed)
elle	*she*	elles	*they* (all female)
on	*one* (people in general)		

2 Je changes to j' before a verb beginning with a vowel sound.

J'ai quinze ans.   *I am 15 years old.*

3 The subject pronouns **tu** and **vous** both mean *you.* Either of these pronouns could be used to address one person depending on your relationship with him or her. **Vous** is used to address more than one person.

a friend, a family member or someone your own age } **tu**

vous { *more than one person or an adult who is not a family member*

4 The pronoun **on** has no direct equivalent in English. It can mean *we, they* as in *people in general* or *one.* The meaning of **on** will depend on the context.

En France, **on** parle français.
In France, they (people in general) speak French.

Vocabulaire et grammaire, *pp. 5–6*
Cahier d'activités, *pp. 1–3*

Online workbooks

En anglais

In English, the subject pronoun *you* is used with anyone, regardless of their age or relationship to you.

Do you use the pronoun *you* to talk to one person, more than one person, or both?

In French, there are two different words for *you.* You'll learn the appropriate use of each word depending on the situation.

21 **Tu ou vous?**

Parlons Tell whether you would use **tu** or **vous** to talk to the people pictured below.

1. Florence

2. M. Amblard

3. Pheng

4. M. et Mme Cordier

22 Écoutons

Listen to Odile and decide if she is talking about **a) herself, b) a female friend** or **c) a male friend.**

23 On se présente

Lisons Chloé and Stéphane meet a new exchange student. Complete their conversation with the correct subject pronouns.

—Salut. ____1____ m'appelle Chloé Dubois. ____2____ te présente Stéphane. C'est un ami. ____3____ t'appelles comment?

—Salut. ____4____ m'appelle Hélène Fournier. ____5____ ai quinze ans. ____6____ as quel âge? Et Stéphane?

—Moi, ____7____ ai seize ans. Et Stéphane, ____8____ a quinze ans.

24 Les présentations

Écrivons/Parlons Use a word from each column to create as many sentences and questions as you can.

Je/J'	ai	seize ans
Il	t'appelles	Christophe
Elle	a	quinze ans
Tu	m'appelle	quel âge
	s'appelle	Monique
	as	Mme Dumont

Communication

25 Interview

Parlons You work for the school newspaper and you're interviewing new students for the next issue of the paper. In each interview:

1. greet the person you're interviewing and introduce yourself.
2. ask what his or her name is.
3. ask how old he or she is.
4. say goodbye.

MODÈLE Bonjour. Je m'appelle...

J. Fillol, joueur de rugby français

Super!

To show that you're doing fine or that you like something, give a "thumbs up".

Comme ci comme ça

To show that you are doing so-so, hold your hand palm down and rock it back and forth.

C'est nul!

To show that you don't like something, make a "thumbs down" gesture.

Culture appliquée

Les gestes

The use of gestures to communicate is common practice in many cultures. Here are some gestures to express opinions that are commonly used in the U.S. and in France. Which gestures are similar in both countries, and which are different?

Un

To indicate the number **un**, hold up your thumb.

Deux

To indicate the number **deux**, use your thumb and index finger.

Trois

To indicate the number **trois**, use your thumb, index finger and middle finger.

Ça va?

You're meeting a new French student. Unfortunately, the new student has lost his/her voice today. You're asking him/her a series of questions. The new student should answer using gestures only. Think of some questions you could ask and then role play the scene with a partner.

 **Recherches** Can you think of gestures that you use? Research what their equivalent would be in France.

Culture

Comparaisons

Les salutations au Sénégal

Greetings

You're visiting with your friend Adama Ndiaye in Saint-Louis, Senegal. How does he greet you?

a. He just says: **Salut!**

b. He gives you a hug.

c. He asks you how your whole family is doing, first in Arabic, then in Wolof.

In Africa, greetings can take up to 15 minutes. The person not only asks "How are you doing?" but also, "And your mom, your dad, your husband, your children, your sister, your brother? . . ." Then one goes on to inquire about a person's health, job, vehicle, and so on.

In Senegal, even though French is the official language, the custom is to greet a person first in Arabic: **"Salam aleykoum"** (Peace be with you), then in Wolof: **"Na nga def?"** (How are you?), **"Naka sa wa kër?"** (How is the family?)

ET TOI?

1. What do you say or do when you greet a friend? How does it differ from a Senegalese greeting?

2. Can you think of a situation in the United States in which a greeting might occur in two languages?

Communauté

Join a French club

There are probably clubs at your school where you can meet new people and take part in a variety of activities. Can you think of a place in your community where you could meet French speakers? The **Alliance française** is usually a good source of information. Is there one in your area? What activities do they offer? What would be the advantages of meeting native French speakers or joining a French-speaking association or club?

Des élèves à la bibliothèque

Vocabulaire
à l'œuvre 2

DVD
Télé-vocab

Objectifs
- to ask about things in a classroom
- to use classroom expressions
- to ask and tell how words are spelled

Dans la salle de classe

une télé(vision)

un poster

une porte

un tableau

un lecteur de CD/DVD

une fenêtre

un(e) prof(esseur)

une fille

une carte

un bureau

un garçon

un ordinateur

une table

un CD/ un DVD

une chaise

Quelle est la capitale de la France?

Exprimons-nous!

To ask about things in a classroom	To respond
Il y a un poster/des posters **dans la salle de classe?** *Is there/Are there . . . in the classroom?*	**Oui, il y a** un poster/des posters. *Yes, there is/are . . .* **Non, il n'y a pas de** poster. *No, there isn't a/aren't any . . .*
Combien d'élèves il y a dans la classe? *How many students are there in the class?*	**Il y en a** cinq. **Il n'y en a pas.** *There are . . . (of them).* *There aren't any.*

Interactive TUTOR

Vocabulaire et grammaire, *pp. 7–10*

Online workbooks

26 **Écoutons**

Listen as Julien describes his classroom. Based on the photo, decide if each statement you hear is **a) true** or **b) false.**

27 **Ma classe**

Écrivons Using complete sentences, first tell if these items are in your classroom. Then tell how many of each there are.

MODÈLE Des CD? **Oui, il y en a sept./Non, il n'y en a pas.**

1. Des ordinateurs?
2. Des élèves?
3. Des fenêtres?

4. Des bureaux?
5. Des télévisions?
6. Des posters?

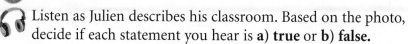 **Communication**

 HOLT **SoundBooth** ONLINE RECORDING

28 **Opinions personnelles**

Parlons Take turns with a partner to describe what you think an ideal classroom looks like.

MODÈLE **Dans la salle de classe, il y a un ordinateur, une télé...**

29 **Devine!**

Parlons Take turns asking your partner about specific things in the classroom. Your partner will answer without looking around.

MODÈLE **—Il y a un poster dans la classe? ...**

À l'école

To give classroom commands	**To ask the teacher something**
Asseyez-vous!/Levez-vous! *Sit down!/Stand up!*	**Monsieur/Madame/** **Mademoiselle,...** *Sir, . . . /Ma'am, . . . /Miss . . .*
Silence!/Faites attention! *Silence!/Pay attention!*	**Je ne comprends pas.** *I don't understand.*
Écoutez et répétez après moi! *Listen and repeat after me!*	**Répétez, s'il vous plaît?** *Could you please repeat that?*
Prenez une feuille de papier! *Take out a sheet of paper!*	**Comment dit-on... en français?** *How do you say . . . in French?*
Allez au tableau! *Go to the blackboard!*	**Qu'est-ce que ça veut dire...?** *What does . . . mean?*
Regardez (la carte)! *Look (at the map)!*	
Retournez à vos places! *Go back to your seats!*	
Ouvrez vos livres (m.) **à la page...** *Open your books to page . . .*	
Fermez vos cahiers. *Close your notebooks.*	

Interactive TUTOR

30 Écoutons

Tell whether a) **un professeur** or b) **un(e) élève** would most likely say each sentence you hear.

31 Quelle photo?

Lisons Match each sentence below with the correct photo.

a. Ouvrez vos livres à la page vingt-six!

b. Regardez la carte!

c. Fermez vos cahiers!

d. Écoutez le CD!

1.

2.

3.

4.

32 En classe

Lisons Select the correct completion for each sentence.

1. Regardez...
2. Comment dit-on *pen...*
3. Fermez...
4. Qu'est-ce que...
5. Allez...

a. en français?
b. au tableau!
c. ça veut dire «fille»?
d. la carte!
e. vos cahiers!

33 Associations

Écrivons Write as many classroom items as you can think of associated with each command below.

MODÈLE prenez: **livres, cahiers, feuille de papier**

1. ouvrez
2. regardez
3. écoutez
4. asseyez-vous
5. allez
6. fermez

34 Donnez des ordres!

Parlons You're the teacher in charge of getting this classroom back in order. How would you tell these students what to do?

35 Scénario

Parlons Work in groups of three. One person is the teacher and gives commands to the students (the other group members). If, and <u>only</u> if, the teacher says **Jacques a dit** (*Simon says*) before a command, the group members must comply and do as told. Take turns playing the teacher and the students.

MODÈLE **Jacques a dit: Asseyez-vous!**
Group members playing the students must sit down.

Les accents et les signes graphiques

You've seen special marks over some French letters. These are called accents and they're very important to the spelling, the pronunciation, and even the meaning of French words.

é The **accent aigu** (´) tells you to pronounce an *e* similar to the *a* in the English word *date:*

éléphant   Sénégal

è The **accent grave** (`) tells you to pronounce an *e* like the *e* in the English word *jet:*

zèbre   zèle

ù An **accent grave** over an *a* or *u* doesn't change the sound of these letters. It does however change the meaning.

où   à

ê The **accent circonflexe** (ˆ) can appear over any vowel, and it doesn't change the sound of the letter:

pâté   forêt   île   hôtel   flûte

ç The **cédille** (¸) under a *c* tells you to pronounce the *c* like an *s:*

français   ça

ï When two vowels appear next to each other, a **tréma** (¨) over the second one tells you to pronounce each vowel separately:

Noël   Haïti

When you spell a word aloud, be sure to say the accent after the letter on which it goes.

*For **L'Alphabet**, see p. xvi.*

Exprimons-nous!

To ask how words are spelled	To tell how words are spelled
Comment ça s'écrit, zèbre? *How do you write . . . ?*	**Ça s'écrit** z-e accent grave-b-r-e. *It is written/spelled . . .*
Comment tu épelles girafe? *How do you spell . . . ?*	
To ask for someone's e-mail address	**To give one's e-mail address**
Quelle est ton adresse e-mail? *What is your e-mail address?*	**C'est** a-l-i-c-e **arobase** b-l-a **point** f-r. (alice@bla.fr) *It's . . . at . . . dot . . .*

Interactive TUTOR

Vocabulaire et grammaire, pp. 7–10

Online workbooks

36 Mais où sont les accents?

Lisons/Écrivons Marlene is writing you an e-mail about her school but she doesn't know how to type accents or special characters. Rewrite her message with the missing accents.

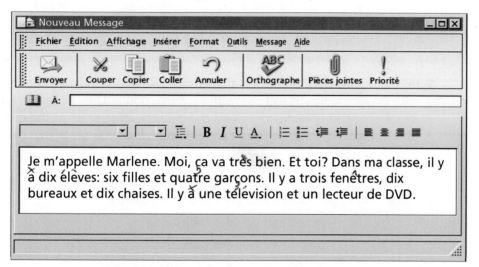

Je m'appelle Marlene. Moi, ça va très bien. Et toi? Dans ma classe, il y a dix élèves: six filles et quatre garçons. Il y a trois fenêtres, dix bureaux et dix chaises. Il y a une télévision et un lecteur de DVD.

37 Écoutons

Listen to these students spell their names and write them down. Don't forget to include all the accents.

38 Une première rencontre

Écrivons You've been asked to welcome a new French exchange student in your school. You know nothing about the student, not even his or her name! Make a list of five questions you could ask when you first meet the new student.

Communication

39 Interview

Parlons A summer camp near Paris is looking for students who could work at the camp next summer. You and a friend (your classmate) have decided to apply. Prepare for the interview by asking each other questions you might be asked during the interview (i.e., your name, how it is spelled, your age, your e-mail address, etc.).

MODÈLE —Tu as quel âge?
—J'ai seize ans.

CAMP DE VACANCES
LE BALLON ROND

Formulaire d'inscription

Informations personnelles
Nom de famille_____Prénom_____
Date de naissance_____ Âge____
Adresse_____
Ville _____Code postal_____
Numéro de téléphone_____
e-mail_____

Niveau de football
☐ débutant ☐ intermédiaire ☐ avancé

Objectifs
- indefinite articles and plural of nouns
- the verb *avoir* and negation

DVD
Grammavision

Grammaire *à l'œuvre* 2

Interactive
TUTOR

Indefinite articles and plural of nouns

1 In French, there are two words that mean *a* or *an*: **un** and **une**. Use **un** with **masculine** nouns and **une** with **feminine** nouns. Use **des** *(some)* with plural nouns. In general, to make a noun plural, add an "**s**" at the end of the word. The final "**s**" is not pronounced when you say the word.

un **garçon**   une **fenêtre**   des **poster**s

2 Some nouns have plurals that are formed differently:

un tableau → **des tableaux**
un bureau → **des bureaux**
un CD/DVD → **des CD/DVD** *(no change)*
un lecteur de CD/DVD → **des lecteurs de CD/DVD**

3 To say there aren't any of an item, remember to use **Il n'y a pas de.**

Il y a **des** cartes dans la classe. → Il n'y a pas **de** cartes dans la classe.

Vocabulaire et grammaire, *pp. 11–12*
Cahier d'activités, *pp. 5–7*
Online workbooks

40 Écoutons

Listen as Louis describes his classroom. In each statement, tell if he is talking about **a) a masculine singular noun, b) a feminine singular noun,** or **c) a plural noun.**

41 Choisis le bon article

Écrivons Complete the following sentences with **un, une, des,** or **de.**

1. Il y a _____ télé et _____ ordinateur.
2. Il y a _____ chaises dans la classe?
3. Il n'y a pas _____ fenêtres dans la classe de Mia.
4. Il y a _____ filles mais il n'y a pas _____ garçons.
5. Est-ce qu'il y a _____ lecteur de DVD dans la classe?
6. Il n'y a pas _____ bureaux dans la classe.
7. Il y a _____ cartes et _____ tableau dans la classe.
8. Il y a _____ élèves mais il n'y a pas _____ professeur.
9. Il n'y a pas _____ DVD.

42 La chambre de Josette

Parlons This is your friend Josette's room. Name at least five things that you see in her room.

MODÈLE   Il y a une porte...

Communication

HOLT **SoundBooth**
ONLINE RECORDING

43 Expérience personnelle

Parlons Take turns with a classmate to describe your classroom. Name at least five things that are in the classroom and your classmate names five things that are not in the classroom.

44 Informations personnelles

Parlons Take turns sharing information about yourself with a classmate. Spell each item aloud in French while your classmate writes it out.

MODÈLE   cé-ache-a-èr-èl-o-té-té-e (Charlotte)

1. your name
2. your e-mail address
3. the name of the town or city where you were born
4. your best friend's full name
5. your best friend's e-mail address
6. your teacher's name

Charlotte Dupuis

Téléphone:
01-13-04-19-28

adresse e-mail:
charlotte@pre.hrw.tra

anniversaire:
12 mars

The verb *avoir* and negation

1 Here are the forms of the verb avoir *(to have):*

avoir	
j' ai	nous avons
tu as	vous avez
il/elle/on a	ils/elles ont

2 Noun subjects (for example, Suzanne or Pierre et Jean) use the same verb form as the pronouns you would use to replace them.

Pierre et Jean **ont** deux chaises. → Ils **ont** deux chaises.

3 To make any sentence negative, add **ne... pas** around the verb. Notice that **ne** becomes **n'** before a verb that begins with a vowel sound. **Un**, **une**, and **des** all change to **de** in a negative sentence.

Ça va.
It's going fine.

Ça **ne** va **pas**.
It's not going fine.

Cléa a **un** poster.
Cléa has a poster.

Cléa **n'**a **pas de** poster.
Cléa doesn't have any posters.

Vocabulaire et grammaire, *pp. 11–12*
Cahier d'activités, *pp. 5–7*
Online workbooks

Interactive
TUTOR

En anglais

In English, when you form a verb in the present tense, most subject pronouns take the same form except for the third person singular: e.g., *I have, she has, we have, they have.*

Can you think of a verb that has more than one different form in the present tense?

In French, verbs often have at least five different forms in a given tense.

45 **On rappe!**

🎧 Listen to the song **Salut!** What different ways did you hear to **1) greet someone and say goodbye** and **2) ask how someone is and respond?** How old are Jérémy, Adèle and Émilie?

46 **Mon copain et moi**

Lisons Complete each of Thierry's sentences by choosing the appropriate form of the verb **avoir**.

1. J' (ai / as) quinze ans.
2. Mon ami Samir, il (ai / a) seize ans.
3. Samir et moi, nous (avez / avons) un prof de maths super.
4. Vous (avez / ont) des ordinateurs dans la classe de français?

47 **Quelle forme?**

Écrivons Use the correct form of **avoir** to complete these phrases.

1. Tu _____ douze ans?
2. Qu'est-ce que le professeur _____ dans la classe?
3. Nous _____ un ordinateur et une télé.
4. Claude et Benoît ne/n' _____ pas de CD.
5. Vous _____ l'adresse e-mail de Simone?

Flash culture

In France, people only say "hello" to each other once a day, not every time they see a person. Saying "hello" a second time would make it seem like you forgot the first time! The French tend not to smile at people they don't know or say "hello" to strangers in the street.

Do Americans interact with strangers in a similar fashion?

48 Et vous avez quoi?

✏️ **Parlons/Écrivons** Use complete sentences to tell what the following people have.

MODÈLE Le professeur a un bureau.

le professeur

1. je

2. les élèves

3. Mme Mayer

4. vous

49 Dans mon lycée

✏️ **Écrivons/Parlons** Use a word or phrase from each column to create complete sentences.

Mon prof	(ne) avoir (pas)	ordinateur
Je		chaise
Tu		télévision
Mes copains		lecteur de DVD
Nous		bureau

Communication

50 Histoire à raconter

Parlons Today is the first day of school. With a partner, create a brief conversation for each scene. Then, perform a scene for the class and have your classmates guess which scene it is.

a.

b.

Français 1
M. Préjean

c.

vincent@tra.hrw.wal

Télé-roman

Que le meilleur gagne!
Épisode 1

STRATÉGIE

Analyzing the opening In any story, there usually is an incident at the beginning that sets the plot rolling. The main characters are faced with a problem or discover something that sets them off on a journey to solve it. As you watch the first episode, think about what the problem and/or the discovered element might be. Based on that problem or element, can you predict what the story will be about? Why do you think that?

Au lycée, le jour de la rentrée...

1

Adrien Salut, Laurie. Ça va?
Laurie Ça va. Et toi?

2

Adrien Bonjour, Kevin. Ça va?
Kevin Bof, tu sais... c'est la rentrée...

3

Yasmina Et lui, qui c'est?
Laurie Kevin Granieri. Il a dix-huit ans. Il est en terminale.
Il n'est pas très sympa.

4

Adrien Rendez-vous à quatre heures à la sortie.

À quatre heures...

Adrien Alors, Yasmina, qu'est-ce que tu penses du lycée?
Yasmina Il est super.

Laurie Eh, regardez!
Ça parle d'un concours.

GAGNEZ LE GRAND PRIX
Un voyage dans le pays de notre lycée frère!!!

Où est notre lycée frère?

notre lycée   le lycée frère

DÉCOUVREZ: 1. SON **CONTINENT**
2. SON **PAYS**
3. SA **VILLE**

Adrien Si vous voulez, on peut participer. Ma prof de géo, Mlle N'Guyen, peut nous envoyer les énigmes.
Laurie Oui! Génial!

Adrien Alors, c'est bon. Mlle N'Guyen nous envoie la première énigme immédiatement. Rendez-vous au café des Arts dans une heure.

AS-TU COMPRIS?

1. Where are the characters meeting?

2. How old is Kevin? Does Laurie like him?

3. What time is it when the three friends meet again at school?

4. What do they see posted in the hallway?

5. Where do they all agree to meet in an hour?

Prochain épisode:
Based on what you already know, what do you think the three friends will do in the next episode?

Lecture et écriture

Recognizing cognates Cognates are words that look alike and have similar meanings in two languages. Recognizing these words will help you understand what a reading passage is about.

A Avant la lecture

Look at the homepage for the school's French Club. Write all the cognates that you can find on a piece of paper and try to guess what each word means.

Fichier   Édition   Affichage   Outils   Aide

Précédente   Suivante   Actualiser   Arrêter   Démarrage   Rechercher   Favoris   Courrier   Imprimer

Adresse: http://www.clubdefrançais.hrw.ggechange.fr   GO

Salut !

Café français
Tu aimes parler français ?
Viens au café Bleu
le samedi[1] de 14h à 16h.

Nouveau Message

Correspond en français

À : clubdefrançais@hrw.ggechange.fr
De : Clotilde@hrw.ggechange.fr

Bonjour. Je m'appelle Clotilde.
J'ai quinze ans. J'habite à Paris.
Le week-end, j'aime aller au cinéma ;
je regarde aussi des films français
et américains sur DVD. J'adore la
musique et le sport. Je joue au tennis
et au volley. Je fais partie[5] du club
de français et je cherche une
correspondante. Écris-moi vite.
Clotilde

Activités artistiques
La photo, c'est ton truc ?
Profite de l'atelier[2] photo le
samedi de 16h à 18h. Tu
préfères le théâtre ? Le club de
français va présenter « L'Avare »
de Molière. Répétition[3] le mardi[4]
de 18h à 20h.

Activités sportives
Match de football samedi
après-midi à 16h au stade
municipal.
Du 21 au
27 mars,
tournoi de
tennis.

Pour plus d'informations, appelle le club au 01.23.45.67.89
ou envoie un e-mail à clubdefrancais@hrw.ggexchange.fr

---

1. Saturdays   **2.** workshop   **3.** rehearsal   **4.** Tuesdays   **5.** I am a member

B Compréhension

Answer the following questions.

1. Where do the French club members meet to practice French?
2. Can you learn theater if you join the French club?
3. Can you play baseball with the members of the French club?
4. Can you correspond with French students by e-mail?
5. Does the club offer tennis?

C Après la lecture

Would you like to become a member of this club? Why or why not? Which actitivies would you participate in if you were a member? Why? What other activities would you suggest if you were a member?

Espace écriture

1. greeting
2. your name
3.

STRATÉGIE pour écrire

Making a list can help you get ideas for writing. List everything you would like to include in your work even if you don't know how to say it in French. You can get help later from the dictionary if you need to find a specific word or phrase.

Le site Internet du club de français

You have joined the French Club and would like to meet some of the other members before the next meeting. Write a short e-mail about yourself to post on the club's Web site. In your e-mail, include a greeting, your name, your age, your e-mail address, and a closing.

1 Plan

Make a list of the information you will need for your e-mail. You may use English or French for this step.

2 Rédaction

Write your e-mail using complete sentences.

3 Correction

Read your sentences twice. Make sure you have included all the information you want to post on the Web site. Exchange your e-mail with a partner and check all spelling and punctuation.

4 Application

Post your completed e-mail on your class bulletin board or Web site.

Prépare-toi pour l'examen

Interactive
TUTOR

① **Vocabulaire 1**
- to greet someone and say goodbye
- to ask how someone is and respond
- to introduce someone and respond to an introduction
  pp. 6–11

1 You meet each of the people below on your way home from school with a friend. Greet each person and ask how he or she is. Then, introduce your friend Camille to each of them.

1. Nasira (quinze ans)
2. Monsieur Roger (un professeur)
3. Madame Tautou (trente ans)
4. Mia et José (douze ans)

2 Fill in the blanks with the correct subject pronoun. Then, for each pair of sentences, identify the verbs.

② **Grammaire 1**
- subjects and verbs
- subject pronouns
  pp. 12–15

1. Il s'appelle Jérôme. _____ a seize ans.
2. Je te présente Emmanuel. _____ a quinze ans.
3. Je m'appelle Samuel. _____ ai dix-sept ans.
4. Comment tu t'appelles? Et _____ as quel âge?
5. Je vous présente Estelle. _____ a dix-sept ans.
6. Gérard et moi, _____ avons vingt ans.
7. _____ as une adresse e-mail?

3 Alexandre is trying to tell what's in his classroom, but he forgot how to say some words. Complete the following sentences by replacing the images with the correct words.

③ **Vocabulaire 2**
- to ask and tell about things in a classroom
- to use classroom expressions
- to ask and tell how words are spelled
  pp. 18–23

Dans la classe, il y a six _____ et huit _____.

Il y a quatre _____ et dix-sept _____.

Il n'y a pas d' _____, mais il y a une _____ _____.

Prépare-toi pour l'examen

④ Élodie is a new student. She is talking to Manon about herself and some other students. Complete their conversation with the correct forms of **avoir.**

—Élodie, tu ___1___ quel âge?

—J'___2___ quatorze ans. Et toi?

—Moi, j'___3___ quinze ans.

—Et Paul? Il ___4___ quel âge?

—Il ___5___ treize ans. Et Marine et Sandrine, elles ___6___ quinze ans.

④ **Grammaire 2**
• indefinite articles
• the verb *avoir* and negation
pp. 24–27

⑤ Answer the following questions.

1. How do people in France greet each other?
2. In what two languages would you hear greetings in Senegal?
3. Would you be on a first name basis with a salesperson in France when you first meet?

⑤ **Culture**
• Comparaisons p. 17
• Flash culture pp. 12, 15, 26

⑥ Listen to the following conversations. For each conversation, tell whether the speakers are **a) greeting each other, b) talking about someone's age, c) introducing someone,** or **d) asking how a word is spelled.**

⑦ Create a short conversation between Béatrice, David, and Vincent based on the illustrations.

Grammaire 1
- subjects and verbs
- subject pronouns
pp. 12–15

Résumé: Grammaire 1

Most sentences have a subject and a verb. The verb tells what the subject does or links the subject to a description.

These are the subject pronouns in French.

je/j'	*I*	nous	*we*
tu	*you*	vous	*you*
il/elle/on	*he/she/one*	ils/elles	*they*

Grammaire 2
- indefinite articles
- the verb *avoir* and negation
pp. 24–27

Résumé: Grammaire 2

In French, there are two words that mean *a* or *an*: un and une.
 Use un with masculine nouns and une with feminine nouns.
 Use des *(some)* with plural nouns.
 Un, une, and des all change to de in a negative sentence.

Here are the forms of the verb **avoir.**

avoir *(to have)*			
j'	ai	nous	avons
tu	as	vous	avez
il/elle/on	a	il/elles	ont

To make a sentence negative, add **ne... pas** around the verb.
Ne becomes **n'** before a verb that begins with a vowel sound.

🎧 Lettres et sons

L'intonation

As you speak, your voice rises and falls. This is called **intonation.**

In French, your voice rises at the end of each group of words within a statement and falls at the end of a statement.

Il aime le football,

mais il n'aime pas la natation.

If you want to change a statement into a question, raise your voice at the end of the sentence.

Tu aimes l'anglais?

Jeux de langue

Tes laitues naissent-elles?
Oui, mes laitues naissent.
Si tes laitues naissent,
mes laitues naîtront.

Dictée

Écris les phrases de la dictée.

To greet someone and say goodbye

Bonjour.	*Good morning.*
Bonsoir.	*Good evening.*
Salut!	*Hi!*
À bientôt.	*See you soon.*
À demain.	*See you tomorrow.*
À plus tard. /À tout à l'heure.	*See you later.*
Au revoir.	*Goodbye.*

To ask and tell someone's name

Comment il/elle s'appelle?	*What is his/her name?*
Comment tu t'appelles?	*What is your name?*
Il/Elle s'appelle...	*His/Her name is . . .*
Je m'appelle...	*My name is . . .*

To ask how someone is

Ça va?/Comment ça va?	*Are you doing OK?/ How's it going?*
Comment allez-vous?	*How are you doing?*
Et toi/vous?	*And you?*
Bien.	*Fine.*

Non, pas très bien.	*No, not too well.*
Oui, ça va. Merci.	*Yes, fine. Thank you.*
Pas mal.	*Not bad.*
Plus ou moins.	*So-so.*
Très bien.	*Very well.*

To introduce and respond to an introduction

C'est un ami/une amie.	*He/She's a friend.*
Ça, c'est...	*This is . . .*
Enchanté(e)!	*Delighted!*
Je te/vous présente...	*I'd like to introduce you to . . .*

To ask and tell how old someone is

Il/Elle a quel âge?	*How old is he/she?*
Il/Elle a... ans.	*He/She is . . . years old.*
J'ai... ans.	*I am . . . years old.*
Tu as quel âge?	*How old are you?*

Les nombres 0–30 .... *see p. 10*

Résumé: Vocabulaire 2

To ask and tell about things in a classroom

un **bureau**	*desk*
une **carte**	*map*
un **CD**/un **DVD**	*CD/DVD*
une **chaise**	*chair*
un/une **élève**	*student*
une **fenêtre**	*window*
une **fille**	*girl*
un **garçon**	*boy*
un **lecteur de CD/DVD**	*CD/DVD player*
un **ordinateur**	*computer*
une **porte**	*door*
un **poster**	*poster*
un/une **prof(esseur)**	*teacher*
la **salle de classe**	*the classroom*
une **table**	*table*
un **tableau**	*blackboard*
une **télé(vision)**	*television*
Il y a...?	*Is/Are there . . . ?*

Non, il n'y a pas de...	*No, there isn't/aren't any . . .*
Oui, il y a...	*Yes, there is/are . . .*
Combien d'élèves il y a dans la classe?	*How many students are there in class?*
Il y en a...	*There is/are . . . (of them).*
Il n'y en a pas.	*There aren't any.*

To give classroom commands and ask the teacher something .... *see p. 20*

To ask and say how words are spelled

Comment ça s'écrit, ...?	*How do you write . . .?*
Comment tu épelles...?	*How do you spell . . .?*
Ça s'écrit...	*It is written/spelled . . .*

To exchange e-mail addresses

Quelle est ton adresse e-mail?	*What is your e-mail address?*
C'est... arobase... point...	*It's . . . at . . . dot . . .*

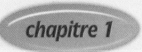

Révisions cumulatives

🎧 **1** Listen to each conversation and match it with the corresponding image.

a.

b.

c.

d.

2 Read Isabelle's e-mail to her pen pal, and tell if the questions that follow are **a) true** or **b) false.**

Bonjour Emmanuel! Ça va? Moi, je m'appelle Isabelle Martin. J'ai quinze ans. Sur la photo, c'est moi et Paul. Paul, c'est un ami. Il a seize ans. Et toi? Tu as quel âge? Mon e-mail, c'est martin55@bla.hrw.fr. Écris-moi très vite!
Isabelle

1. Isabelle and Emmanuel are good friends.
2. Paul and Isabelle are good friends.
3. Isabelle is 16 years old.
4. Paul is 16 years old.
5. Isabelle gives Emmanuel her e-mail address.

 3 You're managing the student exchange program to France. Greet three students who want to participate in the program, ask their names, ages and e-mail addresses. Give them your name and e-mail in case they need to contact you for more information.

4 Study the painting by Duverger and make a list in French of all the classroom objects you see. Then, compare the classroom in the painting to yours. What similarities and differences do you see? Compare the style of this painting to the one by Claude Monet on page 2. Which painting holds your interest more? Why?

Duverger, Theophile (1821–98). In the Schoolroom. Galerie Mensing

Dans la classe de Théophile Duverger

5 You're writing a letter to a new pen pal in France. Introduce yourself, give your age and e-mail address, and ask two other questions you'd like your pen pal to answer. Check your letter for correct punctuation, spelling, and accent marks.

6 À ton tour

Les présentations The French club at your school is organizing a party so that the new members can get to know each other. Introduce yourself to one person, tell him or her your name and age, and ask how he or she is doing. Then, introduce this person to someone else. Try to speak to at least four people.

chapitre **2**

Qu'est-ce qui te plaît?

▶ *Que vois-tu sur la photo?*

Où sont ces personnes?

Et toi, est-ce que tu aimes les parcs?
Et la musique?

Le jardin du **Luxembourg**, à Paris

Objectifs
• to ask about likes and dislikes
• to agree and disagree

Vocabulaire
à l'œuvre 1

DVD

Télé-vocab

Qu'est-ce que tu aimes?

Moi, j'aime manger.

J'aime bien dessiner.

le chocolat

la glace

un crayon (de couleur)

un dessin

les frites

Moi, j'aime l'école.

J'adore lire!

un journal

les mathématiques

un roman

le français

l'anglais

une bande dessinée (une BD)

un magazine

Vocabulaire 1

On aime beaucoup de choses!

écouter de la musique

téléphoner (à des amis)

chanter

surfer sur Internet

les écouteurs

le baladeur (MP3)

la musique moderne

la radio

la musique classique

Salut,
Tu préfères jouer au tennis ou aller au ciné? Anne-Laure et Léa préfèrent jouer au tennis.
Alex

envoyer un e-mail

Café Jade, 7h30? jb

envoyer un SMS/ un texto

D'autres mots utiles

les vacances (f.)	*vacation*
la voiture de sport	*sports car*
dormir	*to sleep*
travailler	*to work*
étudier	*to study*
parler français/anglais	*to speak French/English*
regarder la télé(vision)	*to watch T.V.*

Exprimons-nous!

To ask about likes and dislikes	To respond
Tu aimes étudier? *Do you like . . . ?*	**Oui, j'aime** étudier. *Yes, I like . . .* **Non, je n'aime pas** étudier. *No, I don't like . . .* **Non, je déteste** étudier. *No, I hate . . .*
Qu'est-ce que tu aimes faire? *What do you like to do?*	**J'aime bien/J'adore** dessiner. *I really like/I love . . .*

Interactive TUTOR

Vocabulaire et grammaire, pp. 13–15

Online workbooks

▶ Vocabulaire supplémentaire—Les matières, p. R10

1 Écoutons

You overhear the following conversations in the cafeteria. Select the photo that corresponds to each conversation you hear.

 a.

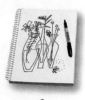 b.

 c.

 d.

 e.

2 Associations

Lisons Select the item in the right column that you would logically associate with each activity on the left.

1. dessiner
2. lire
3. surfer sur Internet
4. écouter de la musique
5. étudier

a. un ordinateur
b. un crayon de couleur
c. l'école
d. une bande dessinée
e. un baladeur MP3

3 Tu aimes ou pas?

Lisons/Parlons How do you feel about these activities?

MODÈLE Tu aimes surfer sur Internet?
Non, je déteste surfer sur Internet.

1. Tu aimes écouter de la musique classique?
2. Tu aimes lire le journal?
3. Tu aimes étudier le français?
4. Tu aimes regarder la télé?
5. Tu aimes envoyer des SMS?

Exprimons-nous!

To agree and disagree	
Moi, j'aime la musique moderne. **Et toi?** *I like . . . And you?*	**Moi aussi.** *Me too.* **Pas moi.** *Not me.*
Moi, je n'aime pas chanter. *I don't like . . .*	**Moi, si.** J'adore chanter. *I do.* **Moi non plus.** Je n'aime pas chanter. *Me neither.*

Interactive TUTOR

Vocabulaire et grammaire, pp. 13–15

Online workbooks

4 On est différent!

Lisons/Écrivons Complete this conversation between Lin and Tran with the expressions from the box.

> Moi non plus. Moi, si. Pas moi!
> Moi aussi Et toi?

LIN   Moi, je n'aime pas l'école. ___1___

TRAN   ___2___ J'aime beaucoup l'école. J'adore le français, mais je n'aime pas les mathématiques.

LIN   ___3___ Je déteste les maths. J'aime beaucoup l'anglais.

TRAN   ___4___ Je n'aime pas l'anglais. Moi, j'aime bien la musique. Et toi?

LIN   ___5___, j'adore la musique!

5 La lettre de Noémie

Lisons/Écrivons Read this letter from your new pen pal, Noémie. First, indicate whether Noémie would be **a) likely** or **b) unlikely** to make each statement that follows. Then, write a response to Noémie's letter.

1. J'adore la musique classique.
2. Je déteste envoyer des SMS.
3. J'adore discuter avec des amis.
4. Je n'aime pas les ordinateurs.
5. J'aime écouter la radio.

> Bonjour,
> Ça va? Je m'appelle Noémie. Et toi, tu t'appelles comment? J'ai quinze ans. J'adore surfer sur Internet. Tu aimes surfer sur Internet? J'aime bien envoyer des e-mails. J'adore aussi écouter de la musique moderne, mais je n'aime pas la musique classique. J'aime bien téléphoner à des amis et j'aime bien envoyer des SMS. Et toi, qu'est-ce que tu aimes faire?
>
> À plus, Noémie

Communication

6 Opinions personnelles

Parlons Take turns asking your partner about three things and activities that he or she likes. For each activity that your partner mentions, be sure to tell him or her how you feel about it as well.

MODÈLE   —Tu aimes écouter de la musique?
—Oui, j'adore la musique moderne.
—Moi aussi. Tu aimes... ?

Grammaire
à l'œuvre 1

Grammavision

Interactive TUTOR

Definite articles

In French, there are four different words, **le, la, l'** and **les**, that mean *the*. You'll choose one of these four words depending on the gender and number of the noun it goes with.

	MASCULINE (BEGINNING WITH A CONSONANT)	FEMININE (BEGINNING WITH A CONSONANT)	MASCULINE OR FEMININE (BEGINNING WITH A VOWEL)
SINGULAR	le	la	l'
PLURAL	les	les	les

Nathalie aime bien l'école.

Patrick adore les bandes dessinées.

There are no set rules to determine which nouns are masculine and which are feminine, so you'll need to memorize the gender of new words as you learn them.

Vocabulaire et grammaire, *pp. 16–17*
Cahier d'activités, *pp. 11–13*

Online workbooks

En anglais

In English, when you say that you like something in general, you omit the article before the noun.

I like music.

Can you think of instances where you need to use the definite article before the noun?

In French, you must always use the definite article before a noun.

J'aime **la** musique.

7 **Chacun ses goûts!**

Lisons Select the correct definite articles to complete these sentences about what Amina and her friends like and dislike.

1. Amina adore (l' / le) anglais.
2. J'aime bien (la / les) glace.
3. Nous aimons (la / les) vacances.
4. Xavier n'aime pas (le / la) chocolat.
5. David et moi, nous aimons regarder (le / la) télé.

8 **Les préférences**

Écrivons Fill in the blanks with the correct definite article.

1. J'adore _____ frites.
2. Tu aimes écouter _____ radio?
3. Moi, j'aime bien _____ école.
4. Je déteste étudier _____ mathématiques.
5. Tu aimes _____ roman *Le Comte de Monte Cristo*?

Online Practice

go.hrw.com

Grammaire 1 practice

KEYWORD: BD1 CH2

9 Et toi?

Parlons You're writing a short scene for a play. Complete the scene below using expressions from the box. Add definite articles where needed.

Moi aussi	vacances	lire
bandes dessinées	romans	école

LUDIVINE   Est-ce que tu aimes ___1___?

SACHA   Oui, j'adore ___2___! Et toi?

LUDIVINE   ___3___. J'aime Alexandre Dumas. Et j'adore ___4___ d'Astérix!

SACHA   Pas moi. Je n'aime pas les BD.

LUDIVINE   Dis, tu aimes ___5___?

SACHA   Non, moi, j'aime ___6___!

10 On aime?

Écrivons Based on the cues, tell whether these people like or don't like the following things. Use the correct definite articles.

1. Julien

2. Charlotte et Claire

3. nous

4. tu

5. vous

6. Théo et Alexia

Flash culture

The first comic strip book was published by a Swiss named Rodolphe Töpffer in the mid 1800s. Some comic books popular among French teens are Astérix, Lucky Luke and Gaston Lagaffe (humor); Tintin and Spirou (adventure); Blake et Mortimer and Yoko Tsuno (science-fiction). Every year, comic book fans gather at the **Festival International de la bande dessinée d'Angoulème** where they can meet their favorite authors and new ones.

What genres of comic books are popular among American teens?

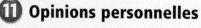

Communication

HOLT **SoundBooth** ONLINE RECORDING

11 Opinions personnelles

Parlons Take turns with a classmate telling whether you like or dislike each of these items and ask your classmate's opinion. He/She will agree or disagree.

1. school
2. chocolate
3. magazines
4. sports cars
5. English
6. modern music

-er verbs

Interactive TUTOR

1 There are three groups of verbs in French: verbs that end in **-er**, **-ir**, and **-re**. To form regular verbs that end in **-er**, drop the **-er** and add the appropriate ending that goes with each subject. Notice that you need to pronounce the **s** in **nous**, **vous**, **ils** and **elles** when the verb form begins with a vowel sound.

aimer *(to like)*	
j' aim**e**	nous aim**ons**
tu aim**es**	vous aim**ez**
il/elle/on aim**e**	ils/elles aim**ent**

Tu **aimes** la glace?

Ils **téléphonent** à des amis.

Nous ne **regardons** pas la télé.

2 Use the appropriate form of aimer plus the infinitive of another verb to say what you and others *like* or *don't like to do*.

Elle aime lire.
She likes to read.

Vous n'aimez pas travailler?
You don't like to work?

Vocabulaire et grammaire, *pp. 16–17*
Cahier d'activités, *pp. 11–13*

Online workbooks

12 Mes amis et moi

Lisons Yves is telling what he and his friends do or like to do. Complete his statements by matching elements from the two columns.

1. J'
2. Hélène et Mia
3. Nous
4. Tu
5. Et Patrick,

a. aimons le chocolat.
b. surfes sur Internet.
c. il adore lire.
d. aiment bien la glace.
e. étudie le français.

13 Écoutons

Sophie's talking to her friends on the phone, but the battery is running low so parts of her conversations are not clear. Choose the word that best completes each statement you hear.

a. écoute
b. téléphonons
c. aimez

d. lire
e. aimes
f. dessinent

À la francophone

In spoken language, French speakers will often leave out the **ne** in a negative sentence.

Moi, j'aime pas chanter.

In writing, you should always include the **ne** in negative sentences.

14 Et le week-end?

 Parlons/Écrivons Create six complete sentences using a word from each of the boxes below.

Je	ne… pas	à des amis
Tu	aimer	sur Internet
Monique	étudier	lire un magazine
Nous	surfer	le français
Vous	téléphoner	travailler
Ils	adorer	étudier

15 Après l'école

Écrivons Eva has taken photos of her friends doing various activities. Write captions telling what activities her friends do after school.

1. elles

2. Léo et Laure

3. il

4. tu

5. vous

6. nous

Communication

16 Sondage

Parlons Work in groups of three to find out what activities you and your partners like or don't like to do. Then, take turns reporting the likes and dislikes of your group to the rest of the class.

MODÈLE —Moi, j'aime bien… Et toi, David?

—Moi aussi, j'adore… Et toi, Michelle?

—Moi, non. Je n'aime pas…

(To the class) David et moi, nous aimons…

Michelle n'aime pas…

Application 1

17 Écoutons

Océane and her friends are giving their opinions about things and activities. For each conversation, decide if Océane **a) agrees** or **b) disagrees** with her friend's opinion.

18 Une lettre à Clément

Lisons/Écrivons Help your classmate Romane send an e-mail to her new e-pal by inserting the correct definite articles.

> Cher Clément,
> Je m'appelle Romane Bourrigault. J'ai quinze ans. Et toi?
> Tu as quel âge? Tu aimes __1__ école? Moi, j'aime bien __2__ maths
> et __3__ anglais. Tu aimes lire? J'aime bien lire __4__ journal,
> mais je n'aime pas __5__ bandes dessinées. J'adore __6__ musique
> moderne et j'aime écouter __7__ radio. Et toi?
> À plus tard!
> Romane

Un peu plus

Irregular plurals

1. You already know that to form the plural of most nouns in French, you add **-s** to the end of the singular form.

> le magazine → les magazine**s**

2. If the singular noun ends in **-eau** or **-eu,** add **-x** to form the plural. The pronunciation of the word does not change.

> le tabl**eau** → les tabl**eaux**   le j**eu** (game) → les jeu**x**

3. If the singular noun ends in **-al**, replace **-al** with **-aux**.

> le journ**al** → les journ**aux**   l'anim**al** → les anim**aux**

Vocabulaire et grammaire, *p. 18*
Cahier d'activités, *pp. 11–13*

Application 1

19 Fais des phrases

Écrivons Write complete sentences using the words below. Make all the necessary changes.

Souviens-toi! Irregular plurals, see p. 24

1. trois / dans la classe / bureau / il y a
2. animal / aimer / Marie / les
3. de musique classique / ils / CD / écouter / des
4. deux / dans la classe / tableau / il y a
5. aimer / les / Hélène / ne / et / journal / pas / lire / Jeanne

20 Mes passe-temps

Écrivons What do you like to do when you have free time? Write a paragraph telling about some of the activities you enjoy. Mention a few activities you don't like.

Communication

HOLT **SoundBooth** ONLINE RECORDING

21 Scénario

Parlons You've received a brochure for a French store in the mail. With your classmate, take turns commenting on what items you like or dislike.

Culture

Culture appliquée
Danses traditionnelles

Each region of France has its own traditional dance. In Brittany, the **danses bretonnes,** which have their origins in the Celtic traditions, are still very popular. In the South, the traditional dances are the **farandole** and the **rigaudon.** The **bourrée** is another traditional French dance, which is danced in many parts of France and varies greatly from one region to another. The **bourrée** was introduced to the French court in the late 16th century. Later on, operas and ballets started incorporating a more elegant form of the **bourrée.**

Une danse traditionnelle bretonne

Danse la bourrée!

The **bourrée** is one of the more simple of traditional French dances. The basic steps are based on walking steps. However, the steps are quick and lively. The rhythm of the music is in double time.

Step 1 Face your partner three to four feet apart. Take a fairly long step forward with your left foot moving towards your partner.

Step 2 Lift your right foot and place it just behind your left foot. Repeat four times.

Step 3 Move forward again toward your partner, this time turning slightly left.

Step 4 Cross your partner's path and take his or her place, turning again to face him or her.

Step 5 Start over. With the **bourrée,** there is always room for improvisation. You can add extra turns and spins as well as many other variations.

 **Recherches** Research the steps of another dance mentioned in the introductory paragraph and teach the dance to the class.

Comparaisons

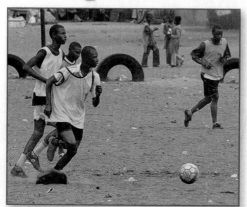

De jeunes Sénégalais jouant au football.

On joue au foot?

You are in Saly, Senegal, and your friend Naago asks you: **On joue au football?**

Do you expect to play:

    a. football?

    b. a video game?

    c. soccer?

"**L**e football" in French-speaking Africa and Europe means soccer. Most Europeans and Africans are passionate soccer fans. Everywhere you go in Africa you'll see young boys playing soccer in the streets or in parks.

French World Cup winner Patrick Vieira, born in Senegal, is co-founder of the Diambars Institute, which provides excellent training in the sport and a balanced academic education at their academy in Saly. In recent years, African women have begun forming soccer teams.

ET TOI?

1. Are there soccer teams in your area? Where do they play? Do you play soccer?

2. What opportunities are available for high school and college soccer players in the United States?

Communauté

Folk dances

Many cultures express themselves through traditional folk dancing. Which folk dances represent the different cultures in your community? Find out if there are any folk dance troops or French music groups in your city or town and ask them to visit your French club or class. You could also arrange a field trip to see one of their performances.

La danse western

Objectifs
- to ask how often you do an activity
- to ask how well you do something and to ask about preferences

Vocabulaire
à l'œuvre 2

Télé-vocab

Les goûts des jeunes Français

faire les magasins (m.)

Avec les copains, j'aime…

aller au cinéma

voir un film

faire la fête

danser

faire un pique-nique

jouer…

aux cartes (f.)

aux échecs (m.)

J'adore faire du sport!

jouer au base-ball

la batte

la balle

aller à la piscine

nager

jouer au football

le ballon

D'autres mots utiles

aller au café	*to go to a café*
sortir	*to go out*
discuter avec des amis	*to chat with friends*
la bibliothèque	*library*
la Maison des jeunes et de la culture (MJC)	*recreation center*
le stade	*stadium*
le centre commercial	*mall*
le lycée	*high school*
le parc	*park*

Exprimons-nous!

To ask how often you do an activity	To respond
Tu aimes aller au cinéma **régulièrement**? *Do you like to . . . on a regular basis?*	**Oui, souvent.** *Yes, often.*
	De temps en temps. *From time to time.*
	Non, rarement. *No, rarely.*
	Non, jamais. *No, never.*

Interactive
TUTOR

▸ Vocabulaire et grammaire, pp. 19–21

Online workbooks

▸ Vocabulaire supplémentaire—Les sports et les passe-temps, p. R11

22 Écoutons

Listen to Ludovic describe his likes and dislikes and decide which bedroom is most likely his.

a.

b.

23 Une question de goût

Lisons/Écrivons Magali is chatting online with a new classmate, telling about her friends and herself. Complete her statements with the correct word from the box below.

~~fête~~	~~jamais~~	~~voir~~	~~souvent~~
télévision	échecs	rarement	~~jouer~~

1. J'aime faire la _échecs_ mais je n'aime pas danser. Je danse _jamais_.
2. Henri aime _jouer_ au base-ball. Il joue _souvent_ avec ses copains.
3. Isabelle aime regarder la _télévision_ mais elle adore _voir_ les films au cinéma!
4. Gilles et Marie jouent souvent aux _fête_.
5. Tristan? Jouer aux cartes? _rarement_!

24 Souvent ou pas souvent?

Parlons Answer these questions, telling how often you do the activities mentioned. Give reasons to support your answers.

MODÈLE Tu joues au football?
Oui, souvent. J'adore le football.

1. Tu discutes régulièrement avec des amis? _oui. Je discutes régulièrement_
2. Tu étudies souvent avec des amis? _oui. J'étudies aves mes amis_
3. Tu joues au base-ball? _no. Je ne pas joue au base ball_
4. Tu nages souvent? _parfois Je nage_
5. Tu danses souvent? _no. Je ne pa danse souvent_

Chapitre 2 • Qu'est-ce qui te plaît?

Exprimons-nous!

To ask how well you do something	To respond
Tu parles **bien** français? *Do you . . . well?*	Oui, je parle **assez bien/bien/très bien** français. *. . . rather well/well/very well.* Non, je parle **mal/très mal** français. *. . . badly/very badly.*
To ask about preferences	**To respond**
Tu préfères/aimes mieux nager **ou** aller au café? *Do you prefer . . . or . . . ?*	J'aime bien nager **mais** je préfère aller au café. *. . . but . . .*
Quelles sont tes activités préférées? *What are your favorite activities?*	J'aime chanter **et** dormir. *. . . and . . .*

Vocabulaire et grammaire, pp. 19–21 · Online workbooks

25 Et toi?

Écrivons Tell whether you like these activities or if you prefer to do something else. Tell how well you do each of these activities.

1.

2.

3.

4.

Communication

HOLT **SoundBooth** ONLINE RECORDING

26 Scénario

Parlons You're applying for a job at a **Maison des jeunes et de la culture** in France. At your interview, the director (your classmate) will ask about sports you play and additional activities you enjoy. Role-play this interview with your classmate. Be sure to tell how well you play or do the sports and activities you mention.

MODÈLE —Quelles sont tes activités préférées?
—J'adore le sport. Je joue au...
—Tu joues bien au...?

Grammavision

TUTOR

Contractions with *à*

The preposition *à* usually means *to* or *at*.

1 When you use *à* with the definite articles **le** or **les**, make the following contractions.

à + **le**	→	**au**	J'aime aller **au** cinéma.
à + **les**	→	**aux**	Tu aimes parler **aux** professeurs?

2 When *à* appears before **la** or **l'**, there is no contraction.

à + **la**	→	**à la**	Tu aimes aller **à la** piscine?
à + **l'**	→	**à l'**	Marie adore aller **à l'**école.

Vocabulaire et grammaire, pp. 22–23
Cahier d'activités, pp. 15–17

Online workbooks

27 **Quelle préposition?**

Lisons Select the correct preposition to complete each of the sentences below.

1. Paul aime manger (à l' / au) café.
2. Moi, je regarde le film (à la / au) télé.
3. Madame Rivière, est-ce que vous travaillez (à la / à l') école?
4. Les élèves ne jouent pas (aux / au) base-ball.
5. Aziz adore jouer (aux / à l') échecs.
6. Nous aimons aller (à la / au) cinéma.

28 **Tous les samedis**

Écrivons Use the phrases below to write complete sentences about what you and your friends do every Saturday.

MODÈLE Valérie / chanter / MJC
Valérie chante à la MJC.

1. Antoine / étudier / bibliothèque
2. Rachida / manger / café avec Luc
3. Marie et Philippe / travailler / centre commercial
4. Je / jouer / cartes / avec des amis / MJC
5. Tu / nager / piscine
6. Vous / jouer au base-ball / parc

Flash culture

French schools generally don't have clubs such as those you find in most American schools. Many French cities have a **Maison des jeunes et de la culture**, a kind of youth center with a variety of activities such as photography, theater and ceramics. Depending on the location of the **MJC**, activities like skiing or sailing might be offered at the center.

Do you have something similar to the **MJC** in your community?

Maison des jeunes et de la culture

LA PAILLETTE

Grammaire 2

 **29 Où on va?**

Lisons/Parlons Complete these sentences with the logical place that goes with each of these activities.

1. Pour manger, Yasmina aime aller _____.

2. Pour étudier, j'aime aller _____.

3. Pour faire du sport, Samuel et Lucas aiment aller _____.

4. Pour faire les magasins, Andréa aime aller _____.

5. Pour faire un pique-nique, vous aimez aller _____.

6. Pour nager, Étienne et moi, nous aimons aller _____.

7. Pour faire du théâtre, nous aimons aller _____.

30 Associations logiques

Écrivons Tell where these people like to go based on the images. Be sure to include the correct preposition in your answer.

1. Thierry et Ming

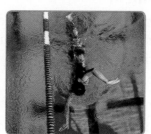
2. tu

3. Eva

4. nous

5. les élèves

6. vous

Communication

HOLT **SoundBooth** ONLINE RECORDING

 **31 Opinions personnelles**

Parlons You're at a French club party where you meet a new student from your school. First introduce yourself. Tell him or her about the things and activities you like and places you like to go. Try to find out what he or she likes to do and where he or she likes to go. Role-play this conversation with your classmate.

MODÈLE —Bonjour, je m'appelle... J'adore... et j'aime aller... Et toi?

Conjunctions

TUTOR

Use conjunctions like **et** *(and)*, **mais** *(but)*, and **ou** *(or)* to link two ideas or two sentences together.

> J'aime le football. J'aime le base-ball.
> J'aime le football **et** le base-ball.
>
> J'aime chanter. Je préfère dessiner.
> J'aime chanter **mais** je préfère dessiner.
>
> Tu préfères danser? Tu préfères regarder la télé?
> Tu préfères danser **ou** regarder la télé?

Vocabulaire et grammaire, pp. 22–23
Cahier d'activités, pp. 15–17

Online workbooks

En anglais

In English, conjunctions like *and* and *but* are used to link ideas together. You use conjunctions to create longer, more sophisticated sentences.

I like to play chess, *but* I hate to play cards.

What other conjunctions can you think of in English?

In French too, conjunctions are used to link ideas together.

J'aime jouer aux échecs **mais** je déteste jouer aux cartes.

32 **Ce qu'ils aiment**

Lisons Annick sent you some text messsages about mutual friends. Use the phrases in the second column to complete what she wrote about each friend.

1. Sébastien aime faire la fête
2. Léo aime aller à la piscine
3. Théa et moi, nous aimons sortir
4. Pauline aime la glace
5. Philippe n'aime pas le sport,

a. mais nous n'aimons pas faire les magasins.
b. et il adore danser.
c. et nager.
d. mais il adore jouer aux échecs et aux cartes.
e. mais elle préfère les frites.

33 **Écoutons**

Sophie's in charge of the local French pen pal club. Listen to the messages that students interested in joining left on her answering machine. Match each message with the appropriate image.

a.   b.   c.   d.

34 Mes préférences à moi

Parlons Tell how you feel about each pair of activities listed below. Use **et** and **mais** in your sentences.

MODÈLE nager / jouer aux échecs
J'aime nager mais je n'aime pas jouer aux échecs.

1. jouer aux cartes / jouer au football
2. chanter / danser
3. faire les magasins au centre commercial / aller à la piscine
4. faire la fête avec les copains / aller au stade
5. étudier à la bibliothèque / étudier avec des amis au café
6. regarder la télévision / aller au cinéma

35 Les activités de Richard

Lisons/Écrivons Use the information from Richard's survey to tell about things he likes and dislikes. Write two questions you could ask him about his preferences. Use **et, mais** and **ou**.

MODÈLE **Il aime faire la fête. Il n'aime pas...**

NOM: DUBOIS Richard	J'adore	J'aime	Je n'aime pas
discuter avec des amis	✓		
aller au cinéma	✓		
faire la fête		✓	
écouter de la musique	✓		
faire les magasins			✓
faire du sport	✓		
faire un pique-nique		✓	
manger au café		✓	
nager			✓
jouer aux échecs			✓

Communication

HOLT **SoundBooth**
ONLINE RECORDING

36 Sondage

Parlons Make a list of different activities in a chart like the one in Activity 35. Survey your classmates about activities they like, love or dislike and record their answers in the chart. Present the results of your survey in the form of a graph or pie chart to the class.

MODÈLE **—Tu aimes faire du sport?**
—Oui, j'adore... mais je n'aime pas...

Application 2

37 **On rappe!**

Listen to the song **Qu'est-ce que tu aimes faire?** Answer that question by adding one more stanza of four lines to the rap song. Talk about things or activities that you like to do.

38 **Il faut décoder!**

Lisons Tanguy's online chat session with his friend, Amélie, got scrambled out of order when he tried to save it. Reconstruct the session by numbering the phrases in order from 1–6.

—Pas moi. Je n'aime pas les films. Je préfère dessiner ou lire.

—Moi aussi, j'adore lire mais je n'aime pas dessiner.

—Qu'est-ce que tu aimes lire?

—Amélie, Cléo et toi, vous aimez aller au cinéma?

—Oui, nous adorons aller au cinéma! Et toi?

—J'adore lire des romans!

Un peu plus

TUTOR

Est-ce que

You've already learned to make a yes-no question by raising the pitch of your voice at the end of a sentence.

Another way to make a yes-no question is to add **Est-ce que** before a statement and raise your voice at the very end. **Est-ce que** becomes **Est-ce qu'** if the following word begins with a vowel sound.

Est-ce que tu aimes sortir?
Do you like to go out?

Est-ce **qu'**ils aiment nager?
Do they like to swim?

Vocabulaire et grammaire, *p. 24*
Cahier d'activités, *pp. 15–17*

Online
workbooks

39 **Rencontre avec Nathalia**

Écrivons Imagine that you've won a backstage pass to meet your favorite music star Nathalia. Make a list of eight questions you'd like to ask her to find out about her likes and dislikes.

MODÈLE   Est-ce que vous aimez aller au cinéma?

40 **Je cherche des correspondant(e)s**

Lisons/Écrivons Read these ads for pen pals in the French
magazine *Monde jeune*. Write a response to one of them giving
similar information about yourself.

Online Practice
go.hrw.com
Application 2 practice

KEYWORD: BD1 CH2

La musique, c'est ma passion!!

Salut! Je cherche quelqu'un
qui parle américain.
J'aime bien le rock, le rap
et la pop. J'adore Daara J!
La danse me fait délirer!
Répondez vite! Réponse
assurée à 110%!

Cléa

Tu aimes le shopping?

Coucou!!! J'adore faire les
magasins. J'aime les jeans et
les tee-shirts très cool. J'aime
aussi aller au ciné, faire la
fête et parler au téléphone.
J'attends vos lettres avec
impatience!

Lise

Malik **Fana de football américain!**

J'adore le sport et surtout le football
américain! Avec mes copains, on regarde
tous les matchs à la télé. J'aime aussi
surfer sur Internet. Si tu as les mêmes
goûts, écris-moi!

Application 2

Communication

HOLT **SoundBooth**
ONLINE RECORDING

41 **Histoire à raconter**

Parlons Margot and Damien-Jean are talking about their likes
and dislikes. Work with a classmate to create their conversation.

L'Île-de-France

Que le meilleur gagne!

Épisode 2

DVD

STRATÉGIE

Gathering information As a viewer, it is important to gather as much information as possible from the characters' exchanges. As you watch the video, write down each bit of important information that you receive from each exchange between Yasmina, Laurie, and Adrien. What new information did you gather in this episode? Have the three friends made any progress in the contest? Have they learned anything new? If so, what?

Les trois amis reçoivent la première énigme...

1

Adrien Voici la première énigme. On doit découvrir le continent où est le lycée.

Yasmina C'est un message codé...

2

Adrien Il y a trois phrases... Regardez!

Laurie À mon avis, chaque lettre de l'alphabet correspond à une autre lettre.

ÉNIGME NUMÉRO 1

DÉCHIFFREZ CETTE ÉNIGME.
EZ TROUVER LE CONTINENT DU LYCÉE

BONNE CHANCE !

3

4

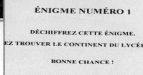

5

Laurie C'est assez simple, en fait. C'est l'alphabet à l'envers. Le A correspond au Z et le B au Y.

Laurie Voici le message décodé.

Le jeune homme "Vous, jeunes Français, de la vie il faut toujours profiter."

Chapitre 2 • Qu'est-ce qui te plaît?

6

Adrien Pardon?
Le jeune homme C'est la dernière phrase de la chanson de Blue Babylon, "Jeunes Français."

7

Laurie Ah oui! Le groupe Blue Babylon! Et ils sont d'où déjà?
Le jeune homme De différents pays d'Afrique.

8

Laurie D'Afrique! D'Afrique! Le lycée est en Afrique!

9

Yasmina Il est à vous, ce cahier?
Le jeune homme Non, non. Il n'est pas à moi.

10 *Il y a une adresse dans le cahier trouvé.*

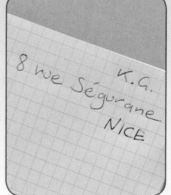

8, rue Ségurane
NICE
K.G.

AS-TU COMPRIS?

1. What kind of code is used in the secret message?
2. Who decodes the message?
3. What does the young man do that helps the three solve the clue?
4. On what continent is their sister school?
5. What does Yasmina find at the café?

Prochain épisode:
Yasmina just found an object that will play an important role in the next episode. Why do you think that is?

A **Avant la lecture**

Look at the photos and charts in the article below. Based on what you see, what do you think you are about to read? What kind of information do you expect to find?

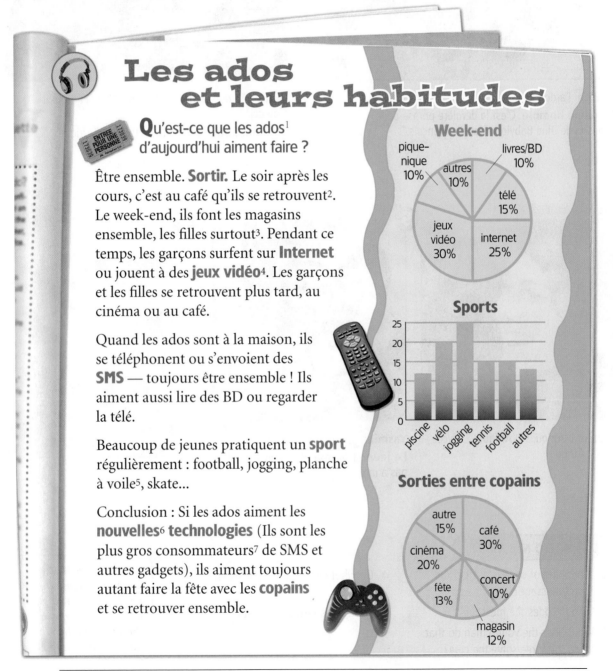

Les ados et leurs habitudes

Qu'est-ce que les ados[1] d'aujourd'hui aiment faire ?

Être ensemble. **Sortir.** Le soir après les cours, c'est au café qu'ils se retrouvent[2]. Le week-end, ils font les magasins ensemble, les filles surtout[3]. Pendant ce temps, les garçons surfent sur **Internet** ou jouent à des **jeux vidéo**[4]. Les garçons et les filles se retrouvent plus tard, au cinéma ou au café.

Quand les ados sont à la maison, ils se téléphonent ou s'envoient des **SMS** — toujours être ensemble ! Ils aiment aussi lire des BD ou regarder la télé.

Beaucoup de jeunes pratiquent un **sport** régulièrement : football, jogging, planche à voile[5], skate...

Conclusion : Si les ados aiment les **nouvelles**[6] **technologies** (Ils sont les plus gros consommateurs[7] de SMS et autres gadgets), ils aiment toujours autant faire la fête avec les **copains** et se retrouver ensemble.

Week-end

- pique-nique 10%
- autres 10%
- livres/BD 10%
- télé 15%
- internet 25%
- jeux vidéo 30%

Sports

piscine, vélo, jogging, tennis, football, autres

Sorties entre copains

- autre 15%
- café 30%
- cinéma 20%
- concert 10%
- fête 13%
- magasin 12%

1. teens 2. get together 3. especially 4. video games 5. wind-surf 6. new 7. consumers

B Compréhension

Complete the following sentences according to **Les ados et leurs habitudes.**

1. En général, les ados aiment beaucoup…
2. Les trois activités préférées des ados pendant le week-end sont…
3. Un des sports que les ados ne pratiquent pas beaucoup est…
4. Les ados aiment souvent aller au…
5. Les technologies que les ados adorent sont…

C Après la lecture

How do your interests compare with those of the teens surveyed? Which interests do you share with them? Is socializing as important to you as it is to the teens in the survey? Why or why not?

Espace écriture

danser · faire la fête · J'aime

STRATÉGIE pour écrire

Cluster diagrams can help you organize your ideas around a particular theme or topic. You can draw bubbles containing information related to your topic, then connect the bubbles to help you see your writing plan more clearly.

Dossier personnel

Every month the school newspaper has a special feature about a different student. They have asked you to write a paragraph about yourself and the activities you like and dislike. In your paragraph, include your name, age, what you like and dislike doing, and how often you do these activities.

1 Plan

Draw two bubbles. Write **J'aime** in one bubble and **Je n'aime pas** in the other. Then draw more bubbles, each with an activity that you like or dislike doing. Connect the bubbles based on your likes and dislikes.

2 Rédaction

Start your paragraph by introducing yourself and telling how old you are. Then, use your cluster diagram to organize the information for your paragraph. Include all the information in your bubbles.

3 Correction

Read your sentences at least twice. Make sure you have included all the necessary information you wanted to include in your paragraph. Exchange your paragraph with a classmate to check spelling and punctuation.

4 Application

You may want to attach a photo of yourself doing your favorite activity to your paragraph. Post your **dossier personnel** on the bulletin board. How well do you know your classmates? Read their paragraphs and find out.

Prépare-toi pour l'examen

Interactive
TUTOR

① Say whether you like or dislike these things or activities.

① Vocabulaire 1
- to ask about likes and dislikes
- to agree and disagree
  pp. 40–43

1.

2.

3.

4.

5.

6.

② Use the correct form of the verbs to complete Vincent's journal entry.

② Grammaire 1
- definite articles
- *-er* verbs
Un peu plus
- irregular plurals
  pp. 44–49

> Je m'appelle Vincent. Mes amis Karim, François et moi,
> nous_____ (aimer) les BD et les magazines. Karim
> aime_____ (lire) le journal. François et moi, nous
> n'_____(aimer) pas lire le journal. Moi, j'adore_____
> (dessiner). Je_____ (dessiner) bien. Karim et François
> n'_____ (aimer) pas dessiner. Ils _____(dessiner) mal.
> Ils préfèrent_____ (écouter) de la musique. Et ils_____
> (adorer) chanter!

③ Vocabulaire 2
- to ask how often you do an activity
- to ask how well you do something and ask about preferences
  pp. 52–55

③ Tell whether these sentences are **a) logical** or **b) illogical**.

1. Sarah adore jouer aux échecs. Elle ne joue jamais aux échecs.
2. Caroline aime manger. Elle préfère manger au café.
3. Pascaline ne joue pas au base-ball. Elle n'aime pas le base-ball.
4. Sylvestre nage souvent. Il déteste nager.
5. Farida adore les romans et les bandes dessinées. Elle n'aime pas lire.

④ Complete this conversation between Rémy and Louise with the correct contractions with **à.**

—Qu'est-ce que tu aimes faire comme sport?

—J'aime nager ___1___ piscine et j'aime aussi aller ___2___ parc ou ___3___ stade pour jouer ___4___ foot.

—Est-ce que tu étudies souvent ___5___ bibliothèque?

—Non, je préfère étudier ___6___ lycée.

⑤ Answer the following questions.

1. Name three French comic books.
2. What kind of North African music is popular in France?
3. What kinds of activities can you do at an **MJC?**

⑥ Listen to this conversation, then say whether the statements that follow are **a) vrai** *(true)* or **b) faux** *(false)*.

1. Thomas' favorite activity is reading.
2. Manon is not a very good soccer player.
3. Thomas plays soccer a lot.
4. Manon only likes activities that she can do with friends.
5. Thomas and Manon both prefer to read magazines.

⑦ Create a conversation between Margot and Adèle.

④ **Grammaire 2**
- contractions with *à*
- conjunctions
Un peu plus
- *est-ce que*
  pp. 56–61

⑤ **Culture**
- Comparaisons
  p. 51
- Flash culture
  pp. 42, 45, 54, 56

Prépare-toi pour l'examen

Grammaire 1
- definite articles
- *-er* verbs

Un peu plus
- irregular plurals
  pp. 44–49

Résumé: Grammaire 1

In French there are four definite articles that mean *the*: **le, la, l',** and **les**.

Here is the conjugation of a regular **-er** verb.

aimer *(to like)*			
j'	aim**e**	nous	aim**ons**
tu	aim**es**	vous	aim**ez**
il/elle/on	aim**e**	ils/elles	aim**ent**

Use the appropriate form of **aimer** plus the **infinitive** of another verb to say what you and others *like* or *don't like to do*.

To form the plurals of nouns that end in **-eau** or **-eu**, add **-x**. If the singular noun ends in **-al**, replace **-al** with **-aux**.

Grammaire 2
- contractions with *à*
- conjunctions

Un peu plus
- *est-ce que*
  pp. 56–61

Résumé: Grammaire 2

The preposition à usually means *to* or *at*. When you use à with definite articles, make the following contractions:

à + le → au   à + les → aux

When à appears before **la** or **l'**, there is no contraction. It remains as à la or à l'.

Use conjunctions like **et** *(and)*, **mais** *(but)* and **ou** *(or)* to link two ideas or two sentences together.

To ask a yes-no question, add **est-ce que** before a statement and raise your voice at the end of the question.

Est-ce qu'il aime danser?

🎧 Lettres et sons

La liaison

In French, you don't usually pronounce consonants at the end of a word, such as the **s** in **les** and the **t** in **c'est**. But, you do pronounce the final consonant if the word that follows it begins with a vowel sound. The linking of the final consonant of one word with the beginning vowel of the next word is called **liaison**.

les élèves   vous avez   C'est un copain.
     z   z   t

There are some exceptions: you never do the **liaison** with **et** or with a proper name.

un journal et un livre   Lucas et Élise
       no liaison   no liaison

Jeux de langue
Loïs et Léo sont deux amis. Ils aiment jouer aux échecs et manger des escargots.

Dictée
Écris les phrases de la dictée.

Résumé: Vocabulaire 1

To ask about likes and dislikes

l'anglais (m.)	*English*
le baladeur (MP3)	*MP3 player*
une bande dessinée (une BD)	*comic strip/comic book*
chanter	*to sing*
le chocolat	*chocolate*
un crayon (de couleur)	*(colored) pencil*
un dessin/dessiner	*drawing/to draw*
dormir	*to sleep*
l'école (f.)	*school*
écouter de la musique	*to listen to music*
les écouteurs (m.)	*headphones*
envoyer un e-mail (m.)	*to send e-mail*
étudier/lire	*to study/to read*
le français	*French*
les frites (f.)	*french fries*
la glace	*ice cream*
un journal	*newspaper*
un magazine	*magazine*
manger	*to eat*

les mathématiques (maths) (f.)	*mathematics (math)*
la musique classique/moderne	*classical/modern music*
parler anglais/français	*to speak English/French*
la radio	*radio*
regarder la télé(vision)	*to watch T.V.*
un roman	*novel*
un SMS (un texto)	*text message*
surfer sur Internet	*to surf the Internet*
téléphoner (à des amis)	*to telephone friends*
travailler	*to work*
les vacances (f.)	*vacation*
la voiture de sport	*sports car*
Tu aimes…?	*Do you like . . .?*
Qu'est-ce que tu aimes (faire)?	*What do you like (to do)?*
Oui, J'adore/J'aime bien…	*Yes, I love/I rather like . . .*
J'aime mieux/Je préfère…	*I prefer . . .*
Non, je déteste…	*No, I hate . . .*
Je n'aime pas...	*I don't like . . .*

To agree and disagree . . . . *see p. 42*

Résumé: Vocabulaire 2

To ask how often you do an activity

aller à la piscine	*to go to the pool*
aller au café	*to go to a café*
aller au cinéma	*to go to the movie theater*
la balle/le ballon	*ball*
la batte	*bat*
la bibliothèque	*library*
le centre commercial	*mall*
danser	*to dance*
discuter (avec des amis)	*to chat (with friends)*
faire du sport	*to play sports*
faire la fête	*to party*
faire les magasins (m.)	*to go shopping*
faire un pique-nique	*to have a picnic*
jouer au base-ball/foot(ball)	*to play baseball/soccer*
jouer aux cartes/aux échecs	*to play cards/chess*
le lycée	*high school*
la Maison des jeunes et de la Culture (MJC)	*recreation center*
nager	*to swim*

le parc	*park*
le stade	*stadium*
sortir	*to go out*
voir un film	*to see a movie*
Tu aimes... régulièrement?	*Do you usually like to . . . ?*
Oui, souvent.	*Yes, often.*
De temps en temps.	*From time to time.*
Non, rarement./Non, jamais.	*No, rarely./No, never.*

To ask how well
you do something. . . . . *see p. 55*

To ask about preferences . . . . *see p. 55*

Révisions cumulatives

1 Match each photo with the appropriate description.

a.

b.

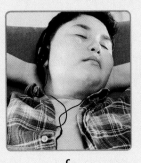
c.

d.

2 You want to meet an e-pal. Read these ads posted on the Web and answer the questions that follow.

Correspondants électroniques

Ahmed Mimouni

14 ans • amimouni@hrw.ma

Salut! Moi, j'aime bien faire du sport. Je joue bien au foot et j'adore nager. J'aime aller à la piscine avec les copains. Nous aimons aussi aller au café. J'adore la glace, le chocolat et les frites.

Simon Gracin

16 ans • sgracin@hrw.net

Salut! J'aime bien sortir avec les copains! Nous aimons faire la fête et écouter de la musique. Nous aimons discuter et danser mais nous n'aimons pas faire du sport.

Mireille Leparc

16 ans • mleparc@hrw.fr

Je m'appelle Mireille. J'adore lire. J'aime lire des magazines, mais je préfère les BD. J'aime aussi dessiner. Je n'aime pas le sport. Je parle bien anglais. Et toi? Qu'est-ce que tu aimes faire?

1. Quelle est l'adresse e-mail de Simon?
2. Ahmed a quel âge?
3. Qui (Who) aime la musique?
4. Qu'est-ce que Mireille aime? Qu'est-ce qu'elle n'aime pas?
5. Qui parle anglais?
6. Qui aime manger?

 3 Take the role of Ahmed, Mireille, or Simon from Activity 2. Your group members will take turns asking you questions in French to guess who you are. Obviously, they cannot ask your name, but they can ask about your age, e-mail address and interests. The first person to guess who you are takes the next turn.

4 Imagine that you're one of the people in the painting. Write a journal entry about the people around you. Include their name, age and one thing that each person likes or dislikes. Read your descriptions to a classmate and see if he/she can guess whom you're talking about. Finally, your classmate might also guess which person in the painting you represent.

Une baignade, Asnières de Georges Seurat

5 Write your own ad for a **correspondant(e) électronique.** Give your name, age, and e-mail address. Tell some of the things you like and don't like so you will get an e-pal with similar interests.

6 À ton tour **Les activités du club** The French Club is planning a meeting. They want to have activities that many people will enjoy. In groups of three, create a survey to find out about your classmates' likes and dislikes. Ask your classmates to complete your survey. Then, tally the results to find out which activities the French Club should plan to include at their next meeting.

DVD
Géoculture

Géoculture
La province de Québec

▲ **La Gaspésie**
The eastern tip of the Gaspe Peninsula is known for its enormous limestone rock formation, **le Rocher Percé**.

Almanac

Population
Over 7 million

Cities
Montreal, Quebec, Laval

Industries
natural resources, aerospace, tourism, pharmaceuticals, information technology

▲ **Les Laurentides**
The Laurentides region, north of Montreal, has spectacular foliage in the fall.

➤ **Le hockey**
Ice hockey is the most popular sport in Quebec.

Savais-tu que...?
Quebec, Canada's largest province, is four times the size of California but nearly half of its inhabitants live on less than 1% of the total land area.

➤ Le Nord du Québec
Wildlife, like the caribous and moose, have adapted to the conditions of this harsh landscape.

⏶ Les aurores boréales
In July, you can enjoy the remarkable phenomenon of the northern lights from the Mount Cosmos Observatory, south of Quebec City.

Baie d'Ungava

Baie d'Hudson

Terre-Neuve

Baie James

QUÉBEC

Ontario

Laurentides

Gaspésie

Gaspé

Golfe du Saint-Laurent

QUÉBEC

Saint-Laurent

Nouveau-Brunswick

Observatoire du mont Cosmos

Laval

Montréal

ÉTATS-UNIS

⏶ Montréal is the second largest French-speaking city in the world, after Paris.

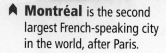

⏷ Le Saint-Laurent
You can see a great variety of large sea mammals like whales, dolphins, and sea lions in this river.

Géo-quiz
Which is the largest French-speaking city in the world? In Canada?

Découvre la province de Québec

Gastronomie

◄ La cipâte aux bleuets
This traditional pie is made with a kind of blueberry found in Canada.

➤ La tourtière
This Quebec specialty is a meat pie, usually made from minced pork and spices.

▲ Le sirop d'érable
In early spring, many people go to a **cabane à sucre** to enjoy the traditional hot maple syrup poured onto a bed of fresh snow and scooped up with wooden sticks.

Sports

➤ La pêche blanche
This sport was handed down from the Inuits and Amerindians. People fish through holes cut in the thick ice that covers rivers and lakes in the winter.

▲ Le canoë
In the summer, people enjoy canoeing on the many waterways that Quebec has to offer.

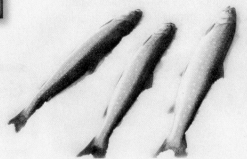

▲ Les traîneaux à chiens
Dogsledding provided transportation to the Inuits, settlers, and fur traders for hundreds of years. Today, "mushing" (traveling on snow with a dog sled) provides ecoadventures through the wilderness.

Fêtes et festivals

Online Practice
go.hrw.com
Photo Tour

KEYWORD: BD1 CH3

➤ **L'International de montgolfières**
This festival in Saint-Jean lasts for ten days. You can admire hot air balloons of all shapes and colors here.

Savais-tu que...?
The name **Québec** comes from the Algonquian word **Kebec,** meaning *narrowing of the river.*

Interactive
TUTOR

▼ **Le Festival international de jazz de Montréal**
Jazz musicians from all over the world participate in over 400 concerts every summer during this festival.

▲ **Le Carnaval de Québec**
This is the biggest winter carnival in the world. Among the numerous festivities, an ice palace is built for **Bonhomme Carnaval,** the mascot of the carnival.

Histoire

◄ **Samuel de Champlain,** sent by the king of France to map the St. Lawrence River, made the fur trade flourish and established ties with native peoples. He founded Quebec City in 1608.

©Bettmann/CORBIS

▲ **Jacques Cartier** explored the St. Lawrence River in the 1530s while searching for a route to Asia. He claimed the area for France, landing on the sites that later became Quebec City and Montreal.

Activité

1. **Gastronomie:** What product is associated with the **cabane à sucre?**
2. **Sports:** What sport was handed down from the Inuits?
3. **Fêtes et festivals:** Who is **Bonhomme Carnaval?**
4. **Histoire:** When was Quebec City founded?

La province de Québec

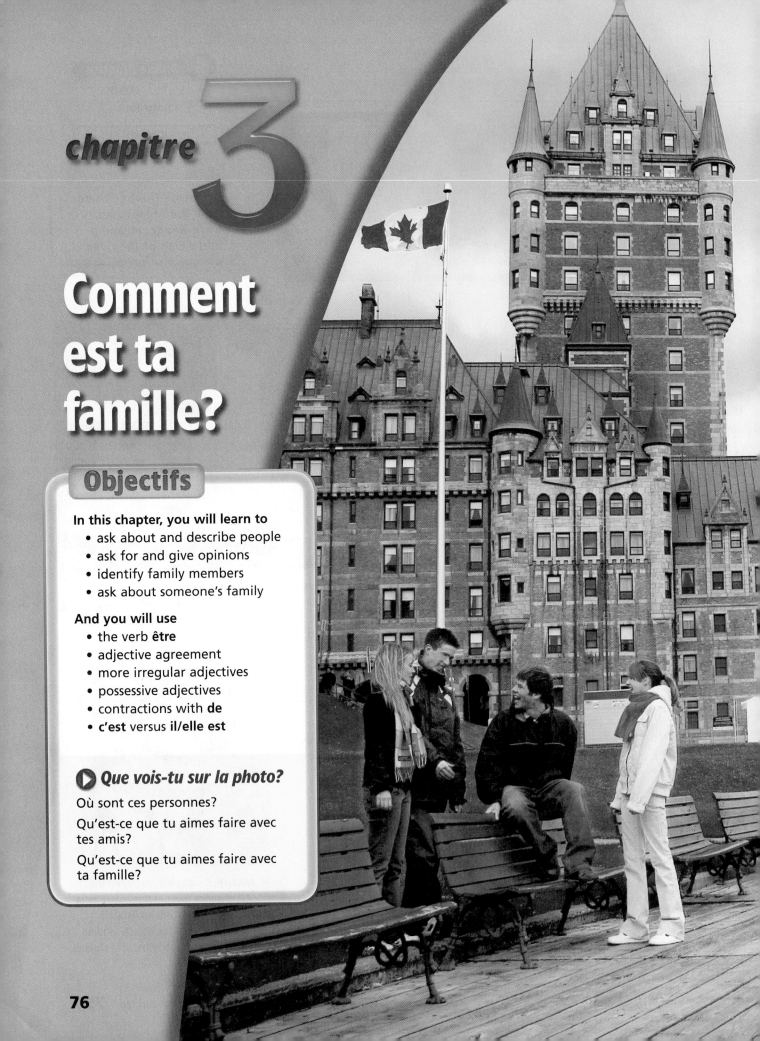

chapitre **3**

Comment est ta famille?

Objectifs

In this chapter, you will learn to
- ask about and describe people
- ask for and give opinions
- identify family members
- ask about someone's family

And you will use
- the verb **être**
- adjective agreement
- more irregular adjectives
- possessive adjectives
- contractions with **de**
- **c'est** versus **il/elle est**

▶ *Que vois-tu sur la photo?*

Où sont ces personnes?

Qu'est-ce que tu aimes faire avec tes amis?

Qu'est-ce que tu aimes faire avec ta famille?

La terrasse Dufferin et le château Frontenac, à Québec

Vocabulaire

à l'œuvre **1**

Télé-vocab

Mon ami(e) est...

blond

blonde

fort

forte

intelligent

intelligente

roux

rousse

timide

timide

généreux

généreuse

grand

grande

créatif

créative

brun

brune

petit

petite

sportif

sportive

Il/Elle a les cheveux...

châtains

blancs

Il/Elle a les yeux...

noirs

marron

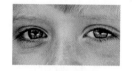

bleus

verts

longs

courts

D'autres mots utiles

génial(e)	*awesome*	**marrant(e)**	*funny*
gentil(le)	*kind*	**pénible**	*tiresome*
méchant(e)	*mean*	**sympa(thique)**	*nice*
mince	*thin*	**sérieux/sérieuse**	*serious*
gros/grosse	*fat*	**paresseux/paresseuse**	*lazy*

Exprimons-nous!

To ask about people	To describe people
Comment est le/la prof de français?	**Il/Elle est très** sympathique.
Il/Elle est comment, Thomas/Séverine? *What is . . . like?*	*He/She is very . . .* **Il/Elle n'**est **ni** grand(e) **ni** petit(e). *He/She is neither . . . nor . . .*
Comment sont Rachid et Isabelle?	**Ils/Elles sont assez** marrant(e)s.
Ils/Elles sont comment, tes ami(e)s? *What are . . . like?*	*They are quite . . .*

Interactive TUTOR

Vocabulaire et grammaire, *pp. 25–27*

Online workbooks

▶ Vocabulaire supplémentaire—Les mots descriptifs, **p. R11**

D'autres mots utiles

jeune	*young*
âgé(e)	*elderly*
la tête	*head*
le nez	*nose*
la bouche	*mouth*
les oreilles (f.)	*ears*

À la créole

In Haiti, as well as in the French Indies, the words often used for *friend* are **compère** for a male and **commère** for a female.

1 Ça veut dire la même chose!

Lisons M. Lafitte tends to repeat everything he says. Decide what would follow each of his statements in the right column.

1. Corinne est grande.
2. Mon ami est sérieux.
3. Les copines de Marie sont sympas.
4. Luc n'est pas gentil.
5. Sandrine est pénible.
6. Paul et Lucien sont minces.
7. David a les cheveux noirs.
8. Mme Duval a les cheveux roux.

a. Il n'est pas blond.
b. Elle n'est pas petite.
c. Il n'est pas marrant.
d. Ils ne sont pas gros.
e. Elle n'est pas blonde.
f. Elle n'est pas géniale.
g. Il est méchant.
h. Elles sont gentilles.

2 Écoutons

Baptiste parle de ses amis. Choisis l'image qui correspond à chaque description.

a.

b.

c.

d.

e.

f.

Exprimons-nous!

To ask for an opinion	To give an opinion
Comment tu trouves Bastien/Yasmina?	**Je le/la trouve** gentil(le). *I think he/she is . . .*
Qu'est-ce que tu penses d'Ousmane/ **de** Marie? *What do you think of . . .?*	**À mon avis,** il/elle est timide. *In my opinion, . . .*

Interactive **TUTOR**

Vocabulaire et grammaire, pp. 25–27

Online workbooks

3 Comment tu trouves...?

Lisons/Écrivons Regarde l'image et complète la conversation entre Laure et Karine d'une façon logique.

LAURE	Comment tu trouves Pauline?
KARINE	Je la trouve ___1___ et ___2___.
LAURE	Et qu'est-ce que tu penses de François?
KARINE	François? Il est ___3___ et ___4___, mais il est ___5___.
LAURE	Et Hubert?
KARINE	À mon avis, il est ___6___. Et je le trouve ___7___ aussi.

4 À mon avis...

Écrivons An online teen magazine from Montreal is conducting an opinion survey. Answer the questions below.

1. Comment tu trouves le professeur de français?
2. Qu'est-ce que tu penses de Homer Simpson?
3. Il est comment, ton acteur préféré *(your favorite actor)*?
4. Comment est le président des États-Unis *(U.S.)*?
5. Comment est ton athlète préféré(e) *(your favorite athlete)*?

Communication

HOLT **SoundBooth**
ONLINE RECORDING

5 Opinions personnelles

Parlons Take turns describing your best friend to your partner. First, tell his or her name and age. Then, give a physical description and mention some of your friend's personality traits. Be sure to also mention some of your friend's likes and dislikes.

MODÈLE Mon ami(e) s'appelle... Il/Elle a... ans. Il/Elle est...

Objectifs
- the verb *être*
- adjective agreement

Grammaire à l'œuvre 1

Grammavision

The verb *être*

Interactive TUTOR

Like **avoir,** the verb **être** is an irregular verb. This means that it does not follow the pattern of other verbs. You will have to memorize its forms individually.

être *(to be)*			
je	**suis**	nous	**sommes**
tu	**es**	vous	**êtes**
il/elle/on	**est**	ils/elles	**sont**

Je ne **suis** pas très sportive.

Est-ce qu'ils **sont** marrants?

Vocabulaire et grammaire, *pp. 28–29*
Cahier d'activités, *pp. 21–23*
Online workbooks

Flash culture

There are only about 400 different last names of French origin in Quebec. The most common ones are Tremblay and Roy. Other common last names are: Gagnon, Gauthier, Charbonneau, Lalonde and Lapointe. The lack of diversity in last names is made up by the variety of first names, with some old-fashioned French ones like Ovide, Adélard or Delima. In Quebec, a child may often be given the mother's maiden name as a first name.

What are some common last names in your area? What is the origin of your last name?

6 Dans la classe de français

Lisons Complète les phrases avec la forme appropriée du verbe **être.**

1. Je (es / suis) sympathique.
2. Le professeur (est / es) créatif.
3. Les élèves (sommes / sont) intelligents.
4. Marine et Jacques (êtes / sont) pénibles.
5. Mes amis et moi, nous (sont / sommes) gentils.
6. Et vous, mademoiselle Leclerc, vous (êtes / est) géniale!

7 Mes copains

Lisons/Parlons Danielle is describing herself and her classmates to a pen pal. Complete her note with the correct forms of the verb **être.**

Ma copine Juliette et moi, nous __1__ brunes. Juliette __2__ petite, mais moi, je __3__ grande. Elle __4__ mince et elle __5__ très intelligente. Et Julien et Pierre? Ils __6__ bruns aussi. Pierre __7__ génial! Julien __8__ un peu timide, mais il __9__ super-cool! Et toi? Tu __10__ comment?

8 À l'école

Parlons Florence always says good things about everyone.
What would she say about the following people?

MODÈLE tu / intelligent → **Tu es intelligent.**
Marie / méchante → **Marie n'est pas méchante.**

1. Clara / paresseuse
2. Jules / gros
3. Nous / généreuses
4. Annick et Laure / pénibles

5. Tu / sympathique
6. Nous / intelligents
7. Gilbert / marrant
8. Vous / gentils

9 On est tous différents!

Écrivons Mélodie is an artist, and she likes drawing her friends.
Write two sentences to describe each of her friends, including
physical descriptions as well as personality traits.

1. Simon

2. Éléa

3. Marius

4. Bernard

Communication

HOLT **SoundBooth**
ONLINE RECORDING

10 Opinions personnelles

Parlons Some say that you are what you do. Using words from
the box, tell what somebody does or likes to do. Feel free to add
other expressions if you'd like. Then, have your classmate use
adjectives to describe the person.

| aime | étudier | dessiner | le chocolat |
| les fêtes | n'aime pas | nager | parler |

MODÈLE **Elle aime beaucoup nager et jouer au base-ball.**
Elle est sportive.

Adjective agreement

1 Adjectives agree in number and gender with the nouns they describe. Unless an adjective already ends in an unaccented **-e,** to make most adjectives feminine, add **-e** to the masculine singular form.

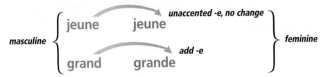

masculine
jeune → jeune *unaccented -e, no change*
grand → grande *add -e*
feminine

2 To form the feminine of adjectives ending in **-eux** or **-if,** make the following spelling changes before adding **-e.**

séri**eux** → séri**euse**

spor**tif** → spor**tive**

3 These adjectives have irregular feminine forms.

lon**g**	→	lon**gue**	gro**s** → gro**sse**	
blan**c**	→	blan**che**	genti**l** → genti**lle**	
bo**n**	→	bo**nne**	migno**n** → migno**nne**	

4 Adjectives come after the noun unless they describe beauty, age, goodness, or size.

before   *after*
Martin est un **bon** ami et un étudiant **sérieux.**

5 Unless its singular form already ends in **-s** (**gros**), to make an adjective plural, add **-s.**

	MASCULINE	**FEMININE**
SINGULAR	intelligent	intelligent**e**
PLURAL	intelligent**s**	intelligent**es**

6 **Des** becomes **de** when the adjective comes before the noun.

Est-ce qu'il y a **de jeunes** professeurs dans ton école?

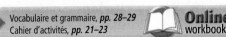

Vocabulaire et grammaire, *pp. 28–29*
Cahier d'activités, *pp. 21–23*

Online workbooks

11 **Mon ami Bruno**

Lisons Complète le paragraphe avec la forme appropriée de chaque adjectif.

Mon ami Bruno n'est ni (grand / grande) ni (petit / petite). Comme moi *(like me)*, il a les yeux (bleu / bleus). Nous sommes (brunes / bruns). Il est assez (marrant / marrante). Il n'est pas (timide / timides)! Bruno est super- (gentil / gentilles). C'est un très (bonne / bon) copain.

12 Écoutons

Danielle is describing her friends Michèle (a girl) and Michel (a boy). Listen to each sentence and say if Danielle is talking about **a) Michèle, b) Michel,** or **c) if it is impossible to tell.**

13 Alain et Amélie

Parlons/Écrivons Alain and Amélie are twins and identical in every way. Describe Amélie based on these statements about Alain.

> **MODÈLE** Alain est brun.
> **Amélie est brune aussi.**

1. Alain est fort.
2. Alain est assez timide.
3. Alain est génial.
4. Alain est assez grand.
5. Alain est créatif.
6. Alain est très généreux.
7. Alain est un bon élève.
8. Alain est paresseux.

14 Mes camarades de classe

Écrivons Look at the picture that Monique drew during a camping trip with friends. Describe each person in the sketch.

Communication

15 Scénario

Parlons Ask your partner to think of a classmate. Guess who he or she is by asking questions that can be answered with **oui** or **non.**

> **MODÈLE** —C'est un garçon?
> —Non, c'est une fille.
> —Elle est grande? etc.

Application 1

16 **Écoutons**

Félix is always saying negative things about his classmates. Listen to each of these statements and decide if Félix is **a) likely** or **b) unlikely** to have said them.

Un peu plus

More irregular adjectives

1. Some adjectives like cool *(cool)*, chic, orange, and marron are invariable. They never change form.

> Les profs sont cool.   La mère de Mathieu est très chic.

2. The adjectives **beau** *(beautiful)*, **nouveau** *(new)*, and **vieux** *(old)* are irregular. They also come before the nouns they describe.

MASCULINE Singular (before a consonant)	MASCULINE Singular (before a vowel)	MASCULINE Plural	FEMININE Singular	FEMININE Plural
beau	bel	beaux	belle	belles
nouveau	nouvel	nouveaux	nouvelle	nouvelles
vieux	vieil	vieux	vieille	vieilles

> Mme Boursier a une belle voiture.
>
> Alain a de vieux posters.

Vocabulaire et grammaire, *p. 30*
Cahier d'activités, *pp. 21–23*

Online workbooks

17 **Les copains d'Emmanuel**

Lisons Some of Emmanuel's instant messages are jumbled. Can you figure out what he's saying about his classmates?

1. Patricia a…
2. Thomas a un…
3. Corinne et Emma…
4. Caroline est une…
5. Guillaume et Paul sont…
6. Alexandre a une…

a. vieille télévision.
b. beaux.
c. de beaux yeux.
d. nouvel ordinateur.
e. belle fille.
f. ont les yeux marron.

Flash culture

«**Je me souviens**» *(I remember)* is the official motto of Québec. It can be seen on automobiles all over Québec, as the official license plate proudly displays the motto. Though Quebeckers are not quite sure about what they are to remember, most agree that it is to remember their historical French roots.

Does your state have a motto? If so, what does it mean? Is the state motto on your family car's license plate?

Chapitre 3 • Comment est ta famille?

Application 1

18 **À l'école de Valentine**

Lisons/Parlons Valentine is talking about people and things at her school. Add the appropriate forms of the adjectives in parentheses.

1. Éric et Ali sont _____. (beau)

2. Il y a un _____ élève à l'école. (nouveau)

3. Marielle a les yeux _____. (marron)

4. Alice a une _____ voiture de sport. (nouveau)

5. Il y a de _____ livres à la bibliothèque. (vieux)

6. Marcel a un _____ ordinateur. (vieux)

19 **Auto-portrait**

Écrivons Use the words in the box below to describe yourself. Use other adjectives if necessary.

grand	mince	vieux	mignon	gentil
généreux	fort	roux	timide	cool
ni grand ni petit	sportif	sympa	intelligent	beau

Communication

HOLT **SoundBooth** ONLINE RECORDING

20 **Opinions personnelles**

Parlons With a classmate, take turns describing different kids pictured below and guessing who is being described.

Papoum   Anna   Gwendoline   Christophe   Samuel   Mariana

Culture appliquée

Le blason familial

The **blason familial,** or family coat of arms, is a symbol originally used to identify knights in combat. It began to appear in Europe in the eleventh century and became popular among the nobility during the twelfth and thirteenth centuries. The official elements of a coat of arms are the motto, the crest, and the shield.

Le blason de l'université McGill, à Montréal

Ton blason

Materials:

- poster board or heavy stock paper
- scissors
- pen or pencil
- crayons, markers, or colored pencils

Create your own **blason!** Before starting, think about your favorite subject, hobby, or sport. How would you illustrate it?

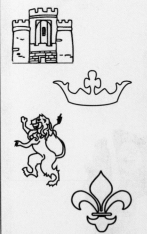

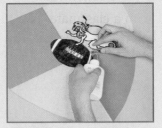

Step 1 Choose a shape for the shield and draw it on the poster board. Cut it out.

Step 2 Choose colors for the background.

Step 3 Pick a symbol that would best illustrate your favorite subject, hobby, or sport. Place it in the middle of your shield.

Step 4 Pick one or two other symbols to go on either side of the shield.

Step 5 Choose a crest to go at the top of the shield.

Step 6 Create a motto of three words in French that describes who you are. Place it at the bottom of the shield.

Recherches Research the coat of arms of the following French royal families: the Capets, the Valois, and the Bourbons. Do these coat of arms have something in common? What is it? Why?

Comparaisons

Les courses en famille

En famille

Imagine you're an exchange student staying with a French family. Which of the following would you expect to do:

a. help yourself to the fridge and be able to snack whenever you like?

b. eat dinner in front of any one of the three TV sets?

c. spend Sunday with your family?

If you stay with a French family, you'll notice that children usually have dinner every evening with their parents. Except for the **goûter**, they don't eat between meals. The family will most likely have dinner in the dining room. Some families might watch the 8 o'clock news together while eating dinner around the dinner table. Boys and girls help with grocery shopping, meal preparation, cooking, and setting or clearing the table. French teenagers rarely have parties at home; they meet their friends at a **café** or at a movie theatre. They usually go out on Wednesday afternoons, since school ends early that day, and on Saturday nights. Sunday is often spent with the family.

ET TOI?

1. Do you always have lunch or dinner with your family?

2. Do American students usually go out on Wednesdays and on Saturdays?

Communauté

Your city's coat of arms

Do you know if your city has a coat of arms? If so, what are the symbols and why were they chosen? What do they mean? You may find some information at the town hall of your city. Then, you may also go to your neighborhood library or on the Internet to do some research on your family's name and see if it has ever been associated with a coat of arms.

Un blason familial

La province de Québec

Objectifs
- to identify family members
- to ask about someone's family

Vocabulaire
à l'œuvre **2**

Télé-vocab

Une famille québécoise

Voilà ma famille, les Michaud.

mon grand-père
Victor **ma grand-mère**
Odile

ma mère
Nathalie **mon père**
Yves **ma tante**
Agnès **mon oncle**
André **ma tante**
Jocelyne

ma sœur
Aurore **C'est moi,**
Vincent! **mon frère**
Guillaume **ma cousine**
Perrine **ma cousine**
Claire **mon cousin**
Maxime

mon chien
Boris **mon chat**
Nikita

Vocabulaire 2

Ma tante Agnès est **divorcée** et **remariée**.

Voici Charles, **le mari** de ma tante.

Voilà tante Agnès avec Arnaud et Sophie, **le fils** et **la fille** de Charles.

Perrine avec **son beau-père**, **son demi-frère** et **sa demi-sœur**.

D'autres mots utiles

les parents	*parents*
l'enfant (m./f.)	*child*
les grands-parents	*grandparents*
les petits-enfants	*grandchildren*
le petit-fils	*grandson*
la petite-fille	*granddaughter*
le neveu	*nephew*
la nièce	*niece*
la femme	*wife*
la belle-mère	*stepmother*

Exprimons-nous!

To identify family members

Qui c'est, ça?
Who is that?

Ça, c'est la cousine **de** Mathieu.
This is Mathieu's . . .

Ça, ce sont les frères **de** Youssef.
These are Youssef's . . .

Interactive

TUTOR

Vocabulaire et grammaire, pp. 31–33

Online workbooks

▶ Vocabulaire supplémentaire—La famille, p. R9

21 **Écoutons**

Clothilde décrit sa famille. Regarde l'arbre généalogique *(family tree)* et décide si les phrases sont **a) vraies** ou **b) fausses.**

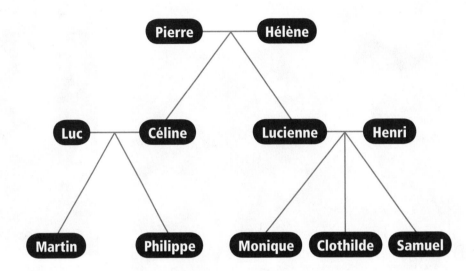

22 **La famille de Clothilde**

Parlons Réponds aux questions suivantes d'après l'arbre généalogique de Clothilde (Activité 21).

1. Comment s'appelle le neveu de Céline?
2. Comment s'appellent les cousines de Martin?
3. Qui est l'oncle de Clothilde?
4. Comment s'appelle le mari d'Hélène?
5. Qui est la tante de Clothilde?
6. Qui est le frère de Martin?
7. Qui est le cousin de Philippe?
8. Qui sont les enfants de Lucienne?

23 **Devinettes**

Lisons/Écrivons Qui sont les personnes suivantes?

MODÈLE **Le fils de ma tante, c'est mon <u>cousin</u>.**

1. La mère de ma mère, c'est ma _____.
2. Le fils de mon beau-père et de ma mère, c'est mon _____.
3. Les frères de ma mère, ce sont mes _____.
4. Le père de mon père, c'est mon _____.
5. La sœur de mon fils, c'est ma _____.
6. Les fils et les filles de mes enfants, ce sont mes _____.
7. Le fils de mon frère, c'est mon _____.

Exprimons-nous!

To ask about someone's family	To respond
Tu as des frères et des sœurs? *Do you have brothers and sisters?*	**Non, je suis fils/fille unique.** *No, I'm an only child.*
Tu as combien de frères et de sœurs? *How many . . . do you have?*	**J'ai** deux sœurs **et** un demi-frère. *I have . . . and . . .*
	Je n'ai pas de frères **mais** j'ai une sœur. *I don't have any . . . but . . .*
Vous êtes combien dans ta famille? *How many people are there in your family?*	**Nous sommes** cinq. *There are . . . of us.*
Tu as un animal domestique? *Do you have a pet?*	**Oui, j'ai trois chats et un chien.** *Yes, I have . . .*

Vocabulaire et grammaire, pp. 31–33

Online workbooks

Vocabulaire 2

24 Un portrait de famille

Écrivons Imagine que tu es Ronan et que tu as pris *(took)* cette photo. Décris ta famille.

Entre copains

branché(e)	*hip*
chouette	*cool/nice*
un(e) gamin(e)	*a kid*
un(e) frangin(e)	*a brother/ a sister*
mes vieux	*my parents*
mamie	*grandma*
papi	*grandpa*

Communication

HOLT **SoundBooth** ONLINE RECORDING

25 Interview

Parlons Ask three of your classmates the questions below. Based on their answers, see if there are any similarities between their families and yours. Report your findings to the class.

1. Vous êtes combien dans ta famille?

2. Comment s'appelle ton père? Et ta mère?

3. Tu as des frères ou des sœurs?

4. Est-ce que tu as un animal domestique?

Grammaire
à l'œuvre 2

Grammavision

Possessive adjectives

Interactive TUTOR

1 Here are the possessive adjectives in French. Notice that the possessive adjectives agree in gender and number **with what is possessed.**

	MASCULINE Singular	**FEMININE** Singular	**PLURAL**
my	mon	ma	mes
your (tu)	ton	ta	tes
his/her/its	son	sa	ses
our	notre	notre	nos
your (vous)	votre	votre	vos
their	leur	leur	leurs

Mon père est petit.   **Ses frères** sont sportifs.

2 For singular nouns beginning with a vowel, use the masculine form of the possessive adjective, even if the thing possessed is feminine.

Ça, c'est **mon** amie, Claudine.

3 Another way to indicate possession is with the preposition **de.** **De/D'** plus a person's name is used in the same way as *'s* in English.

J'aime bien le frère **d'**André.   *I really like André's brother.*

Vocabulaire et grammaire, *pp. 34–35*
Cahier d'activités, *pp. 25–27*

Online workbooks

26 Chez moi

Lisons Choose the correct possessive adjective in each case.

Voilà (mon / ma) frère Olivier. Il adore faire du sport. Ça, c'est (nos / notre) chat Zola. Il est gentil. Voilà (son / mon) grand-père Raoul et (ma / mon) grand-mère Thérèse. Voilà (ses / mes) petits frères Adrien et Romain. Ils sont pénibles!

27 Écoutons

Denise and Christophe are showing each other family photos. Tell whether each statement refers to someone in a) **Denise's family** or b) **Christophe's family.**

Grammaire 2

28 Dans ma famille

Lisons/Écrivons Fernand is asking Élodie about her family.
Fill in the blanks with the appropriate possessive adjective.

—Élodie, vous êtes combien dans ___1___ famille?

—Nous sommes sept: ___2___ père, ___3___ mère,
___4___ petit frère et ___5___ trois sœurs.

—Comment s'appelle ___6___ frère?

—Il s'appelle Olivier.

—Elles sont comment, ___7___ sœurs?

—___8___ sœurs sont belles et super-gentilles!

29 Mon journal

Écrivons Écris un paragraphe pour décrire les membres de ta famille.
Dis aussi ce que chaque personne aime ou n'aime pas faire.

Communication

HOLT **SoundBooth** ONLINE RECORDING

30 Scénario

Parlons You and a friend are cleaning out your garage.
Before throwing anything away, your friend asks to whom
each item belongs. Respond by telling which family member owns
each item.

MODÈLE —Est-ce que c'est le ballon de ton frère?

—Non, ce n'est pas son ballon. C'est le ballon
de mon neveu.

Contractions with *de*

Interactive TUTOR

1 De contracts with the definite article **le** to form **du**.

de + le → du

Le bureau **du** professeur est marron.

2 De contracts with the definite article **les** to form **des**.

de + les → des

Comment est le père **des** sœurs Lebrun?

3 When **de** appears before **la** or **l'**, there is no contraction.

de + la → de la

de + l' → de l'

Ils sont comment, les frères **de la** copine de Guy?

Elle est comment, la mère **de l'**ami de Charles?

Vocabulaire et grammaire, *pp. 34–35*
Cahier d'activités, *pp. 25–27*

Online workbooks

31 Les nouveaux voisins

Lisons/Parlons M. Robert and Mlle Lebrun are talking about the new people who moved into their neighborhood. Complete their exchanges with **du, de la, de l'**, or **des**.

M. ROBERT   Il est comment, le père ____1____ frères Dubois?

MLLE LEBRUN   Il est grand et brun.

MLLE LEBRUN   Et la mère ____2____ amie de Clarisse Duchesne, comment elle s'appelle?

M. ROBERT   Elle s'appelle Colette Leroy.

MLLE LEBRUN   Comment elle s'appelle, la sœur ____3____ frères Martin?

M. ROBERT   Elle s'appelle Alice.

M. ROBERT   Il est comment, le frère ____4____ garçon blond?

MLLE LEBRUN   Il est roux et pénible!

MLLE LEBRUN   La grand-mère ____5____ fille blonde, elle est comment?

M. ROBERT   Elle est très gentille!

M. ROBERT   Et le père ____6____ garçon roux, comment il s'appelle ?

MLLE LEBRUN   Il s'appelle M. Bonnet.

Flash culture

In February, Quebeckers celebrate the **Carnaval de Québec**. This carnival, which began in 1894, lasts the two weeks before Lent and is the world's largest winter carnival. Families can participate in activities like canoe and dogsled races, a snow bath, ice fishing, snow rafting, a soapbox derby race, and skating with **Bonhomme Carnaval** (the mascot of the carnival). The carnival is famous for its ice palace, night parades, and international ice sculpture show.

Do you know of any other carnivals that take place just before Lent?

32 Devinettes

Lisons/Écrivons Complete the following riddles with **du, de la, de l',** or **des.** Then supply the answer to each riddle.

1. La mère _____ père de ma sœur, c'est _____.
2. La fille _____ sœur de mon père, c'est _____.
3. Le père _____ frère de mon père, c'est _____.
4. Le frère _____ fille de ma tante, c'est _____.
5. Le mari _____ mère de mes cousins, c'est _____.
6. La mère _____ frères de ma cousine, c'est _____.

33 C'est à qui?

Parlons/Écrivons Your friend Aimée is organizing a garage sale. Tell to which of Aimée's family members each of these items belongs.

MODÈLE —C'est la radio du grand-père d'Aimée.

le grand-père

1. la sœur

2. les parents

3. le frère

4. la grand-mère

5. les cousins

6. l'oncle

Communication

HOLT **SoundBooth** ONLINE RECORDING

34 Scénario

Parlons Bring a family picture or a picture of a famous family to share with your classmate. Your classmate will ask you about the people in the picture. Answer by saying who they are and by describing them.

MODÈLE —C'est qui, le garçon blond?
—C'est…
—Il est comment?
—Il est… mais très…

Application 2

35 On rappe!

Listen to the song **Comment est-il?** Write four family members mentioned in the song. Write one description you heard for each family member you picked.

36 Mon animal domestique

Écrivons Jessica et Luc parlent de leurs animaux domestiques. Complète leurs phrases avec des adjectifs possessifs.

—Il a quel âge, ____1____ chien, Luc?

— ____2____ chien? Je n'ai pas de chien mais j'ai trois chats.

—C'est cool! Ils s'appellent comment, ____3____ chats?

—Athos, Porthos et Aramis. Tu as des chats?

—Non, mais ____4____ sœur a un chien et un serpent.

—Whoa! Est-ce que ____5____ parents aiment les animaux?

—Oui, ____6____ parents adorent les animaux!

Un peu plus

C'est versus Il/Elle est

1. Use c'est

- with **a person's name,**

    C'est **Norbert.**

- with **an article/possessive adjective + a noun**

    C'est **une élève.**

    C'est **mon père.**

- with **an article + a noun + an adjective.**

    C'est **un homme intelligent.**

To form a negative sentence, use the expression ce n'est pas.

2. Use il est/elle est

- with an **adjective by itself**

    Elle est **blonde.**

Vocabulaire et grammaire, *p. 36*
Cahier d'activités, *pp. 25–27*

Online workbooks

37 Fais le bon choix

Écrivons Fill in the blanks with **c'est, il est,** or **elle est.**

1. Monique? _____ très belle.

2. _____ un petit garçon.

3. Et M. Poiret, _____ roux?

4. Comment tu trouves Mia? _____ sympa, non?

5. Ça, _____ mon cousin Jacques.

6. _____ très intelligent, ton frère!

38 Je l'adore!

Écrivons Write an e-mail to your Canadian pen pal about your favorite celebrity or your favorite character from a famous television show. Be sure to describe the person or character in detail.

Application 2

39 Qui est Caillou?

Lisons/Écrivons You're surfing the Web to buy your five-year-old Quebecois cousin a video of his favorite cartoon, Caillou. Read about Caillou and answer the questions that follow.

Personnages | Jeux | Activités | Écris à Caillou

Description des personnages

Caillou est un petit garçon de 4 ans. Il est adorable, innocent, enjoué, curieux, et il aime beaucoup les aventures. Il a une sœur qui s'appelle Mousseline. Elle a 2 ans. Caillou a un chat qui s'appelle Gilbert.

Caillou aime beaucoup sa maman et son papa. Ils sont très sympathiques et affectueux et aiment faire les aventures avec Caillou. Grand-maman est artiste et elle aime la nature. Grand-papa est très marrant!

1. Quel âge a Mousseline?
2. Comment s'appelle le chat de Caillou?
3. Comment est Caillou?
4. Comment est Grand-papa?

Communication

HOLT **SoundBooth**
ONLINE RECORDING

40 Histoire à raconter

Parlons Look at Jean-François' family album. With a partner, take turns describing Jean-François and his family.

a.

b.

c.
$10^2 = 100$

Télé-roman

Que le meilleur gagne!

Épisode 3

Au café, Yasmina a trouvé un cahier avec une adresse...

1

Yasmina Regardez! Il y a des initiales et une adresse.

2

Yasmina Oh! Je sais où c'est. Mon oncle et ma tante habitent près de là. On y va?

3

Adrien Moi, je t'accompagne si tu veux.

Adrien et Yasmina traversent un parc...

4

Yasmina Dis, Adrien, on peut se reposer un peu? Je suis crevée.
Adrien Oui, moi aussi.

5

Yasmina Tu as des sœurs et des frères?
Adrien J'ai un frère. Il s'appelle Tristan.

Télé-roman

⑥

⑦

⑧

Adrien Et ça, c'est ma mère. Elle est très sportive.

Yasmina Tiens! Bonjour, tante Zora!
Tante Zora Salut, Yasmina! Ça va?

Tante Zora Oh là là! Mon mari m'attend! Bon alors, à bientôt, toi.

Adrien et Yasmina reprennent la route...

⑨ *Adrien et Yasmina arrivent chez la personne au cahier mystérieux.*

⑩ *La personne ouvre la porte et Adrien et Yasmina sont surpris.*

AS-TU COMPRIS?

1. What do Yasmina and Adrien decide to do at the beginning of the episode?

2. What do they talk about at the park?

3. Does Adrien have any brothers or sisters?

4. Whom do they see at the park?

5. Where are they at the end of the episode?

Prochain épisode:
Who do you think opens the door at the end? What makes you think so?

STRATÉGIE pour lire

Using genre to set expectations Consider the *genre* of a text before you read it. The *genre* can tell you what kind of writing to expect. Some examples of different genres are short story, novel, poem, essay, and play.

A **Avant la lecture**

Look at the following text. What type of reading do you think this is? What should you expect to find in this type of reading? Make a list.

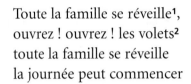

Toute la famille
de Pierre Lozère

Toute la famille se réveille[1],
ouvrez ! ouvrez ! les volets[2]
toute la famille se réveille
la journée peut commencer

5 Papa fait sa gymnastique
un, deux, trois, quatre,
Maman met de la musique
les enfants attrapent[3] le chat !

Toute la famille se réveille,
10 ouvrez ! ouvrez ! les volets
toute la famille se réveille
la journée peut commencer

Papa démarre[4] la voiture
un, deux, trois, quatre,
15 Grand-mère fait des confitures[5]
les enfants attrapent le chat !

Toute la famille se réveille,
ouvrez ! ouvrez ! les volets
toute la famille se réveille
20 la journée peut commencer

Grand-père est parti à pied[6]
un, deux, trois, quatre,
la confiture est brûlée[7]
les enfants attrapent le chat !

25 Toute la famille se réveille,
ouvrez ! ouvrez ! les volets
toute la famille se réveille
la journée peut commencer

---

1. wakes up **2.** shutters **3.** catch **4.** starts
5. jam **6.** went for a walk **7.** burned

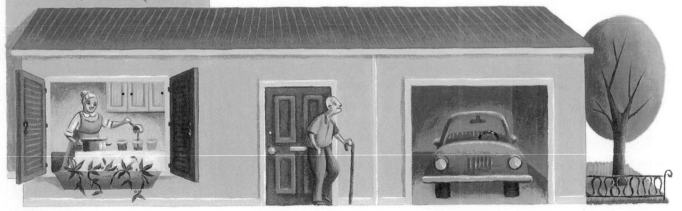

B Compréhension

Match each family member with the sentence that best describes him or her.

1. papa
2. maman
3. le fils ou la fille
4. grand-mère
5. grand-père

a. Il/Elle aime préparer à manger.
b. Il/Elle est sportif.
c. Il/Elle est petit(e) et pénible.
d. Il/Elle aime sortir.
e. Il/Elle aime écouter la radio.

C Après la lecture

1. Compare the list you made in **Avant la lecture** with what you noticed while reading the poem. Is the poem different from what you expected? Does this poem remind you of the way songs are written? Why?

2. How is this family's routine similar to or different from your family's routine?

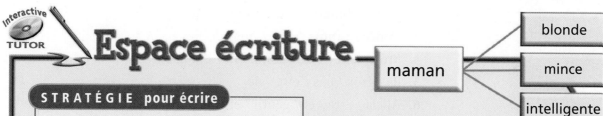

Interactive TUTOR

Espace écriture

STRATÉGIE pour écrire

Graphic organizers can help you remember details that you might otherwise forget. You can draw a square containing the thing you wish to describe, then draw lines extending out from the square to its characteristics.

Portrait de famille

Create a portrait of your family or of an imaginary one. Draw, cut out magazine pictures, or find photos of four family members. Write a caption for each image. Tell who each person is and what he or she is like.

1 Plan

Draw four squares with lines extending out from each square. Write the names of family members in the squares and their relationship to you (**maman**). Then, write adjectives to describe them on the lines (**blonde, mince, intelligente**).

2 Rédaction

Begin each caption by giving your family member's name and his or her relationship to you. Then describe that person's appearance and personality.

3 Correction

Read each caption to make sure that you have all the required information. Read the captions again to check for spelling, punctuation, and adjective agreement.

4 Application

Mount your images and captions on poster board and display your family portrait in class. Read your classmates' posters. Can you guess which family belongs to each of your classmates?

Prépare-toi pour l'examen

Interactive
TUTOR

① Describe the people and pets in the photos. Be sure to use at least two adjectives to describe each person or animal.

❶ **Vocabulaire 1**
- to describe people
- to ask for and give opinions
  pp. 78–81

a.   b.   c.   d.

② Write complete sentences using the elements given. Make all the appropriate changes.

❷ **Grammaire 1**
- the verb *être*
- adjective agreement
Un peu plus
- more irregular adjectives
  pp. 82–87

1. ton frère / toi / être / vous / grand / très / et
2. grand / blond / être / moi / et / je
3. mince / Emma / être / mignon / et
4. professeur / être / comment / d'anglais / le
5. ils / gros / pas / être / ne
6. Alicia / être / et / gentil / et /intelligent / Jeanne
7. être / Eva / être / elle / marrant / timide / mais
8. avoir / je / frère / trois / pénible / beau / mais

③ Réponds aux questions suivantes.

❸ **Vocabulaire 2**
- to identify family members
- to ask about someone's family
  pp. 90–93

1. Vous êtes combien dans ta famille?
2. Comment s'appelle ta mère?
3. Elle est comment?
4. Tu as des frères ou des sœurs?
5. Comment s'appellent tes grands-parents?
6. Ils/Elles sont comment?
7. Tu as un chien ou un chat?
8. Comment il est?
9. Comment sont tes amis?
10. Comment tu trouves le professeur de français?

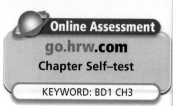
Prépare-toi pour l'examen

4 Complète la conversation entre Luc et Annick avec la forme appropriée de l'adjectif possessif.

LUC   Vous êtes combien dans (ta / notre) famille?

ANNICK   Nous sommes cinq: (ma / votre) grand-mère, (mon / son) père, (ma / ta) mère, (mon / notre) frère et moi.

LUC   Quel âge a (mon / ton) frère?

ANNICK   Il a vingt ans. Il étudie à l'université. (Leur / Son) université est à Montréal.

5 Answer the following questions.

1. Who is **Bonhomme Carnaval?** Where can you see him?
2. What family festival is celebrated in August in Quebec?
3. What is the official motto of Quebec?

6 Listen to Marie-France speaking about her family. Indicate if the following statements are **a) true** or **b) false.**

1. Marie-France a cinq ans.
2. Son chien est très gros.
3. Sa mère est belle et sportive.
4. Son frère s'appelle Valentin.

7 Tell what Jean-François is saying about his family.

4 Grammaire 2
- possessive adjectives
- contractions with **de**

Un peu plus
- **c'est** versus **il/elle est**

pp. 94–99

5 Culture
- Comparaisons p. 89
- Flash culture pp. 82, 86, 92, 96

Grammaire 1

- the verb *être*
- adjective agreement

Un peu plus

- more irregular adjectives
  pp. 82–87

Résumé: Grammaire 1

The verb **être** is irregular.

être *(to be)*		
je suis		nous sommes
tu es		vous êtes
il/elle/on est		ils/elles sont

Adjectives agree in number and gender with the nouns they describe.
To make most adjectives feminine, add **-e** to the masculine form.
To make most adjectives plural, add **-s** to the singular form.
Some adjectives have irregular feminine forms:
blanc (blanche), bon (bonne), gentil (gentille), gros (grosse), mignon (mignonne), long (longue)
Adjectives that end in **-eux** become **-euse** in the feminine forms.
Adjectives that end in **-if** become **-ive** in the feminine forms.

Some adjectives like **cool, chic, orange,** and **marron** are invariable. They never change forms.
The adjectives **beau** *(beautiful),* **nouveau** *(new),* and **vieux** *(old)* have special forms.

Grammaire 2

- possessive adjectives
- contractions with *de*

Un peu plus

- *c'est* versus *il/elle est*
  pp. 94–99

Résumé: Grammaire 2

French **possessive adjectives** agree in gender and number with what is possessed.
They are: **mon, ton, son, ma, ta, sa, mes, tes, ses, notre, votre, leur, nos, vos, leurs**

Contractions with **de:** de + le = du
                            de + les = des
When **de** appears before **la** or **l',** there is no contraction.

Use **c'est** with a person's name, with an article plus a noun, with an article, plus a noun, plus an adjective.
Use **il est/elle est** with an adjective by itself.

Lettres et sons

The r sound

The French **r** is quite different from the American *r.* To pronounce the French **r,** keep the tip of your tongue pressed against your lower front teeth. Arch the back of your tongue upward, almost totally blocking the passage of air in the back of your throat.

Jeux de langue

Mon père est maire, mon frère est masseur, ma tante est sœur et mon cousin est frère.

Dictée

Écris les phrases de la dictée.

Résumé: Vocabulaire 1

To ask about and describe people

âgé(e)	*elderly*	le **nez**	*nose*
beau (belle)	*handsome, beautiful*	noir(e)	*black*
blanc (blanche)	*white*	nouveau (nouvelle)	*new*
bleu(e)	*blue*	les **oreilles** (f.)	*ears*
blond(e)	*blond*	paresseux (paresseuse)	*lazy*
bon/bonne	*good*	pénible	*tiresome/difficult*
la **bouche**	*mouth*	petit(e)/grand(e)	*short/tall*
brun(e)/châtain	*dark-haired/chestnut, light brown*	roux (rousse)	*red-headed*
court(e)/long (longue)	*short/long*	sérieux (sérieuse)	*serious*
créatif (créative)	*creative*	sportif (sportive)	*athletic*
fort(e)	*strong*	la **tête**	*head*
généreux (généreuse)	*generous*	timide	*shy*
génial(e)	*fantastic/awesome*	vert(e)	*green*
gentil(le)	*kind*	Comment est/sont...?	*What is/are . . . like?*
Il/Elle a les cheveux/yeux...	*He/She has . . . hair/eyes.*	Il(s)/Elle(s) est/ sont comment...?	*What is/are . . . like?*
intelligent(e)	*smart*	Il/Elle est très...	*He/She is very . . .*
jeune/vieux (vieille)	*young/old*	Ils/Elles sont assez...	*They are quite . . .*
marrant(e)	*funny*	Il/Elle n'est ni...ni...	*He/She is neither . . . nor . . .*
marron	*brown*		
méchant(e)/sympathique	*mean/nice*		
mince/gros(se)	*thin/fat*		

To ask for and give an opinion .... *see page 80*

Résumé: Vocabulaire 2

To identify family members

le **beau-père**	*stepfather*	le **mari**	*husband*
la **belle-mère**	*stepmother*	la **mère**/ma mère	*mother/my mother*
le **chat**	*cat*	le **neveu**	*nephew*
le **chien**	*dog*	la **nièce**	*niece*
le/la **cousin(e)**	*cousin*	l'**oncle**	*uncle*
le **demi-frère**	*half-brother*	les **parents** (m.)	*parents*
la **demi-sœur**	*half-sister*	le **père**	*father*
divorcé(e)	*divorced*	la **petite-fille**	*granddaughter*
un/une **enfant** (m./f.)	*child*	le **petit-fils**	*grandson*
la **famille**	*family*	les **petits-enfants** (m.)	*grandchildren*
la **femme**	*wife*	la **sœur**	*sister*
la **fille**/le **fils**	*daughter/son*	la **tante**	*aunt*
le **frère**	*brother*	Voici.../Voilà...	*Here is/are . . ./There is/are . . .*
la **grand-mère**	*grandmother*	Ça, c'est/ce sont...	*This is/These are . . .*
le **grand-père**	*grandfather*	Qui c'est, ça?	*Who is that?*
les **grands-parents** (m.)	*grandparents*		

To ask about someone's family .... *see page 93*

chapitres 1-3

Révisions cumulatives

1 Listen as Isabelle and Pauline talk about their families and decide who's talking: **a) Isabelle** or **b) Pauline.**

La famille d'Isabelle

La famille de Pauline

2 You're thinking about getting a pet. Read these advertisements, and then answer the questions that follow with: **a) the cat, b) the dog,** or **c) both.**

EN DIRECT DES REFUGES

César

Beau chien noir et marron de 6 ans. Yeux marron. Je ne peux pas le garder parce que mon père est allergique. Idéal pour famille avec enfants ou chats. Sociable, docile, très intelligent. Déjà vacciné. Il adore jouer à la balle. Contacter **Lise Girard** au **418-555-4625.**

Un minou adorable!

Chaton gris et blanc aux yeux bleus. 3 mois. Petit, gentil, très mignon, un peu timide. Déjà vacciné. Aime beaucoup les enfants. Si vous voulez l'adopter, téléphonez à **Guy Brassard** au **418-555-1359.**

1. Which pet likes children?
2. Which pet is shy?
3. Which pet likes to chase balls?
4. Which pet is smart?
5. Which pet has blue eyes?
6. Which pet needs a new home because of a family member's allergies?

3 Your family is being considered for a reality show. The staff wants to know everything about your family so they can decide if you'd be right for the show. Work with a classmate to create a conversation in which a staff member interviews you about your family: how many of you there are, each person's age, a description, and what each person likes and dislikes.

4 Look at the painting and write a short narrative, in French, about this family. Imagine who the different family members are and describe them in detail. Then, discuss what you think the family is celebrating. How do you know?

Massicotte, Edmond-Joseph. Le Traditionnel Gâteau des Rois, 1926. Lithograph. 20.8 x 31 cm. Musée national des beaux-arts du Québec. 69.402.

Le traditionnel gâteau des Rois d'Edmond-Joseph Massicotte

5 Imagine that you're shooting a short film at school and you're looking for talent. Write ads describing what kind of people you're looking for (man, woman, boy, girl, tall, etc.) Don't forget to mention if you're looking for specific personality traits.

6 À ton tour **Les nouveaux voisins** A new family has moved into your neighborhood, and you notice they have a son about your age. First, introduce yourself and find out about the son's likes and dislikes. Then, ask about his family members. Act out your conversation for the class.

Révisions cumulatives

Mon année scolaire

Objectifs

In this chapter, you will learn to
- ask about classes
- ask for and give an opinion
- ask others what they need and tell what you need
- inquire about and buy something

And you will use
- **-re** verbs
- **-ger** and **-cer** verbs
- **le** with days of the week
- the verbs **préférer** and **acheter**
- adjectives as nouns
- agreement with numbers

▶ *Que vois-tu sur la photo?*

Où sont ces élèves?

Est-ce qu'ils sont contents?

Et toi, est-ce que tu aimes aller au lycée?

1
CÔTE DE LA FABRIQUE

UNIVERSITÉ
LAVAL
École d'architecture

Le Petit Séminaire de Québec, à Québec

Objectifs
- to ask about classes
- to ask for and give opinions

Vocabulaire
à l'œuvre 1

DVD
Télé-vocab

Au Cégep à Québec

Quelle est ta matière préférée?

La biologie

La chimie

La physique

La géographie

L'histoire (f.)

L'informatique (f.)

L'espagnol (m.)

L'allemand (m.)

Les mathématiques (f.)

Les arts (m.) plastiques

L'éducation (f.) musicale

L'EPS (éducation (f.) physique et sportive)

Quelle heure est-il? Il est...

une heure

2:00	2:10
deux heures	deux heures dix

2:15	2:30	12:00 AM
deux heures et quart	deux heures et demie	minuit

2:40	2:45	12:00 PM
trois heures moins vingt	trois heures moins le quart	midi

Vocabulaire 1

Les jours de la semaine

mars
la semaine du 12 au 18   le **week-end**

lundi	mardi	mercredi	jeudi	vendredi	samedi
12	13	14	15	16	17

dimanche 18

D'autres mots utiles

du matin	*in the morning*
de l'après-midi	*in the afternoon*
du soir	*in the evening*
aujourd'hui	*today*
demain	*tomorrow*
maintenant	*now*
la récréation	*break/recess*
la sortie	*dismissal*
l'examen (m.)	*exam*
les devoirs (m.)	*homework*

Exprimons-nous!

To ask about classes	To respond
À quelle heure tu as anglais? *At what time do you have . . . ?*	**J'ai** anglais **à** midi et demi. *I have . . . at . . .*
Tu as quel cours à neuf heures du matin? *What class do you have at . . . ?*	
Quel jour est-ce que tu as maths? *What day do you have . . . ?*	**J'ai** maths **lundi**. *I have . . . on Monday.*
Quand est-ce que tu as maths? *When do you have . . . ?*	**J'ai** maths **le lundi, le mercredi** et **le vendredi**. *. . . on Mondays, Wednesdays . . . Fridays.*

Interactive
TUTOR

Vocabulaire et grammaire, pp. 37–39

Online workbooks

▶ **Vocabulaire supplémentaire**—Les matières, p. R10

La province de Québec

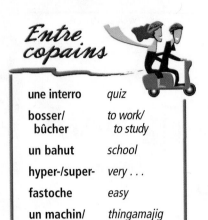

Entre copains

une interro	*quiz*
bosser/ bûcher	*to work/ to study*
un bahut	*school*
hyper-/super-	*very . . .*
fastoche	*easy*
un machin/ un truc	*thingamajig*

1 Quel cours?

Lisons What class will each of these students most likely take based on what they like?

1. Annick aime Shakespeare.
2. Didier aime jouer au foot.
3. Sylvie aime les ordinateurs.
4. Matthieu aime dessiner.
5. Lucille aime chanter.
6. Paul aime les nombres.

   a. les mathématiques
   b. les arts plastiques
   c. l'EPS
   d. l'éducation musicale
   e. l'anglais
   f. l'informatique

2 Écoutons

Émilie parle de ses cours avec son ami Maurice. Est-ce qu'Émilie a les cours suivants **a) le matin** ou **b) l'après-midi?**

1. l'histoire
2. les mathématiques
3. l'anglais

4. l'informatique
5. la géographie
6. les arts plastiques

3 L'heure

Écrivons Écris quelle heure il est avec des phrases complètes.

1.   2.   3.   4.   5.

Exprimons-nous!

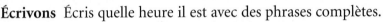

To ask for an opinion	To give an opinion
Comment est ton cours de maths? *What's your . . . class like?*	Il est **difficile/facile.** *. . . hard/easy.*
Comment c'est, l'éducation musicale? *What's . . . like?*	**C'est intéressant/fascinant/ennuyeux.** *It's interesting/fascinating/boring.* **D'après moi, c'est** cool **parce que** j'adore le prof! *In my opinion, it's . . . because . . .*
Ça te plaît, l'informatique? *Do you like . . .?*	**Je trouve ça génial./Ça me plaît beaucoup!** *I think it's awesome./ I like it a lot!*

Vocabulaire et grammaire, pp. 37–39   **Online** workbooks

4 À leur avis...

Parlons Tell what these students might say about their classes.

1.

2.

3.

4.

5.

6.

5 Mes cours

Écrivons Choose four classes from the box below and tell what time you have each of these classes and what you think of them.

physique	EPS	histoire	biologie	maths
français	arts plastiques	anglais	géographie	chimie

Communication

6 Scénario

a. **Parlons** You and your classmate prepare blank schedules showing only the times classes meet at your school. Take turns asking what classes each of you has this week during the times listed. Fill in each other's schedules.

MODÈLE —**Tu as quel cours à neuf heures lundi?**
—**J'ai chimie à neuf heures.**

b. Then, take turns asking your classmate what he or she thinks about any four classes. Your classmate will give reasons why he or she likes or dislikes each class.

Grammaire à l'œuvre 1

Grammavision

Interactive TUTOR

-re verbs

You've already learned about **-er** verbs in French. Here are the forms for a group of verbs that end in **-re**.

attendre (to wait for)			
j'	attend**s**	nous	attend**ons**
tu	attend**s**	vous	attend**ez**
il/elle/on	attend	ils/elles	attend**ent**

Il **attend** Agathe.

Nous **attendons** le bus.

Notice that in the third person singular form, you do not add an ending to the stem.

Vocabulaire et grammaire, *pp. 40–41*
Cahier d'activités, *pp. 31–33*

Online workbooks

More -re verbs:

entendre	to hear
perdre	to lose
répondre (à)	to answer
vendre	to sell
rendre	to return
rendre visite à	to visit (someone)

7 Écoutons

Félix is talking to his friends on his cell phone but the signal is not very good. For each sentence you hear, write the missing subject pronoun.

8 En classe

Écrivons Lise overhears snippets of conversations between her classmates before the bell. Complete these sentences with the appropriate forms of the verbs.

1. Attention! Tu _____ ton livre. (perdre)
2. Est-ce qu'on _____ des écouteurs là-bas? (vendre)
3. Nous _____ Annabelle après la sortie. (attendre)
4. Elles ne _____ pas aux questions du professeur. (répondre)
5. Béa et Léo _____ des tee-shirts. (vendre)
6. Vous _____ Ludovic pour aller en cours? (attendre)
7. Il ne _____ pas visite à sa grand-mère. (rendre)
8. Je _____ toujours mes crayons de couleur. (perdre)
9. Tu _____ la musique? (entendre)
10. Pourquoi vous ne _____ pas à mes e-mails? (répondre)

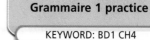
9 **Que se passe-t-il?**

Parlons Décris les photos en faisant une phrase complète. Utilise des verbes en **-re.**

MODÈLE **On vend des magazines ici.**

on

1. Olivier

2. tu

3. je

4. Rémy

5. Jérôme et moi

6. vous

10 **Faisons des phrases**

Écrivons Write complete sentences using different subjects and the words provided. Use an **-re** verb in each sentence.

MODÈLE DVD: **Je rends le DVD à Céline.**

1. des devoirs
2. un e-mail
3. la musique

4. des CD
5. des amis
6. le professeur

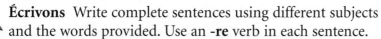

Communication

11 **Informations personnelles**

Parlons With a classmate, take turns asking each other the following questions to find out what you have in common.

1. Est-ce que tu vends tes vieux CD?
2. Est-ce que tes amis répondent toujours à tes e-mails?
3. Ton équipe *(team)* de football préférée perd souvent?
4. Est-ce que tu rends visite à tes grands-parents régulièrement?
5. Tes copains et toi, vous attendez le week-end avec impatience?
6. Est-ce que tu perds souvent tes devoirs?

La province de Québec

-ger and -cer verbs

1 Verbs that end in **-ger** are conjugated like **-er** verbs in every form except the **nous** form. In the **nous** form, you add **e** before the ending **-ons**. This is to keep the soft **ge** sound, as in the other forms.

manger *(to eat)*			
je	mange	nous	mang**e**ons
tu	manges	vous	mangez
il/elle/on	mange	ils/elles	mangent

2 Verbs that end in **-cer** are also conjugated like **-er** verbs in every form except the **nous** form. In the **nous** form, **c** becomes **ç** to keep the soft **s** sound as in the other forms.

commencer *(to begin, to start)*			
je	commence	nous	commen**ç**ons
tu	commences	vous	commencez
il/elle/on	commence	ils/elles	commencent

The verb **commencer** is followed by the preposition à and another verb in the infinitive to mean *to start to do something.*

Nous **commençons** à travailler après le week-end.

We start working after the weekend.

Vocabulaire et grammaire, *pp. 40–41*
Cahier d'activités, *pp. 31–33*

More -ger verbs:

changer	*to change*
échanger	*to exchange*
corriger	*to correct*
déranger	*to disturb*
encourager	*to encourage*
voyager	*to travel*

More -cer verbs:

placer	*to place, put*
prononcer	*to pronounce*
remplacer	*to replace*
avancer	*to go forward*
lancer	*to throw*

À la québécoise

In Quebec, people use the term **la fin de semaine** rather than **le week-end.**

⑫ Quelle forme choisir?

Lisons Complète les phrases avec le verbe approprié.

1. Elles _____ le cours de biologie à 2h.
   a. changeons   **b.** commencent   **c.** prononcent

2. Monsieur Dumas _____ les devoirs de ses élèves.
   a. corrige   **b.** encourage   **c.** encourageons

3. Pauline et moi, nous _____ pendant les vacances.
   a. encourageons   **b.** voyagez   **c.** voyageons

4. Tu _____ bien l'espagnol, Ludo!
   a. déranges   **b.** prononces   **c.** prononce

5. Nous _____ à quelle heure, aujourd'hui?
   a. changent   **b.** commençons   **c.** mange

6. J' _____ mes vieux CD.
   a. échange   **b.** avancent   **c.** encourage

7. Vous _____ visite à vos parents pendant le week-end?
   a. commencez   **b.** avancez   **c.** rendez

À remplir

Lisons/Écrivons Complete each sentence with the correct form of the verb in parentheses.

1. Est-ce que Jason _____ la classe? (déranger)
2. Je _____ mon cours d'art par un cours d'anglais. (remplacer)
3. Mia et moi, nous _____ les cours à dix heures. (commencer)
4. Nous _____ le CD. (changer)
5. Vous _____ les élèves à parler français. (encourager)
6. Nous _____ à la piscine après l'école. (nager)

14 Les illustrations parlent

Écrivons/Parlons Describe what these people are doing in the photos using an appropriate **-cer** or **-ger** verb and the subject.

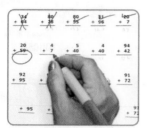
1. le professeur

2. mes copains

3. la petite fille

4. vous

5. nous

6. tu

Communication

15 Scénario

Parlons Work with a classmate to create a conversation using as many expressions from the box as you can. Act out your conversation to the rest of the class. Your classmates will vote to determine who came up with the best, most logical conversation. Be creative!

À quelle heure...?	vendredi	génial	déranger
informatique	professeur	sympa	commencer
ennuyeux	français	aimer	encourager

La province de Québec

cent dix-neuf **119**

Application 1

16 **La journée d'Anne**

Parlons Anne est très occupée *(busy)* aujourd'hui. Quels cours est-ce qu'elle a aux heures indiquées?

1. 8h00

2. 9h15

3. 10h05

4. 11h30

5. 2h45

6. 4h10

Un peu plus

Le with days of the week

To say that you do something **regularly on a certain day of the week,** put **le** before the day of the week.

> J'ai anglais **le** vendredi.
> *I have English class on Fridays.*

To say that you are doing something **on one particular day of the week,** do not use the article in front of the day of the week.

> J'ai un examen jeudi.
> *I have an exam on (this) Thursday.*

Vocabulaire et grammaire, *p. 42*
Cahier d'activités, *pp. 31–33*

Online workbooks

17 **Écoutons**

Listen as Farid's friends talk about their school schedules. For each statement, decide if they are talking about something that happens a) **every week** or b) **only on a specific day.**

Flash culture

The 24-hour time system (**l'heure officielle**) is used to give schedules for transportation, schools, stores, and movies. School generally begins at 8h00 (**huit heures**) and lets out (**la sortie**) around 17h00 (**dix-sept heures**) or 18h00 (**dix-huit heures**). Be careful not to mix the two systems, for instance; you must say **seize heures quinze**, never **seize heures et quart**. The expressions **et demie, et quart** and **moins le quart** are not used in official time.

Do you know of a context when the 24 hour clock is used in the U.S.?

18 **Ma semaine**

Écrivons Complète les phrases suivantes pour décrire ta semaine.

1. Je commence les cours à…

2. Le vendredi soir, mes copains et moi, nous…

3. Le lundi matin, j'ai…

4. Après l'école, mes amis et moi, nous…

5. Le week-end, je…

19 **Un emploi du temps idéal**

Écrivons The French club is doing a survey on how students picture an ideal week. You've been asked to contribute by describing your ideal weekly schedule.

MODÈLE   **Le lundi, je surfe sur Internet. Le mardi et le jeudi, je dessine…**

Communication

HOLT **SoundBooth**
ONLINE RECORDING

20 **Interview**

Parlons Imagine that you're an exchange student at the **Lycée Corneille** in France. The school newspaper reporter (your classmate) is interviewing you about your class schedule. Tell what days and times (use the **heure officielle**) you have each class and give your opinion of your classes.

EMPLOI DU TEMPS

	LUNDI	MARDI	MERCREDI	JEUDI	VENDREDI	SAMEDI	DIMANCHE
8h00	Anglais	Biologie	Anglais	Géographie	Chimie		LIBRE
9h00	Maths	Allemand	Maths	Français	Maths	Maths	
10h00	Récréation	Récréation	Récréation	Récréation	Récréation	EPS	
10h15	Histoire	Physique	Histoire	Physique	Arts plastiques		
11h15	Informatique		Informatique	Musique	Informatique	**Sortie**	
12h15	**Déjeuner**	**Déjeuner**	**Sortie**	**Déjeuner**	**Déjeuner**		
14h00	Arts plastiques	Chimie		Chimie	Biologie		
15h00	Chimie	Français		Informatique	Allemand		
16h00	Récréation	**Sortie**		Récréation	Récréation		
16h15	Français			Anglais	Histoire		
17h15	**Sortie**			**Sortie**	**Sortie**		

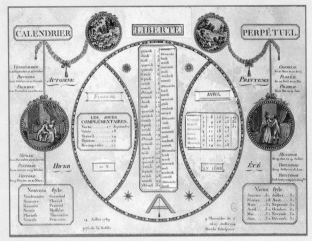

Calendrier révolutionnaire

Culture appliquée
Les jours de la semaine

In French, five out of seven days **(samedi** and **dimanche** being the exceptions) take their name from a Roman god or goddess: **lundi,** "day of the moon" **(la lune), mardi,** "day of Mars," **mercredi,** "day of Mercury," **jeudi,** "day of Jupiter" and **vendredi,** "day of Venus." But, following the French revolution, the newly formed Republic created its own calendar, renaming the days and the months. The calendar was in use for about twelve years.

Ton calendrier

Create a French calendar for the current school year.

Step 1 On twelve different sheets of paper, write the months and days of the week in French. Remember that the first day of the French week is Monday. The months in French are: **janvier, février, mars, avril, mai, juin, juillet, août, septembre, octobre, novembre,** and **décembre.**

Step 2 After you have created your calendar, look up the school vacation schedule for France and Quebec on the Internet. Mark the French vacation dates in red and the Quebec vacation dates in blue. Include all the **jours fériés** (national holidays) for both France and Quebec.

Step 3 Decorate your calendar with photos of francophone countries found in magazines or on the Internet.

Recherches Right after the French revolution in 1789, the French used a different calendar. Research the **calendrier révolutionnaire.** What were the names of the days and months? Were there any other differences?

Comparaisons

Un conseil de classe

Les délégués de classe

You're a high school student in France, and you campaign to be elected student representative so that:

    a. you can help plan the end of the year dance.

    b. you can represent your class at the class council.

    c. you can plan the class fundraiser.

In France, at the beginning of the school year, each class elects its **délégués de classe** *(student representatives).* The **délégués de classe** represent their fellow students during the **conseil de classe** *(class council).* He or she can defend students and also participate in any other conversations at the same level as the teachers and administrators. Teachers, administrators and **délégués de classe** of each grade meet three times a year. Each student's grade and the academic results of the entire class are discussed during those meetings. Other topics discussed may include discipline and classroom logistics. The **délégués de classe** also attend the **conseil de discipline** *(disciplinary council).*

ET TOI?

1. What role does the student representative play at your school?

2. What role does the school council play at your school?

Communauté

Vacations

Are all the schools in your state or county on vacation at the same time? How many weeks of vacation do students at your school get each year? Do public and private schools take the same vacation days? If there is an international school in your community, find out if they follow a different vacation calendar (such as the school vacation calendar of the country of origin) or if their vacation is the same as the other schools in your area.

Vive les vacances!

Vocabulaire
à l'œuvre **2**

DVD
Télé-vocab

Un magasin de fournitures scolaires à Québec

un stylo

un sac (à dos)

un dictionnaire

une trousse

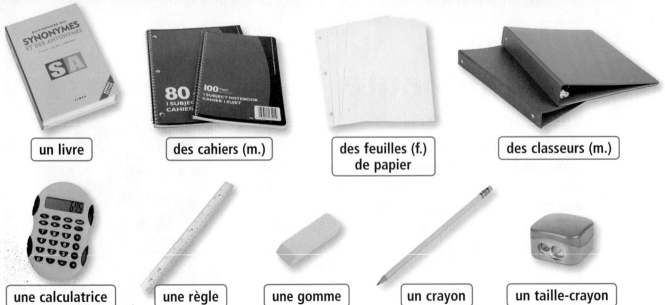

un livre

des cahiers (m.)

des feuilles (f.) de papier

des classeurs (m.)

une calculatrice

une règle

une gomme

un crayon

un taille-crayon

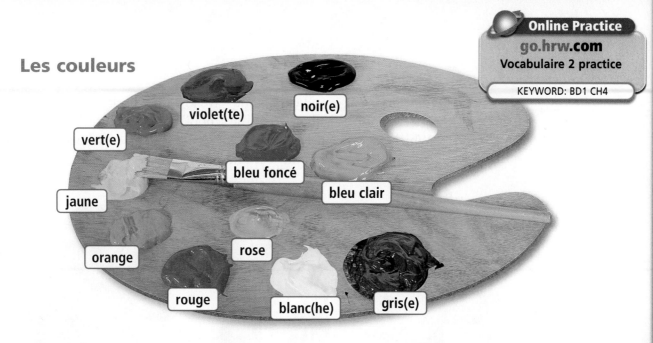

violet(te)

noir(e)

vert(e)

bleu foncé

bleu clair

jaune

orange

rose

rouge

blanc(he)

gris(e)

Vocabulaire 2

Les nombres de 31 à 201

31	40	50	60	70
trente et un	quarante	cinquante	soixante	soixante-dix
71	**72**	**80**	**81**	**90**
soixante et onze	soixante-douze	quatre-vingts	quatre-vingt-un	quatre-vingt-dix
91	**100**	**101**	**200**	**201**
quatre-vingt-onze	cent	cent un	deux cents	deux cent un

D'autres mots utiles

un portable	*laptop computer*	**un short**	*shorts*
un mobile	*cell phone*	**un sweat-shirt**	*sweat-shirt*
des baskets (f.)	*sneakers*	**un tee-shirt**	*T-shirt*

Exprimons-nous!

To ask others what they need and tell what you need	
De quoi tu as besoin? *What do you need?*	**J'ai besoin de** cinq livres et **d'**un stylo.
Qu'est-ce qu'il te faut pour les maths? *What do you need for . . . ?*	**Il me faut** une règle. *I need . . .*
Tu pourrais me prêter ta calculatrice? *Could you lend me . . . ?*	**Tiens./Voilà.** *Here.*
Tu as un dictionnaire **à me prêter?** *. . . that I could borrow?*	**Désolé(e).** Je n'ai pas de dictionnaire. *Sorry.*

Interactive
TUTOR

Vocabulaire et grammaire,
pp. 43–45

Online workbooks

21 Écoutons

Vincent, Denise, and Guillaume have lost their backpacks. Listen to the calls they left at the school's lost-and-found office. Which backpack belongs to which student? Whose backpack was not turned in to the lost-and-found office?

1.   2.   3.

22 La liste de fournitures

Écrivons You're in charge of purchasing school supplies for several classes. Tell what supplies you need for each class.

MODÈLE   français: cahier (82), dictionnaire (31)
   Pour le cours de français, j'ai besoin de quatre-vingt-deux cahiers et de trente et un dictionnaires.

1. maths: règle (48), calculatrice (57), classeur (78)
2. arts plastiques: crayon (63), gomme (95), trousse (100)
3. EPS: tee-shirt (93), short (69)
4. histoire: livre (73), cahier (26)
5. géographie: carte (33), cahier (72)

Exprimons-nous!

To inquire about and buy something	
You might say	*The salesperson might say*
Je cherche une trousse, s'il vous plaît. *I'm looking for . . .*	**De quelle couleur?** *In what color?*
Le sac à dos, **c'est combien?**	**C'est** dix-huit dollars quatre-vingt-cinq.
Il/Elle est à combien, le stylo/la règle? *How much is the . . . ?*	**Il/Elle est à** deux dollars. *It's . . .*
Merci, monsieur. *Thank you, . . .*	**Je vous en prie./À votre service.** *You're welcome.*

Vocabulaire et grammaire, pp. 43–45   **Online workbooks**

23 Au magasin

Lisons/Écrivons Annick is shopping for school supplies with her mother. Complete their conversation logically.

MME MILLET	Alors, tu as besoin de quoi?
ANNICK	Pour les maths, ___1___ une calculatrice.
MME MILLET	Pardon monsieur, ___2___, la calculatrice bleue?
LE VENDEUR	___3___ vingt-quatre dollars.
ANNICK	___4___ un dictionnaire anglais s'il vous plaît.
LE VENDEUR	Oui, voilà les dictionnaires anglais.
ANNICK	Merci, monsieur.
LE VENDEUR	___5___.

24 De quelle couleur est...?

Écrivons Write complete sentences to describe Farid and Amélie's clothing and school supplies. Be sure to include colors in your descriptions.

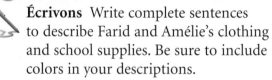

Communication

25 Scénario

Parlons You left home in a hurry today and are missing a lot of school supplies. Take turns asking your classmate if you can borrow school supplies that you need for three of your classes.

MODÈLE —J'ai histoire à neuf heures. Tu as des feuilles de papier à me prêter?
—Oui, voilà… /Non, désolé(e)…

26 Scénario

Parlons You're at a stationery store purchasing items for your different classes. With a classmate, take turns playing the roles of the customer and the salesperson. Buy at least three items and be sure to specify what colors the items should be.

Objectifs
- the verbs *préférer* and *acheter*
- adjectives as nouns

Grammaire
à l'œuvre 2

DVD
Grammavision

The verbs *préférer* and *acheter*

Interactive TUTOR

The verbs **préférer** and **acheter** follow a slightly different pattern from other **-er** verbs.

1 Here are the forms of the verb **préférer** *(to prefer).*

je préfère	nous préférons
tu préfères	vous préférez
il/elle/on préfère	ils/elles préfèrent

Je préfère l'histoire.

Verbs like **préférer:**

espérer	*to hope*
répéter	*to repeat/ to rehearse*

2 Here are the forms of the verb **acheter** *(to buy).*

j' achète	nous achetons
tu achètes	vous achetez
il/elle/on achète	ils/elles achètent

Il achète le journal.

Verbs like **acheter:**

amener	*to bring along someone*
emmener	*to take along someone*
lever	*to raise*
promener	*to take for a walk*

Vocabulaire et grammaire, *pp. 46–47*
Cahier d'activités, *pp. 35–37*

Online workbooks

27 Une petite note

Lisons Your Canadian e-pal wrote you an e-mail telling you about school supplies she's buying, but her e-mail program erased all the accents. Add all the missing accents.

> Aujourd'hui, ma mere et moi, on promene le chien et on fait les magasins. Nous achetons des fournitures scolaires. J'achete trois cahiers. Mes amis et moi, nous preferons les classeurs mais le professeur prefere les cahiers. On achete aussi un dictionnaire et des stylos. Tu as un dictionnaire pour ton cours de francais? Et les eleves de ton ecole, ils achetent beaucoup de fournitures scolaires?
>
> A+
> Arielle

28 Des phrases complètes

Écrivons Create complete sentences using the fragments below. Be sure to make all necessary changes. Add any missing elements.

1. nous / répéter / Hamlet de Shakespeare / lundi et jeudi
2. Madame Rigaud / promener / petit-fils / au parc
3. Kevin / ne pas amener / sœur / au cinéma
4. vous / acheter / trente / gomme
5. tu / préférer / trousse / bleue / ou / rouge / trousse

29 Que font-ils?

Parlons Décris chaque photo en utilisant le verbe donné.

| 1. préférer | 2. acheter | 3. emmener | 4. promener |

30 Des goûts et des couleurs

Lisons/Écrivons You're responding to a survey conducted on your school campus. Answer the following questions.

1. Quelle couleur est-ce que tu préfères pour les sacs à dos?
2. Qu'est-ce que tu achètes pour le cours d'EPS?
3. Tu lèves souvent la main pour répondre en classe?
4. Est-ce qu'on répète souvent en cours de musique?
5. Dans quel cours tu espères avoir de bonnes notes *(grades)*?

Communication

HOLT **SoundBooth**
ONLINE RECORDING

31 Sondage

Écrivons/Parlons Create a survey and ask your classmates their preferences of school supplies for their classes. For example, do they prefer a notebook or a binder for math, or which colors do they prefer their school supplies to be?

MODÈLE **Tu préfères un sac à dos rouge ou jaune?**

Adjectives as nouns

Interactive
TUTOR

1 To avoid repetition, you can drop a **noun,** leaving an **article** and an **adjective** to stand for it. The article and adjective agree in gender and number with the noun that was dropped.

drop the noun ⟶ ⟵ *T-shirt is understood*

le **tee-shirt bleu** ou le **blanc**
the blue T-shirt or the white one

2 You often use this when talking about preferences.

—Est-ce que vous aimez **la grande** télé ou **la petite**?

—J'aime **la grande.**

Vocabulaire et grammaire, *pp. 46–47*
Cahier d'activités, *pp. 35–37*

Online workbooks

En anglais

In English, you can use an adjective as a noun by putting *the* before the adjective and *one* or *ones* after the adjective.

I like *the blue one.*

When someone says "I like the blue one," how do listeners know to what object the person is referring?

In French too, adjectives can be used as nouns.

J'aime **la bleue.**

32 Lesquels?

Lisons/Écrivons Complète les phrases avec **le, la, l'** ou **les.**

1. Il me faut une règle. Tu aimes _____ jaune?
2. Tu aimes le portable gris foncé ou tu préfères _____ blanc?
3. Il aime la nouvelle télé ou _____ vieille?
4. Qui sont les amies de Mia? _____ blondes ou _____ brunes?
5. Les shorts roses sont beaux, mais je préfère _____ violets.

33 Quelle couleur?

Lisons Lise and Aurore are passing each other notes about school supplies they saw earlier at the store. Put their notes in order.

— La rose est adorable!

— Non, je vais prendre les bleus.

— Qu'est-ce que j'achète? Le sac bleu ou le blanc?

— Oui, la verte est mignonne aussi. Et tu as des cahiers?

— Bon, le bleu alors. J'ai aussi besoin d'une trousse.

— Pas le blanc! Je préfère le bleu.

— Non, j'aime mieux la verte.

34 Écoutons

Listen as Coralie and her friends shop for school supplies. For each statement, decide which object the speaker is talking about.

1. a backpack / pens
2. a binder / a calculator
3. TVs / cell phones
4. T-shirts / sneakers
5. erasers / pencils
6. a notebook / a pencil case

35 **C'est à qui?**

Parlons Ton frère Timothée et ta sœur Adèle ont des goûts *(tastes)* très différents. De quelles couleurs sont les fournitures de Timothée et d'Adèle?

MODÈLE   trousse: **la bleue est à** *(belongs to)* **Adèle et la verte est à Timothée.**

1. sac à dos
2. règle
3. baskets

4. dictionnaire
5. tee-shirts
6. short

36 **Préférences**

Écrivons Write a note to your French cousin about school supplies you typically buy at the start of the school year. Tell what supplies you buy, how many of each, and if you're particular about any colors.

Communication

37 **Scénario**

Parlons You're out shopping with a classmate for school supplies. Role-play the scene in the store with your classmate. You should talk about the items you need and exchange opinions about sizes and colors.

MODÈLE   —**Il me faut des baskets pour EPS. J'aime les jaunes.**
—**Pas moi. Je préfère les gris foncé.**
—**Est-ce que tu aimes les grandes trousses noires?**
—**Les grandes? …**

Application 2

38 **On rappe!**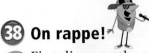

First, listen to the song **De quoi tu as besoin… ?** Then, rewrite the rap song by substituting the various items with ones that you might need. With a classmate, perform your song to the class.

39 **Quel choix!**

Écrivons Look at this brochure you received for a back-to-school sale. Write a note to your parent telling which of these school supplies you need for your classes and what colors you prefer.

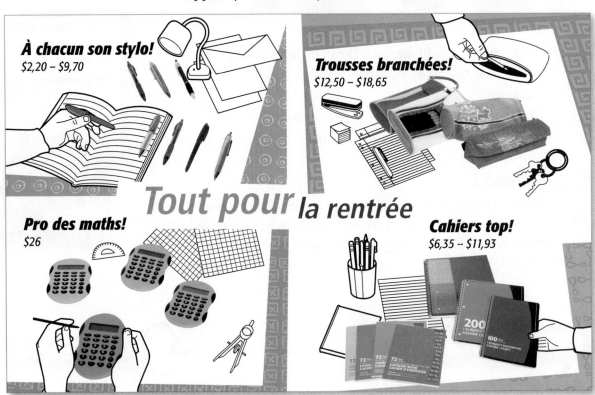

À chacun son stylo!
$2,20 – $9,70

Trousses branchées!
$12,50 – $18,65

Tout pour la rentrée

Pro des maths!
$26

Cahiers top!
$6,35 – $11,93

Un peu plus

Agreement with numbers

You've already learned that the numbers **quatre-vingts** and multiples of **cent** take an **-s** unless they are followed by another number.

The number **un** changes to **une** when followed by a feminine noun.

M. Rocher a **vingt et un** livres. Il a aussi **vingt et une** règles.

Vocabulaire et grammaire, *p. 48*
Cahier d'activités, *pp. 35–37*

Online workbooks

40 L'inventaire

Parlons You're on the phone, confirming an order for a French stationery store, **Papeterie Gailland.** Say the numbers and items listed, in French, to make sure that you have the order right.

Papeterie Gailland			
80	taille-crayons	51	règles
201	cahiers	88	stylos
100	classeurs	72	crayons

À la suisse

In Switzerland, as well as in Belgium, you will hear **septante** and **nonante** rather than **soixante-dix** and **quatre-vingt-dix**. In Switzerland, people also use **octante** or **huitante** instead of **quatre-vingts**, depending on the region.

Communication

HOLT SoundBooth ONLINE RECORDING

41 Sondage

Écrivons/Parlons You're working at a stationery store. Determine which school supplies are most popular by conducting a survey among your classmates to find out what they buy at the beginning of each year. Report the results of your survey in the form of a bar graph or a pie chart.

42 Histoire à raconter

Parlons With a classmate, tell what each person in the illustrations is saying.

La province de Québec

Télé-roman
Que le meilleur gagne!
Épisode 4

DVD

STRATÉGIE

Understanding a character's motives To understand a character, you must first understand his or her motives: why he or she is doing something or acting a certain way. To understand someone's motives, you must watch his or her actions and behavior. In this episode, Yasmina and Kevin interact for the first time. Judging by Yasmina's behavior toward Kevin, can you guess how she feels about him? Is Kevin's behavior the same at the beginning of the episode and toward the end? Why do you think that is? How about Adrien's attitude? What is his motive for being upset?

Yasmina téléphone à Laurie...

1

Laurie Allô?
Yasmina J'ai une histoire incroyable à te raconter!
Laurie Vas-y. Raconte!

3

2 *Yasmina et Adrien sonnent à la mystérieuse adresse.*

Kevin Oui?

4

Adrien Kevin! Quelle surprise! Dis, on a trouvé ce cahier dans un café près du lycée. Il est à toi?
Kevin Oui, c'est mon cahier de géo. Je l'ai perdu hier.

5

Yasmina Je t'ai vu parler avec mademoiselle N'Guyen.
Kevin Ben… oui, c'était pour le concours.
Yasmina Tu fais le concours? Nous aussi, on fait le concours!

6

Kevin On peut manger ensemble. Mardi, ça te va?
Yasmina OK. Ça marche. Voici mon e-mail.

7

Adrien Euh… Vous savez, il y a un match de foot à la télé. Alors…
Kevin Ah oui, c'est vrai! Bon, allez, salut!

8

Adrien Kevin ne voulait pas nous parler et puis… on mentionne le concours et boum! C'est un peu bizarre, tu ne trouves pas?
Yasmina Non. Pas du tout! Toi, par contre, tu es un peu nul! Salut!

9

Yasmina Je vais manger avec Kevin Granieri!
Laurie Oui. Mais, tu sais, Adrien a peut-être raison…

AS-TU COMPRIS?

1. Why does Yasmina call Laurie?
2. Who opens the door to Yasmina and Adrien?
3. What is Yasmina curious about?
4. What do Kevin and Yasmina decide to do?
5. What is Adrien's reaction to Yasmina and Kevin's conversation? Why?

Prochain épisode:
Our characters will get a new clue about the mysterious high school. Who do you think will find the answer?

Lecture et écriture

STRATÉGIE pour lire

Using background knowledge Background knowledge is what you already know about a subject. Taking a moment to recall what you already know about the type of text and the topic will help you with unfamiliar vocabulary and with making predictions as you read.

A **Avant la lecture**

What do you know about the play *Hamlet* by William Shakespeare? Do you know any famous lines from the play? What kind of conversation might take place between a student named Hamlet and a teacher?

L'accent grave
de Jacques Prévert

LE PROFESSEUR —Élève Hamlet!

L'ÉLÈVE HAMLET *(sursautant)* —… Hein…
Quoi… Pardon… Qu'est-ce qui se passe[1]…
Qu'est-ce qu'il y a… Qu'est-ce que c'est ?…

LE PROFESSEUR *(mécontent)* —Vous ne pouvez
pas répondre « présent » comme tout le
monde[2] ? Pas possible, vous êtes encore
dans les nuages[3].

L'ÉLÈVE HAMLET —Être ou ne pas être dans
les nuages !

LE PROFESSEUR —Suffit. Pas tant de
manières. Et conjuguez-moi le verbe
être, comme tout le monde, c'est tout
ce que je vous demande.

L'ÉLÈVE HAMLET —To be…

LE PROFESSEUR —En français,
s'il vous plaît, comme tout
le monde.

L'ÉLÈVE HAMLET —Bien, monsieur.
(Il conjugue :)
Je suis ou je ne suis pas
Tu es ou tu n'es pas
Il est ou il n'est pas
Nous sommes ou nous ne sommes pas…

LE PROFESSEUR *(excessivement mécontent)*
—Mais c'est vous qui n'y êtes pas[4],
mon pauvre ami[5] !

L'ÉLÈVE HAMLET —C'est exact,
monsieur le professeur,
Je suis « où » je ne suis pas
Et, dans le fond, hein, à la réflexion[6],
Être « où » ne pas être
C'est peut-être aussi la question.

---

1. What's happening   2. like everybody else
3. daydreaming   4. you're the one who doesn't get it
5. my poor friend   6. if you really think about it

B Compréhension

Est-ce que les phrases suivantes sont **a) vraies** ou **b) fausses?**

1. Hamlet a cours d'anglais.
2. Il n'écoute pas le professeur.
3. Hamlet est différent des autres *(other)* élèves.
4. Hamlet conjugue bien le verbe «être».
5. Le professeur trouve qu'Hamlet est pénible.

C Après la lecture

Which words in the scene look alike except for an accent? What do the words mean? Why do you think the scene is called **L'accent grave?** What is the connection between the scene and Shakespeare's play, *Hamlet?*

Lecture et écriture

novembre	
lundi	**mardi**
	7h30 musique
8h15 maths	8h15 français
10h30 anglais	10h30 sciences
Informatique:	Géographie:
crayon, cahier,	stylo, cahier,
calculatrice,	atlas, livres
livres, stylo	

Interactive **TUTOR**

Espace écriture

STRATÉGIE pour écrire

Using chronology When describing sequential events or activities, it helps to arrange your ideas chronologically. You can use lists, timelines, or charts.

Emploi du temps

Imagine that you are helping a foreign exchange student who has just arrived at your school. Write a conversation in which you ask what classes he or she has and when, and you tell the student what school supplies he or she needs. Include information in your conversation that would be helpful to a new student.

1 Plan

Divide a sheet of paper into five columns, one for each school day. Write classes and class times for each day in the appropriate column. At the bottom of each column, list the school supplies needed for that day's classes.

2 Rédaction

Using your chart, write your conversation. Introduce yourself and ask what classes the exchange student has. He or she responds, including what time the classes are. Then, tell what school supplies he or she needs. End your conversation by giving the student a way to reach you if needed.

3 Correction

Read your draft at least two times, comparing it to your chart. Check spelling and punctuation.

4 Application

Practice your conversation with a classmate and perform it for the class. You may wish to use props and create a simple set to use during your performance.

Prépare-toi pour l'examen

Interactive
TUTOR

❶ Vocabulaire 1
- to ask about classes
- to ask for and give opinions
pp. 112–115

① Complete the dialogue according to your class schedule.

—Tu as quels cours le jeudi matin?

—J'ai ___1___, ___2___, ___3___ et ___4___.

—Quand est-ce que tu as anglais?

—J'ai anglais ___5___.

—Comment est ton cours d'anglais?

—Il est ___6___.

❷ Grammaire 1
- *-re* verbs
- *-ger* and *-cer* verbs
Un peu plus
- *le* with days of the week
pp. 116–121

② Tu entends les choses suivantes pendant la récréation. Complète chaque phrase avec la forme du verbe approprié.

1. À quelle heure est-ce que le cours d'histoire _____ (commencer)?
2. Est-ce que nous _____ (manger) bientôt?
3. Pierre et Jean-Martin _____ (lancer) des feuilles de papier. Ils _____ (déranger) toujours *(always)* les profs!
4. Est-ce que tu _____ (entendre) le chien?
5. Nous _____ (commencer) à _____ (corriger) les devoirs.
6. Pierre et Jean-Martin _____ (perdre) toujours leurs devoirs.
7. Mireille et moi, nous _____ (répondre) souvent aux questions du prof.
8. Nicole et Élise, qu'est-ce que vous _____ (attendre)?

❸ Vocabulaire 2
- to ask others what they need and tell what you need
- to inquire about and buy something
pp. 124–127

③ The following items belong to your friend Frédéric. Write complete sentences describing the items he owns. Be sure to include the color of each item.

1.

2.

3.

4.

5.

6.

4 Isabelle and her friends are shopping for school supplies. Complete their sentences with the appropriate form of the verb or noun.

1. —Est-ce que tu _____ (préférer) le classeur bleu
   ou _____ (rouge)?

2. —Est-ce que vous _____ (acheter) les feuilles de papier
   jaunes ou _____ (blanc)?

3. —Isabelle, est-ce qu'Alice et Ivan _____ (acheter) les stylos
   noirs ou _____ (violet)?

4. —Est-ce que vous _____ (préférer) la trousse verte ou
   _____ (gris)?

4 Grammaire 2
- the verbs *préférer*
  and *acheter*
- adjectives as nouns
Un peu plus
- agreement with
  numbers
  pp. 128–133

5 Answer the following questions.

1. What's a **Cégep**?
2. What degree do Canadian students get after the **secondaire?**
3. What is **l'heure officielle**? Where is it often used?

5 Culture
- Comparaisons
  p. 123
- Flash culture
  **pp. 116, 118, 120,
  128, 133**

6 Aline et ses amis achètent des fournitures scolaires. Écoute chaque phrase et indique si c'est **a) le vendeur/la vendeuse** ou **b) le client/la cliente** qui parle.

7 Utilise les illustrations pour décrire la journée de Jean-Claude.

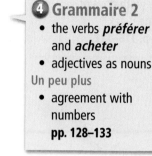

a.

b.

c.

d.

Prépare-toi pour l'examen

Grammaire 1
- *-re* verbs
- *-ger* and *-cer* verbs
Un peu plus
- *le* with days of the week
  pp. 116–121

Résumé: Grammaire 1

Regular **-re** verbs follow a fixed pattern.

attendre			
j'	attends	nous	attendons
tu	attends	vous	attendez
il/elle/on	attend	ils/elles	attendent

Verbs ending in **-ger** and **-cer** have a spelling change in the **nous** form: **nous mangeons** and **nous commençons.** The verb **commencer** + **à** + infinitive means *to start to do something.*

Ma sœur **commence à** étudier à 6h le soir.

To say that you do something regularly on a certain day of the week, use le before the day of the week.

To say that you are doing something on one particular day of the week, don't use the article in front of the day.

Grammaire 2
- the verbs *préférer* and *acheter*
- adjectives as nouns
Un peu plus
- agreement with numbers
  pp. 128–133

Résumé: Grammaire 2

The verbs **préférer** and **acheter** have spelling changes in all forms except the **nous** and **vous** forms.

Tu préfères nager à la piscine?

You can use colors and other adjectives as nouns to avoid repetition. Use the appropriate article **le, la, l',** or **les** in front of the adjective.

J'adore la chemise verte mais j'aime bien la bleue aussi.

Remember these rules with numbers:

- **Quatre-vingts** and multiples of **cent** (**deux cents**) have an -**s** unless they are followed by another number (**deux cent trois**).
- The number **un** changes to **une** when followed by a feminine noun (**trente et une calculatrices**).

🎧 Lettres et sons

The nasal sound [ã]

This sound is called a nasal because you make it by passing the air through the back of your mouth and nose. The nasal sound [ã] has four possible spellings: **an, am, en,** and **em.** These letter combinations don't represent a nasal sound if another vowel follows the **n** or **m,** or if the **n** or **m** is doubled. You have to learn the pronunciation when you learn the word.

Jeux de langue
Ta tante t'attend.
J'ai tant de tantes. Quelle tante m'attend?
Ta tante Antoinette t'attend.

Dictée
Écris les phrases de la dictée.

To ask and tell about classes

l'allemand (m.)	German	la semaine	week
les arts (m.) plastiques	art class	la sortie	dismissal
aujourd'hui	today	le week-end	weekend
la biologie	biology	de l'après-midi (m.)	in the afternoon
la chimie	chemistry	demain	tomorrow
les devoirs	homework	du matin	in the morning
l'examen (m.)	test	du soir	in the evening
l'éducation (f.) musicale	music	Il est... heure(s)	It is . . . o'clock.
l'EPS (éducation (f.) physique et sportive)	physical education	À quelle heure tu as...?	At what time do you have . . . ?
l'espagnol (m.)	Spanish	Quand est-ce que tu as...?	When do you have . . . ?
la géographie	geography	Quelle heure est-il?	What time is it?
l'histoire (f.)	history	Quel jour est-ce que tu as...?	What day do you have . . . ?
l'informatique (f.)	computer science	Tu as quel cours...?	What class do you have . . . ?
le jour	day	J'ai... lundi.	I have . . . on Monday.
maintenant	now	J'ai... le lundi, le mercredi, et...	I have . . . on Mondays, Wednesdays and. . .
les mathématiques (f.)	mathematics	J'ai... à...	I have . . . at . . .
les matières (f.)	school subjects		
la physique	physics	Les jours de la semaine .... see page 113	
la récréation	break	To ask for and give opinions .... see page 114	

Résumé: Vocabulaire 2

To tell what you need

des baskets (f.)	sneakers	De quoi tu as besoin?	What do you need?
un cahier	notebook	Désolé(e).	Sorry.
une calculatrice	calculator	J'ai besoin de/Il me faut...	I need . . .
un classeur	binder	Qu'est-ce qu'il te faut pour...?	What do you need for . . . ?
un crayon (de couleur)	pencil (colored)	Tiens./Voilà./	Here.
un dictionnaire	dictionary	Tu as... à me prêter?	Do you have . . . that I could borrow?
une feuille de papier	sheet of paper		
une gomme	eraser	Tu pourrais me prêter...?	Could you lend me . . . ?
un livre	book	Les couleurs .... see page 125	
un mobile	cell phone	Les nombres de 30 à 201 .... see page 125	
un portable	cell phone or laptop		
une règle	ruler	**To inquire about and buy something**	
un sac (à dos)	backpack	Je cherche...	I'm looking for...
un short	shorts	..., c'est combien? C'est...	How much is the . . . ?/It's . . .
un stylo	pen	Il/Elle est à combien, ...?	How much is the . . . ?
un sweat-shirt/un tee-shirt	sweat-shirt/T-shirt	Il/Elle est à... dollars.	It is . . . dollars.
un taille-crayon	pencil sharpener	De quelle couleur?	In what color?
une trousse	pencil case	À votre service./ Je vous en prie.	You're welcome.

Révisions cumulatives

1 Look at the illustrations below. Match each statement you hear with the appropriate illustration.

a.

b.

c.

d.

2 Adrien, a French-speaking teenager from Montreal has just been accepted as an exchange student in the United States. Read his e-mail to his host parents and then tell whether each statement below is **a) vrai** or **b) faux.** Correct the false statements.

Bonjour! Je m'appelle Adrien Richard. Je suis de Montréal. J'ai une sœur et deux frères. Je suis assez petit et brun. J'ai les yeux bruns. Je ne suis pas timide! J'adore discuter avec des amis, envoyer des e-mails et sortir avec mes copains. J'aime aussi lire des bandes dessinées, aller au cinéma et faire du sport. Au lycée, j'étudie l'anglais, le français, la physique, les maths, l'informatique et l'histoire canadienne. Je n'aime pas les maths. C'est difficile. Je préfère l'informatique. Je trouve ça intéressant. J'aime aussi l'anglais. C'est facile!
J'arrive à l'aéroport le 5 juin à 14h.
À bientôt!
Adrien

1. Adrien n'a pas de sœur.
2. Il aime les cours d'anglais et d'informatique.
3. Il n'aime pas les maths parce que c'est difficile.
4. Il est timide.
5. Il n'aime pas voir des films.

 3 You've just finished your first day of school. Your parents want to know what classes you have and how you like them. Tell your parents about your classes and any school supplies you need.

4 Regarde ce tableau de Matisse et réponds aux questions suivantes.

1. Quelles couleurs est-ce qu'il y a dans ce tableau?
2. Est-ce qu'il y a une personne dans ce tableau?
3. Qu'est-ce que cette personne fait?
4. Ça te plaît, ce tableau?
5. Avec un(e) camarade de classe, discutez en anglais, le style de ce tableau. Présentez vos commentaires à la classe.

Matisse, Henri (1869–1954). Female Creole Dancer. 1950. Cutout, 205 x120 cm. © Succession H. Matisse/ARS, NY.

La Danseuse créole d'Henri Matisse

5 You saw an ad asking for volunteers for peer tutoring on the school bulletin board. Volunteers need to send information about the times they're available. Write a letter to the school counselor telling him/her which classes you have and when you're available. You might mention your favorite classes.

6

À ton tour

Le nouveau Work in groups of three or four to welcome a new exchange student to your school. Start with a greeting and introductions. Describe a typical day at your school. Tell what classes you each have and at what times. Discuss what you and your friends like to do after school. Ask the new student how he/she feels about various school subjects and find out what he/she likes to do after school and on the weekends.

Géoculture

Géoculture
L'Ouest de la France

▲ **La côte de Granit Rose,** dans le nord de la Bretagne, offre un paysage unique.

▼ **À Carnac,** en 4000 avant J.-C., les habitants ont dressé des pierres (*stones*), appelées «menhirs», pour des raisons mystérieuses.

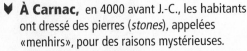

▲ **Le pont de Normandie** est situé au Havre. C'est un des plus grands ponts à haubans (*suspension bridge*) du monde.

Almanach

Population
Plus de 9 millions d'habitants

Villes principales
Rennes, Nantes, Tours, Le Mans, Saumur, Rouen, Le Havre

Économie
agriculture, élevage, industrie automobile, construction navale, tourisme

▼ **Les coiffes bretonnes** sont des bonnets traditionnels. Aujourd'hui, les Bretonnes portent encore la coiffe pour les fêtes folkloriques.

Savais-tu que...?

Les marées (*tides*) de la baie du Mont-Saint-Michel sont très fortes. Leur vitesse peut atteindre (*reach*) 30 km/h (*18 mph*) au printemps.

▼ **La réserve naturelle des Sept-Îles** abrite une grande variété d'oiseaux *(birds)* marins.

▲ **Les maisons troglodytes,** près de Saumur, sont des maisons construites dans la roche calcaire *(limestone)*.

▼ **En Normandie,** on élève des vaches *(cows)* et on cultive des pommes.

Manche

Côte de Granit Rose

Les Sept-Îles

Saint-Malo

BRETAGNE

Fougères •

Rennes •

Carnac •

HAUTE-NORMANDIE

Le Havre •

Bayeux •

BASSE-NORMANDIE

■ Mont-Saint-Michel

Le Mans •

PAYS DE LA LOIRE

Loire

Nantes • Saumur •

• Rouen

Orléans •

• Chambord

Tours •

Villandry • • Chenonceaux

CENTRE

OCÉAN ATLANTIQUE

▼ **Villandry,** un des châteaux de la Loire, est connu pour ses magnifiques jardins à la française.

➤ **Le Mont-Saint-Michel** est une abbaye construite sur un rocher qui devient une île *(island)* pendant les grandes marées.

Géo-quiz
Qu'est-ce que c'est, un «menhir»?

145

Découvre l'Ouest de la France

Histoire

▼ **La tapisserie de Bayeux,** longue de 70 mètres, raconte l'histoire de l'invasion de l'Angleterre par Guillaume le Conquérant en 1066.

Musée de la tapisserie, Bayeux, France

©Bettman/Corbis

◄ **Les cimetières américains** en Normandie rappellent le débarquement des Alliés qui a eu lieu le 6 juin 1944.

▲ **Jeanne d'Arc,** à l'âge de 17 ans, libère Orléans des Anglais pendant la guerre de Cent Ans.

Architecture

➤ **Fougères** est une ville fortifiée de l'est de la Bretagne. Ses remparts et son château sont un bel exemple de l'architecture défensive du Moyen Âge.

▼ **Le château de Chambord** reflète le style de la Renaissance. Ici, les tours ne sont pas défensives mais décoratives.

Gastronomie

➤ **Le plateau de fruits de mer** est composé de crabes, de langoustines, de crevettes, d'huîtres et d'autres coquillages et crustacés.

▲ **Le camembert, le valençay et le pont-l'évêque** sont des fromages très appréciés dans le monde entier.

◀ **Le far breton** est un gâteau traditionnel fait avec des pruneaux *(prunes)* ou des raisins secs.

Savais-tu que...?

On dit que le château d'Ussé, dans la vallée de la Loire, a inspiré le conte de Charles Perrault «La Belle au bois dormant».

Interactive
TUTOR

Sports

▼ **Les 24 heures du Mans**
Cette compétition automobile est une course d'endurance qui a lieu *(takes place)* chaque année depuis 1923.

➤ **La Route du Rhum** est une course de voiliers *(sailboats)*, en solitaire, qui commence à Saint-Malo et se termine à Pointe-à-Pitre, en Guadeloupe.

Activité

1. **Histoire:** Quelle est la date du débarquement en Normandie?
2. **Architecture:** Où est-ce qu'il y a un château du Moyen Âge?
3. **Gastronomie:** Qu'est-ce qu'il y a dans le far breton?
4. **Sports:** Où est-ce que la course du Rhum se termine?

L'Ouest de la France

chapitre 5

Le temps libre

Objectifs

In this chapter, you will learn to
- ask about interests
- ask how often someone does an activity
- extend, accept, and refuse an invitation
- make plans

And you will use
- the verb **faire**
- question words
- adverbs
- the verb **aller** and the **futur proche**
- the verb **venir** and the **passé récent**
- idioms with **avoir**

▶ *Que vois-tu sur la photo?*

Où sont ces personnes?

Qu'est-ce qu'elles font?

Et toi, est-ce que tu aimes faire du vélo? Et quelles autres activités?

Le Mont-Saint-Michel, en Normandie

Objectifs
- to ask and tell about interests
- to ask when someone does an activity

Vocabulaire
à l'œuvre **1**

DVD

Télé-vocab

Les sports et les passe-temps

 En hiver, nous aimons…

faire du ski | faire du patin à glace

Au printemps, j'aime…

jouer au basket-ball | faire de la photo

 En été, nous aimons…

jouer au volley | faire du surf

En automne, j'aime…

faire du vélo | faire du jogging

Les mois	janvier	février	mars	avril	mai	juin
	juillet	août	septembre	octobre	novembre	décembre

Online Practice

go.hrw.com
Vocabulaire 1 practice

KEYWORD: BD1 CH5

Le week-end, j'aime…

jouer au hockey

jouer au tennis

faire du skate(-board)

jouer du piano

jouer de la batterie

jouer de la guitare

faire du théâtre

faire de la vidéo amateur

jouer à des jeux vidéo

D'autres mots utiles

faire de l'athlétisme	*track and field*	la raquette	*racket*
faire de l'aérobic	*to do aerobics*	les skis (m.)	*skis*
le caméscope	*camcorder*	le casque	*helmet*
l'appareil photo (numérique) (m.)	*(digital) camera*	la saison	*season*

Exprimons-nous!

To ask about interests	To tell about interests
Est-ce que tu fais du sport? *Do you play sports?*	**Non, je ne fais pas de sport.** *No, I don't play sports.*
Est-ce que tu joues au basket? *Do you play . . . ?*	Non, **je ne joue pas** au basket. *I don't play . . .*
Qu'est-ce que tu fais comme sport? *What sports do you play?*	**Je joue** au hockey. *I play . . .*
Qu'est-ce que tu fais pour t'amuser? *What do you do for fun?*	**Je fais** du skate. *I do . . .*
Qu'est-ce que tu fais samedi? *What are you doing on . . . ?*	**Je ne fais rien.** *I'm not doing anything.*

Interactive TUTOR

Vocabulaire et grammaire, pp. 49–51

Online workbooks

▶ Vocabulaire supplémentaire—Les sports et les passe-temps, p. R11–12

1 Écoutons

Monsieur Delville's grandchildren are all having birthdays this month. Listen to each conversation and decide which item he is likely to buy for each of them.

1. Marie
2. Charles
3. Corinne
4. Marc
5. Hélène
6. Denis

a. une guitare
b. un casque
c. une raquette
d. un caméscope
e. des skis
f. un ballon

2 Les mois et les saisons

Lisons/Parlons Complete each series logically.

1. mars, _____, mai, _____
2. l'automne, _____, _____, l'été
3. juin, _____, _____, septembre
4. décembre, _____, _____, mars
5. l'été, _____, _____, le printemps

3 Qu'est-ce que tu fais après les cours?

Écrivons Farid et Sylvain parlent des activités qu'ils aiment faire après les cours. Complète leur conversation avec les activités représentées.

♻ *Souviens-toi!* Likes and dislikes, pp. 52–53

SYLVAIN   Est-ce que tu aimes ___1___ après les cours?

FARID   Oui, mais j'aime aussi ___2___ . Et toi?

SYLVAIN   Moi, j'aime ___3___ et ___4___ .

FARID   Pas moi. Je préfère ___5___ . Le week-end,

j'aime ___6___ . Et toi?

SYLVAIN   Moi, j'aime ___7___ avec mon frère.

Exprimons-nous!

To ask when someone does an activity	To respond
Quand est-ce que tu fais du jogging? *When do you . . . ?*	**Je fais** du jogging **en** automne et **au** printemps. *I . . . in the . . .*
En quelle saison tu fais du jogging? *In which season do you . . . ?*	
Tu fais du basket **pendant quels mois**? *What months do you play . . . ?*	**Je fais** du basket **en** juillet et **en** août. *I do/play . . . in . . .*

Interactive TUTOR

Vocabulaire et grammaire, *pp. 49–51* Online workbooks

4 Toute la famille est sportive!

Parlons/Écrivons Describe what sport or activity each member of Benoît's family does and in what season.

1. ses oncles

2. Sam et Benoît

3. vous

4. ses cousines

5. sa grand-mère

6. tu

Communication

HOLT SoundBooth ONLINE RECORDING

5 Sondage

Parlons The sports club where you work received 100,000 euros for new equipment. Do a survey among your classmates to find out which of the sports listed below they play and how regularly they play these sports. Then, decide on what equipment to buy.

jouer au tennis	jouer au basket	faire du vélo
jouer au volley	faire du ski	jouer au base-ball

Grammavision

Grammaire à l'œuvre 1

Interactive TUTOR

The verb *faire*

Faire is an irregular verb. Here are its forms.

faire *(to make, to do)*			
je	fais	nous	faisons
tu	fais	vous	faites
il/elle/on	fait	ils/elles	font

Elle **fait** du jogging.

Est-ce que vous **faites** du vélo?

Vocabulaire et grammaire, *pp. 52–53*
Cahier d'activités, *pp. 41–43*

Online workbooks

6 **Des projets**

Lisons/Écrivons Adèle et Lisette parlent de leurs projets pour le week-end. Complète leur conversation avec les formes correctes de **faire**.

ADÈLE Alors Lisette, qu'est-ce qu'on ___1___ ce soir?

LISETTE Moi, le soir, j'aime ___2___ du vélo. Tu aimes?

ADÈLE Non, je préfère faire du skate. Tu ___3___ du skate?

LISETTE Je déteste le skate. Qu'est-ce que Gilles et toi, vous ___4___ demain?

ADÈLE Ben… Nous ___5___ du patin à glace à dix heures et à midi, je ___6___ du théâtre à la MJC. Et Gilles et Laure ___7___ de la vidéo amateur.

LISETTE Très bien! Je vais ___8___ du théâtre avec toi à midi.

7 **Des phrases à construire**

Écrivons Mets les mots dans le bon ordre et fais des phrases complètes. Fais tous les changements nécessaires.

1. automne / je / athlétisme / faire
2. été / faire / mes copains / aérobic
3. printemps / vous / vélo / faire
4. faire / à l'école / nous / théâtre
5. week-end / mes parents / vidéo amateur / faire
6. patin à glace / au Canada / faire / on / hiver

8 **C'est ma passion!**

Écrivons/Parlons Qu'est-ce que ces personnes font souvent, d'après les images? Utilise les verbes **faire** et **jouer**.

MODÈLE **Martine fait du jogging.**

Martine

1. vous

2. mes cousins

3. je

4. mon grand-père

5. tu

9 **Souvent ou pas?**

Écrivons Regarde ton calendrier. Mentionne cinq activités que tu fais et quels jours tu les fais.

lundi	mardi	mercredi	jeudi	vendredi
1 basket-ball piano	**2** jogging vidéo amateur	**3** basket-ball piano	**4** théâtre à la MJC	**5** hockey
8 basket-ball piano	**9** au Club d'échecs à 5h00	**10** basket-ball patin à glace	**11** théâtre à la MJC	**12** jeux vidéo avec Tristan

Communication

HOLT **SoundBooth**
ONLINE RECORDING

10 **Sondage**

Parlons You're working for a Quebecois polling agency that's conducting a survey among teens to find out about their favorite sports. Use these questions to interview at least five classmates.

1. Qu'est-ce que tu fais pour t'amuser?
2. Est-ce que ton meilleur ami fait du sport?
3. Qu'est-ce que tu aimes faire en hiver?
4. En quelles saisons est-ce qu'on fait du vélo?
5. Toi et tes amis, qu'est-ce que vous faites le week-end?
6. Qu'est-ce que tu aimes faire en été?

Question words

Interactive
TUTOR

1 You've already learned to ask yes-no questions using intonation or **est-ce que.**

> **Tu aimes le base-ball?**
>
> **Est-ce qu'il fait du jogging?**

2 To ask for information, use a question word followed by **est-ce que** plus a subject and verb.

	question word	subject	verb
		↓	↓ ↓
(When)	**Quand est-ce qu'**il fait du théâtre?		
(Why)	**Pourquoi est-ce qu'**il n'aime pas le football?		
(What)	**Qu'est-ce qu'**il fait en automne?		
(Where)	**Où est-ce qu'**il nage?		
(How)	**Comment est-ce qu'**on fait du ski?		
(With whom)	**Avec qui est-ce que** tu joues au tennis?		

3 You don't use **est-ce que** with question words when they are followed by the verb **être.**

> **Où est ton frère?**   **Comment est ton amie?**

4 The question word **Qui** *(Who)* is followed directly by a verb.

> **Qui joue de la guitare?**

Vocabulaire et grammaire, *pp. 52–53*
Cahier d'activités, *pp. 41–43*
Online workbooks

En anglais

In English, in an information question, the question word usually comes at the beginning of the sentence.

> When do you play tennis?

What words do we use in English to ask information questions?

In French, question words can appear in different places in the sentence, depending on the level of formality of the conversation.

> **Quand est-ce que tu vas au ciné?**
>
> **Tu vas au ciné quand?**
> *(less formal)*

11 **Qu'est-ce qu'elles font?**

Lisons/Écrivons Fatima et Cécile parlent de leurs activités de cette semaine. Complète leur conversation de façon logique.

Où	Comment	Quand	Avec qui	Qu'est-ce que

—____1____ est-ce que tu vas jouer au volley?

—Jeudi.

—____2____ est-ce que tu joues?

—Avec mon cousin Dominique. Et toi, ____3____ tu fais jeudi?

—Moi, je joue du piano.

—Tu joues du piano, toi!? ____4____?

—À l'école de musique de Notre-Dame.

—Ah bon? ____5____ est ton prof?

—Il est super!

12 Écoutons

 Écoute chaque question et choisis la réponse logique.

a. Avec Olivia.   d. Oui, j'adore faire du ski.

b. Lundi soir.   e. Du vélo et du surf.

c. À l'école.   f. Ma tante Inès.

13 Scènes de vie

Lisons/Parlons Réponds aux questions d'après les illustrations.

1. Luc   2. Mathieu   3. Marthe

1. Qui fait du patin à glace?
2. Qu'est-ce que Luc fait?
3. Quand est-ce que Luc fait du sport?
4. Qu'est-ce que Mathieu fait? En quelle saison?
5. En quelle saison est-ce que Marthe fait du sport?

14 Mon journal

Écrivons There are several new French exchange students at your school, and you're really curious about them. Write an instant message to your friend who's been helping the new students, asking questions to get more information about them.

Communication

15 Scénario

Parlons You're a parent and your teenage child (your classmate) wants to go out Friday night. Ask your child a lot of questions to find out as many details as you can about his/her plans. Role play this conversation for the rest of the class.

MODÈLE —Où est-ce que tu vas vendredi soir?

Application 1

16 **Écoutons**

Listen to the conversation between Pascal and Ariane. Identify which of these sports or activities Pascal likes and which ones he dislikes.

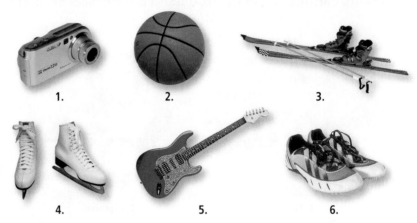

1.   2.   3.

4.   5.   6.

17 **Ton sport préféré**

Parlons Réponds aux questions suivantes.

1. Qu'est-ce que tu fais comme sport ou comme activité?
2. Pourquoi est-ce que tu aimes cette activité?
3. Où est-ce que tu fais cette activité?
4. Quand est-ce que tu fais cette activité?
5. Avec qui est-ce que tu fais cette activité?

Un peu plus

Adverbs

You've already learned some adverbs like **souvent, de temps en temps, rarement** and **régulièrement**. In English, many adverbs end in *-ly: quickly, slowly, etc.* In French, many adverbs end in **-ment.** To form most adverbs in French, take the feminine form of the adjective and add **-ment.** Adverbs are usually placed after the verb.

> **sérieux** → sérieuse → sérieusement
>
> Les élèves travaillent sérieusement.

The adjectives **bon** and **mauvais** have irregular adverbs:

> **bon** → bien *(well)* and **mauvais** → mal *(badly).*
>
> Ma cousine joue bien au hockey.

Vocabulaire et grammaire, *p. 54*
Cahier d'activités, *pp. 41–43*

Online workbooks

Interactive **TUTOR**

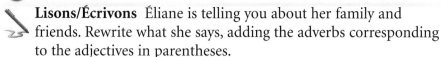

Application 1

18 **Des détails**

Lisons/Écrivons Éliane is telling you about her family and friends. Rewrite what she says, adding the adverbs corresponding to the adjectives in parentheses.

MODÈLE Mon grand-père nage pendant une heure. (facile)
Mon grand-père nage facilement pendant une heure.

1. Ma sœur parle. (timide)
2. Papa travaille. (rapide)
3. Mon frère et moi, nous jouons au tennis. (bon)
4. Je joue au hockey. (mauvais)
5. Ici, en automne, on fait du ski. (rare)

Communication

HOLT **SoundBooth**
ONLINE RECORDING

19 **Scénario**

Parlons You and your friends are looking at a brochure for a summer camp in France. In groups of three, take turns asking your classmates if they like the activities featured in the brochure and how often and how well they do these activities.

Camp Lac Puffin

Des vacances fun!

Passe l'été avec moi, Pierre Puffin au bord d'un lac spectaculaire!

Tennis, natation, volley, randonnée à vélo...

• Tu as entre 12 et 18 ans.
• Le sport, c'est ta passion!
• Tu es libre en juillet ou en août.

Alors, ce camp est fait pour toi!

Inscris-toi sur campuffin@hrw.gt.com

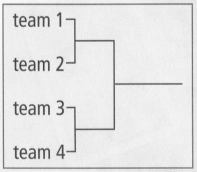

Une partie de pétanque

Culture appliquée

La pétanque

Pétanque is a very popular game in France, especially in the South. The name **pétanque** comes from the Provençal language and means "feet together." The modern version of the game dates back to 1907, but the ancient Romans played a similar game. To play **pétanque,** you need two teams of two or three players each. The goal of the game is to throw several steel balls, called **boules,** the closest possible to the **cochonnet,** which is a smaller wooden ball.

Un tournoi de pétanque

If you don't have **boules** and a **cochonnet,** use tennis balls for the **boules** and a table tennis ball for the **cochonnet.** Mark each team's tennis balls with different colors so that teams can identify which are theirs.

Step 1 Divide the class into teams of three. Teams will compete against one another until one team wins. Draw a chart on which to enter the names of the teams.

Step 2 Draw a line from which the balls are thrown.

Step 3 The first player will throw the **cochonnet** 6–10 meters from the line.

Step 4 Each player will throw the balls toward the **cochonnet.** At the end of the game, the team with the ball closest to the **cochonnet** wins!

Repeat steps 3 and 4 until you have a winning team.

 **Recherches** In what other countries do people play **pétanque** or a similar game? Are the rules the same?

Culture

Comparaisons

Une leçon de tennis

Vive le sport!

You are an exchange student for a year in France. You are talking with your French host family about sports. You have been playing tennis since you were six. Your host family advises you to:

a. join a tennis club.

b. join your school's tennis team.

c. practice tennis at school every day.

Since French high schools are very demanding, with a full day of classes and a lot of homework, sports and cultural activities are unusual within the school. Such activities usually take place outside school, in youth clubs, art schools, sports clubs, etc. Sometimes students join a school sports association **(UNSS, Union Nationale du Sport Scolaire)**, which enables them to train and participate in school sports competitions. It is very common for parents to encourage their children to take part in organized classes outside of school, typically on Wednesdays and Saturdays.

ET TOI?

1. Do you practice sports outside of your school?

2. How different from the French system is your school's approach to sports?

Communauté

Un club de pétanque

Do you know of a group of people that plays **pétanque** in your community? Find out from the **Alliance française** or do research at your local library to get this information. Do you know of any other type of sport or activity that is played in your community that resembles **pétanque**? What is it? What are the rules of that sport?

Un jeu du fer à cheval

Objectifs
- to extend, accept and refuse an invitation
- to make plans

Vocabulaire
à l'œuvre 2

DVD

Télé-vocab

Où vas-tu? Je vais...

à la patinoire

au théâtre/à l'opéra

à la montagne

au lac

à la mer

à la campagne

au cybercafé

au club (de tennis, de foot)

Quel temps fait-il?

Il fait beau.

Il fait chaud.

Il pleut.

Il y a du vent.

Il fait froid.

Il neige.

D'autres mots utiles

le zoo	zoo	Il fait mauvais.	The weather is bad.
la plage	beach	Il y a du soleil.	It's sunny.
le musée	museum	Il y a des nuages.	It's cloudy.

Exprimons-nous!

To extend an invitation	To accept and refuse an invitation
On fait du jogging? *Shall we . . . ?*	**D'accord./Bonne idée!/Pourquoi pas?** *Okay. / Good idea! / Why not?*
On va au lac? *How about going to . . . ?*	**Si tu veux./Si vous voulez.** *If you want.*
Tu as envie de faire du vélo ce soir? **Ça te/vous dit de** jouer au tennis? *Do you feel like . . . ?*	Non, **ça ne me dit rien.** *. . . , I don't feel like it.*
Tu viens au cybercafé avec moi? *You want to come . . . ?*	**Désolé(e), je n'ai pas le temps.** *Sorry, I don't have the time.*

Vocabulaire et grammaire, pp. 55–57

Online workbooks

▶ Vocabulaire supplémentaire—La météorologie, p. R10

Vocabulaire 2

20 Écoutons

Écoute les conversations. Est-ce que les personnes a) **acceptent** ou b) **refusent** d'aller aux endroits suivants?

21 Tu veux faire quoi?

Lisons/Parlons Complète les phrases avec l'endroit le plus approprié pour faire les activités suggérées.

1. On fait du jogging (au musée / au parc / à la bibliothèque).
2. Ça te dit de jouer au tennis (au club / au lac / à la montagne)?
3. Tu aimes nager (au théâtre / au cybercafé / à la mer)?
4. Ça te dit de faire du ski (au stade / au théâtre / à la montagne)?
5. Tu viens faire un pique-nique (à l'opéra / au lac / au musée)?

22 Les activités de saison

Parlons Tell what the weather is like in each photo. Then, extend an invitation to do an activity for each type of weather.

1.

2.

3.

4.

5.

6.

23 Des invitations

Écrivons Anne is inviting Serge to do activities over the weekend. Serge is busy on Saturday but agrees to do something on Sunday. Write their conversation using expressions from the box.

Tu as envie de…?	Désolé, je…	au cybercafé
à la plage	Bonne idée!	Ça te dit de…?

Exprimons-nous!

To make plans	To respond
Qu'est-ce que tu vas faire s'il pleut? *What are you going to do if it . . . ?*	**Je vais** jouer aux cartes. *I will . . .*
Avec qui est-ce que tu joues? *With whom . . . ?*	**Avec** Lili. *With . . .*
Où ça?/Où est-ce qu'on se retrouve? *Where? Where are we meeting?*	À la MJC.
Qu'est-ce qu'on fait mardi? *What are we doing . . . ?*	**On pourrait** aller au café. *We could . . .*
Tu vas faire quoi samedi? *What are you going to do . . . ?*	**Pas grand-chose./Rien de spécial.** *Not much./Nothing special.*
	Samedi, **j'ai trop de choses à faire.** **Je suis très occupé(e).** *. . . I have too many things to do. I'm very busy.*

Vocabulaire et grammaire, pp. 55–57

Interactive TUTOR

Online workbooks

24 **En colonie de vacances**

Écrivons You're at a summer camp and you send an e-mail to your parents telling them what the weather is like, what activities you do each day of the week, and with whom you're doing these activities.

Communication

HOLT SoundBooth ONLINE RECORDING

25 **Scénario**

Parlons With a classmate, take turns inviting each other to do five activities. Imagine different weather situations. Accept or refuse each invitation.

> MODÈLE —Il fait beau. Ça te dit de faire du jogging?
> —Pourquoi pas?

26 **Scénario**

Parlons Ton/Ta camarade veut savoir ce que tu fais samedi. Parle-lui de tes projets.

> MODÈLE —Tu vas faire quoi samedi matin?
> —Je joue au tennis à 10h.
> —Où ça?
> —Au...
> —Avec qui?...

SAMEDI 21 juillet

10h jouer au tennis / Manon / club de tennis
1h jouer au volley / Mathieu, Guillaume, Laure / à la plage
4h surfer sur Internet / Ahmed / cybercafé
6h étudier / Lydia / bibliothèque

Objectifs
- *aller* and the *futur proche*
- *venir* and the *passé récent*

Grammavision

Aller and the *futur proche*

Interactive TUTOR

1 The verb **aller** is irregular. Here are its forms.

aller *(to go)*		
je vais	nous	allons
tu vas	vous	allez
il/elle/on va	ils/elles	vont

—Est-ce que vous **allez** au parc?

2 You can use a form of **aller** plus **an infinitive** to talk about something that is going to happen in the *near future*.

Je **vais jouer** au basket.   Nous **allons étudier** la géo.
I'm going to play basketball.   *We're going to study geography.*

Vocabulaire et grammaire, pp. 58–59
Cahier d'activités, pp. 45–47

Online workbooks

27 **Qui va où?**

Lisons Complète chaque phrase avec la forme qui convient.

1. Juliette et moi, nous (allez / allons) au lac samedi.
2. Est-ce que tu (vas / va) à la bibliothèque ce soir?
3. Les professeurs (va / vont) au théâtre samedi.
4. Pauline et Lucas, vous (allez / vont) au stade?
5. Ma mère (va / vais) travailler au club de tennis.

28 **Tu viens?**

Écrivons Michèle invite sa copine à un pique-nique. Complète sa note.

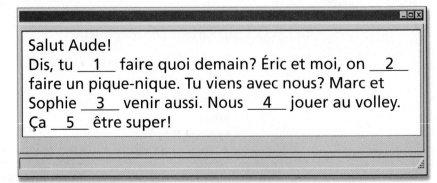

Salut Aude!
Dis, tu __1__ faire quoi demain? Éric et moi, on __2__ faire un pique-nique. Tu viens avec nous? Marc et Sophie __3__ venir aussi. Nous __4__ jouer au volley. Ça __5__ être super!

29 **Logique ou pas logique?**

Parlons Based on the weather, tell whether the following people are going to do these activities. If not, tell what they're going to do instead.

> **MODÈLE** Il neige: Lydia / faire du vélo au parc
> **Lydia ne va pas faire du vélo au parc!**
> **Elle va regarder la télévision.**

1. Il y a du vent: Les enfants / jouer au volley au parc
2. Il neige: Géraldine / faire du ski
3. Il pleut: Toi et ta cousine / faire de l'athlétisme
4. Il fait mauvais: Je / jouer au foot au stade
5. Il y a du soleil: Nous / faire de la vidéo à la campagne

30 **Des projets pour le week-end**

Écrivons Dis ce que ces personnes vont faire et où, d'après les photos.

1. Olivier

2. mon frère et moi

3. vous

4. tu

5. les Renaud

6. je

Communication

31 **Scénario**

Parlons Invite your classmate to do different activities. He/She always has other plans at the times you propose. After several attempts, your classmate finally accepts your invitation.

> **MODÈLE** —**Tu as envie d'aller au parc samedi matin?**
> —**Désolé(e), je vais aller au lac samedi...**

Venir and the *passé récent*

Interactive
TUTOR

1 The verb **venir** is an irregular verb. Here are its forms.

venir *(to come)*		
je **viens**	nous	**venons**
tu **viens**	vous	**venez**
il/elle/on **vient**	ils/elles	**viennent**

Ils **viennent** au théâtre avec Paul.

Est-ce que tu **viens** au parc avec nous?

2 You can use a form of **venir** plus **de** plus the **infinitive** of another verb to say that **something just happened**.

Je **viens** de téléphoner à Ali.
I just phoned Ali.

Il **vient** de pleuvoir.
It just rained.

Vocabulaire et grammaire, *pp. 58–59*
Cahier d'activités, *pp. 45–47*

Online workbooks

32 **Écoutons**

Listen as Guillaume talks to his friends. For each conversation, tell if the friend **a) is going to do something** or **b) just did something.**

33 **On vient?**

Lisons Complète les phrases suivantes logiquement.

1. Nous ___ (d)
2. Patrice, tu ___ (c)
3. Florent et Salima ___ (e)
4. Natasha ___ (b)
5. Vous ___ (a)

a. venez à la plage?
b. ne vient pas au parc.
c. viens à la patinoire?
d. venons au musée avec toi.
e. viennent à la campagne.

34 **Des projets**

Écrivons Complète les phrases avec la bonne forme de **venir.**

1. Je _viens_ au cinéma avec Julie.
2. Nous _venons_ de voir un film français.
3. Tu _viens_ au stade avec moi ce soir?
4. Paul et toi, vous _venez_ à l'opéra demain?
5. Mes parents _viennent_ d'aller en France.

35 Qu'est-ce qui vient d'arriver?

Parlons Qu'est-ce que ces personnes viennent de faire?

1. les filles

2. tu

3. nous

4. je

5. vous

6. le chien

36 Carnet de bord

Écrivons You and your family just returned to your ho[...]
France after an exciting day. Write a short journal entry [...]
about an activity that each person just did, when, with [...]
etc. Mention at least two things that you're going to do. [...]

MODÈLE mardi 8 avril

Je viens de visiter le Louvre avec Caroline c[...]
Le musée est cool! Mes parents viennent de [...]

[Handwritten note:]
1. les filles viennent aller au magasin
2. Tu viens faire les tableux sur la maison
3. Nous venons faire du ski
4. Je viens faire de la natation
5. vous venez faire

Communication

37 Scénario

Parlons You're acting as a host to a visiting French student. Invite him or her to do activities with you and your friends. The student has just done several of the activities you propose, so be sure to offer additional suggestions. Role play this with your classmate.

MODÈLE —Ça te dit d'aller au zoo?
—Je viens d'aller au zoo avec Hector.
—Ben… je vais aller… vendredi. Tu viens avec moi?
—Vendredi, je suis très occupé(e)…

Application 2

38 **On rappe!**

Écoute la chanson rap **Qu'est-ce que tu fais…?** Quelles activités est-ce qu'on fait **a) quand il fait beau, b) quand il fait mauvais** et **c) quand il fait froid?**

39 **Et toi?**

Parlons Réponds aux questions suivantes.

1. Qu'est-ce que tu fais quand il pleut?
2. Ça te dit d'aller au musée?
3. Tu vas faire quoi ce soir?
4. Tu aimes aller au zoo?
5. Avec qui est-ce que tu étudies?
6. Qu'est-ce que tu viens de faire?

40 **La routine quotidienne**

Écrivons What are some things that your family usually does on Saturdays around the same time? For each time given below, describe something that a family member may have just done.

MODÈLE 7h00 du matin: **Mon père vient de lire le journal.**

1. 8h30 du matin
2. midi
3. 1h00 de l'après-midi
4. 4h00 de l'après-midi
5. 7h30 du soir
6. 11h00 du soir

Un peu plus

Idioms with **avoir**

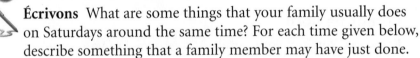

You've already learned the verb **avoir** (to have). Here are some useful expressions with **avoir**.

avoir besoin de	to need
avoir envie de	to feel like
avoir faim	to be hungry
avoir soif	to be thirsty
avoir chaud	to feel hot
avoir froid	to feel cold
avoir sommeil	to feel sleepy

J'ai chaud!	Tu as envie de nager?
I'm hot!	*Do you feel like swimming?*

Vocabulaire et grammaire, *p. 60*
Cahier d'activités, *pp. 45–47*

Online workbooks

41 **Extraits de conversation**

Parlons Complète les phrases en utilisant une expression avec **avoir.**

1. Je/J' _____! Tu as un coca?
2. Nous _____ deux calculatrices pour les maths.
3. On _____ à Boston en hiver.
4. Pauline _____ en été.
5. Pierre et moi, nous _____ manger des frites.
6. Je/J' _____, moi! Je vais manger un hamburger.

42 Il se sent comment?

Écrivons Marie-Line sent you some photos she took with her cell phone. Write a caption for each photo using an expression with **avoir**.

1. Vincent

2. tu

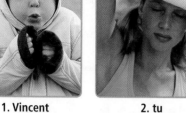
3. je

4. Seydou et Laure

43 Un message pour Bérangère

Parlons You're planning to visit your friend Bérangère in Paris. Leave a message on her answering machine to let her know two things you need to do or feel like doing during your visit. Be sure to invite her to do at least two other activities with you.

MODÈLE   **Salut, Bérangère. Je viens à Paris ce soir. J'ai envie de manger au café Camargue. Tu viens avec moi?…**

Communication

HOLT **SoundBooth**
ONLINE RECORDING

44 Scénario

Parlons Florence is babysitting Flavien who is being very difficult today! Look at the images below and create a conversation between Florence and Flavien for each of them.

a.

b.

c.

Télé-roman

Que le meilleur gagne!
Épisode 5

DVD

STRATÉGIE

Looking for clues Part of being an astute viewer involves looking for clues in the information that is provided in a story. Sometimes the clues are quite obvious and sometimes they are purposely hidden. The clues can also provide some insight into where the story is headed. Think back on the clues presented in the previous episodes and look for clues in this episode. Write down at least three things that you observe about Yasmina, Laurie, Kevin, and Adrien.

Chez Laurie, les deux filles sont en train de faire leurs devoirs...

Laurie C'est quand, ton déjeuner avec Kevin?
Yasmina Demain. On mange à l'Olivier, à côté du lycée.

Adrien Salut, Laurie. C'est Adrien. Ça va?
Laurie Super. Qu'est-ce qui se passe?

Adrien On vient de recevoir un e-mail de mademoiselle N'Guyen avec la deuxième énigme du concours. Vous venez chez moi?

Laurie Ben, tu sais, on fait nos devoirs. Envoie-nous l'énigme et on essaie de trouver la réponse chacun de notre côté.

Yasmina Bon, c'est sur le sport.
Laurie Tu sais, Adrien adore le sport. À mon avis, il va trouver la réponse.

Chez Adrien...

Adrien Maman! J'ai reçu la deuxième énigme pour le concours. C'est sur le sport. Tu peux m'aider?

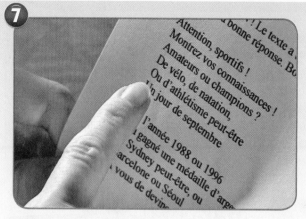

Mme Ortiz Bon, voyons... Vélo, natation ou athlétisme... Ça doit être un de ces trois sports... 1988 ou 1996... Les années des Jeux olympiques...

Adrien Amadou Dia Ba?

Mme Ortiz Ah, mais oui, regarde!
Adrien «Amadou Dia Ba: champion d'athlétisme sénégalais. Gagne une médaille d'argent à Séoul en 1988.»

Adrien Et il est sénégalais. Le pays du lycée, c'est le Sénégal, alors!

AS-TU COMPRIS?

1. Whom is Yasmina going to meet for lunch?

2. What is in the e-mail that Mlle N'Guyen sent to Adrien?

3. Why is Laurie confident that Adrien will find the answer to the clue?

4. Who helps Adrien find the answer to the second clue?

5. What nationality is Amadou Dia Ba? Why is this important to the three friends?

Prochain épisode:
At the beginning of the next episode, Yasmina will be very excited. Can you guess why?

Lecture et écriture

Ⓐ Avant la lecture

Look at the headings, subheadings, and photos in the following ad. What is the ad for? What information do you expect to find? Who do you predict will be interested in the activities in the ad?

CLUB LOISIRS ET VACANCES
Week-end sportif ou voyage organisé

Stages ou colonies de vacances
Choisissez votre élément !

AIR

Parachutisme, parapente, deltaplane[1]

Parachutisme découverte. Stage[2] d'une semaine du 15 mars au 15 octobre.

EAU

Funboard, voile[4], plongée[5], surf, kayak, canoë, kite surf, ski nautique

Stage de voile d'une semaine en mer Méditerranée. Stage le week-end hors-saison[6].

NEIGE

Ski alpin, ski de randonnée, snowboard, alpinisme

Stage Glisse dans les Alpes. Week-end ou à la semaine.

Vous souhaitez partir en vacances avec vos amis ou organiser vos week-ends. Profitez d'un programme « à la carte » ! Notre Club Loisirs et Vacances vous propose la formule Indépendance. Vous organisez votre programme sportif et extra-sportif comme vous le voulez.

TERRE

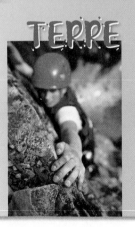

Équitation[7], golf, tennis, VTT[8], randonnée, escalade[9]

Séjour[10] d'intense activité physique en pleine nature. Week-end ou séjour d'une à trois semaines.

Pour plus de renseignements[3], appelez nos bureaux au 01.23.45.67.89. Nous sommes ouverts tous les jours de 7h à 19h.

---

1. hang-gliding   2. training/workshop   3. information   4. sailing   5. diving   6. off-season   7. horseback riding   8. mountain biking
9. rock climbing   10. a stay

B Compréhension

Réponds aux questions suivantes.

1. Quand est-ce qu'on peut téléphoner au club?
2. Combien de temps durent *(last)* les stages du club?
3. Quelle activité est-ce qu'on peut faire en mer Méditerranée?
4. En quelles saisons est-ce qu'on peut faire du parachutisme?
5. Où est-ce qu'on va pour faire du ski?
6. Qu'est-ce qu'on peut faire sur «Terre»?

C Après la lecture

What is the theme around which the activities in the ad revolve? Which set of activities would you prefer to do? Why? Would this club be popular in your state or area? Why or why not?

Espace écriture

1. Activités
   a. tennis
   b. volley
   c. .....

2. Temps
   a. beau

STRATÉGIE pour écrire

An outline is a list that is divided into categories. Creating an outline can help you organize your ideas logically and remember everything that you want to include in your writing.

Ça te dit...?

Imagine that you're vacationing with **Club Loisirs et Vacances**. Write a letter to a friend describing everything that you're doing and asking him or her to join you this weekend.

Tell about the activities you're doing, where and how often you do each one, and what the weather is like. Ask what plans your friend has for this weekend and if he or she wants to come to the vacation club.

1 Plan

List **Activités** and **Temps** on a sheet of paper, skipping several lines between each entry. Then, list specific facts or details that you want to include in your letter under the appropriate heading.

2 Rédaction

Using your outline, write a letter to your friend describing your vacation experience.

3 Correction

Check your letter against the outline you wrote to make sure you included everything. Read your letter a second time, checking it for spelling, grammar, and punctuation.

4 Application

Exchange letters with a classmate. Answer each others' letters, explaining why you accept or decline the invitation.

Prépare-toi pour l'examen

Interactive
TUTOR

① Vocabulaire 1
• to ask about interests
• to ask when someone does an activity
pp. 150–153

① Regarde les illustrations. Est-ce que tu fais ces activités? Réponds avec une phrase complète.

a.

b.

c.

d.

② Emmanuel is interviewing Roger about the activities he likes. Based on Roger's responses, fill in Emmanuel's questions.

② Grammaire 1
• the verb *faire*
• question words
Un peu plus
• adverbs
pp. 154–159

EMMANUEL   ____**1**____

ROGER   Je fais du skate, de l'athlétisme et je joue au hockey.

EMMANUEL   ____**2**____

ROGER   Je fais du skate au printemps, en été et en automne.

EMMANUEL   ____**3**____

ROGER   Je fais du skate avec mon frère.

EMMANUEL   ____**4**____

ROGER   Non. Je fais rarement du vélo.

EMMANUEL   ____**5**____

ROGER   Parce que c'est ennuyeux!

③ Complète les phrases suivantes avec des expressions logiques.

③ Vocabulaire 2
• to extend, accept and refuse an invitation
• to make plans
pp. 162–165

1. On fait du patin à glace à la _____.
2. Quand il _____, je joue à des jeux vidéo ou je regarde la télé.
3. On va _____ pour faire du ski.
4. En _____, j'aime faire du patin à glace et du ski.
5. Quand il fait _____, j'aime jouer au tennis ou faire du jogging.
6. Au _____, on joue au base-ball.
7. On va _____ ou _____ pour faire de la planche à voile.
8. Quand il fait _____, j'aime nager et faire du surf.

Prépare-toi pour l'examen

④ Complète la conversation entre Annick et Rachid avec les verbes **aller** ou **venir**.

RACHID   Qu'est-ce que tu ___1___ faire ce week-end?

ANNICK   Samedi soir, Marina et moi, nous ___2___ au théâtre avec Karim. Dimanche après-midi, je ___3___ au cinéma avec Marina. Tu ___4___ avec nous?

RACHID   Non, Michel et moi, nous ___5___ de voir un film. En plus, je ___6___ travailler ce week-end.

⑤ Answer the following questions.

1. What scale is used in France to measure temperature?

2. Name three sports that can be classified as **sports de glisse.**

3. Do schools in France have team mascots? Why or why not?

⑥ Salima et Farid parlent de sports et de passe-temps. Indique si les phrases suivantes sont **a) vraies** ou **b) fausses.**

1. Farid trouve le skate difficile.

2. Il joue souvent au tennis.

3. Il trouve le base-ball amusant.

4. Farid aime jouer à des jeux vidéo avec ses copains.

⑦ Crée une conversation entre Florence et son amie Patricia.

④ **Grammaire 2**
- *aller* and the *futur proche*
- *venir* and the *passé récent*

Un peu plus
- idioms with *avoir*
  pp. 166–171

⑤ **Culture**
- Comparaisons
  p. 161
- Flash culture
  pp. 152, 154, 158, 164

Grammaire 1
- the verb *faire*
- question words

Un peu plus
- adverbs
  pp. 154–159

Résumé: Grammaire 1

Faire is an irregular verb.

faire *(to make, to do)*	
je fais	nous faisons
tu fais	vous faites
il/elle/on fait	ils/elles font

To ask for information, use the following question words: **quand, pourquoi, qu'est-ce que, où, qui, comment, avec qui.**

To form most adverbs in French, take the feminine form of the adjective and add **-ment: sérieux → sérieusement.**

Some irregular adverbs are **bon → bien** and **mauvais → mal.**

Grammaire 2
- *aller* and the *futur proche*
- *venir* and the *passé récent*

Un peu plus
- idioms with *avoir*
  pp. 166–171

Résumé: Grammaire 2

These are the forms of the verb **aller** *(to go)*.

je vais	nous allons
tu vas	vous allez
il/elle/on va	ils/elles vont

Use a form of **aller** plus **an infinitive** to talk about something that is going to happen in the near future.

· These are the forms of the verb **venir** *(to come)*.

je **viens**	nous **venons**
tu **viens**	vous **venez**
il/elle/on **vient**	ils/elles **viennent**

Use a form of **venir** + de + **infinitive** of another verb to say that something just happened.

For a list of idiomatic expressions with **avoir**, see page 170.

🎧 Lettres et sons

S versus SS

The consonant **s** is pronounced like the sound **[z]** when it is placed between two vowels. To keep the **[s]** sound, we need to double the **s.**

Jeux de langue
Poisson sans boisson, c'est poison!

Dictée
Écris les phrases de la dictée.

Résumé: Vocabulaire 1

To ask and to tell about interests

l'appareil photo numérique	*digital camera*
le **caméscope**	*camcorder*
le **casque**	*helmet*
Faire...	
de l'**aérobic** (f.)	*aerobics*
de l'**athlétisme** (m.)	*track and field*
du **jogging**	*jogging*
du **patin à glace**	*skating*
de la **photo**	*to do photography*
du **skate**(-board)	*skateboarding*
du **ski**	*skiing*
du **surf**	*surfing*
du **théâtre**	*drama*
du **vélo**	*biking*
de la **vidéo amateur**	*make amateur videos*
Jouer...	
au **basket**(-ball)	*basketball*
à des **jeux vidéo** (m.)	*video games*
au **hockey**	*hockey*
au **tennis**	*tennis*
au **volley**	*volleyball*

de la **batterie**	*drums*
de la **guitare**	*guitar*
du **piano**	*piano*
les **passe-temps**	*pastime activities*
la **raquette**	*racket*
les **skis** (m.)	*skis*
Est-ce que tu fais du sport?	*Do you play sports?*
Est-ce que tu joues au...?	*Do you play . . . ?*
Qu'est-ce que tu fais comme sport?	*What sports do you play?*
Qu'est-ce que tu fais pour t'amuser?	*What do you do for fun?*
Qu'est-ce que tu fais...?	*What are you doing on . . . ?*
Je fais/joue.../Je ne joue pas...	*I do/play . . ./I don't play . . .*
Non, je ne fais pas de sport.	*No, I don't play sports.*
Je ne fais rien.	*I'm not doing anything.*

Les mois de l'année ....*see page 150*

Les saisons ....*see page 150*

To ask when someone does an activity ....*see page 153*

Résumé: Vocabulaire 2

To invite; to extend, accept and refuse an invitation

la **campagne**	*countryside*
le **club**	*sports club*
le **cybercafé**	*cybercafé*
le **lac**/la **mer**	*lake/sea*
la **montagne**	*mountain*
le **musée**	*museum*
l'**opéra** (m.)	*opera house*
la **patinoire**	*skating rink*
la **plage**	*beach*
le **théâtre**	*theater*
le **zoo**	*zoo*
Quel temps fait-il?	*What's the weather like?*
Il fait beau.	*The weather is nice.*
Il fait chaud.	*It's hot.*
Il fait froid.	*It's cold.*
Il fait mauvais.	*The weather is bad.*
Il neige.	*It's snowing.*

Il y a des nuages.	*It's cloudy.*
Il pleut.	*It's raining.*
Il y a du vent.	*It's windy.*
Il y a du soleil.	*It is sunny.*
On fait.../On va...?	*Shall we... ?/What about going...?*
Tu as envie de...?/ Ça te/vous dit de...?	*Do you feel like . . . ?*
Tu viens...?	*You want to come . . . ?*
D'accord./Bonne idée!/ Pourquoi pas?	*Okay./Good idea!/ Why not?*
Si tu veux/vous voulez.	*If you want.*
..., ça ne me dit rien.	*. . . , I don't feel like it.*
Désolé(e), je n'ai pas le temps.	*Sorry, I don't have the time.*
J'ai trop de choses à faire. Je suis très occupé(e).	*I have too many things to do. I'm very busy.*

To make plans ....*see page 165*

Idioms with avoir ....*see page 170*

Prépare-toi pour l'examen

Révisions cumulatives

1 Choisis la photo qui correspond à chaque conversation.

a.　　　　b.　　　　c.　　　　d.

2 Read this brochure for a vacation resort in Tunisia. Then, tell whether or not each of the people described below is going to like the resort.

Club Sousse

Bienvenue au *Club Sousse*, une oasis de calme avec des plages dorées et une mer limpide. Le *club* offre des activités pour toute la famille. Services d'accueil, de restauration et de location sur place.

Sports & Loisirs

- Discothèque
- Piscine olympique et piscine enfant
- 2 saunas
- Une salle de gymnastique
- Location de vélos
- Un terrain omnisports: Basket-ball, Volley-ball
- 5 courts de tennis dont 2 éclairés
- 1 salle de jeux vidéo
- cybercafé: 20 ordinateurs

1. Juliette adore la neige.
2. Jean-Michel et moi, nous aimons bien la plage.
3. Anne aime jouer à des jeux vidéo.
4. Monsieur et Madame Dupont ont deux enfants qui adorent nager.
5. J'ai un casque et j'adore faire du vélo.
6. Abdul n'aime pas la mer. Il préfère la montagne.

③ You're interviewing a school athlete for an upcoming issue of the French Club newspaper. Ask the athlete what sports and activities he or she does at different times of the year and in various weather conditions. Find out how often the athlete does each activity.

④ Write a paragraph in French describing the scene below. Include the weather, a description of the woman and the girl, their ages, and what their relationship to each other is. What activities do you think the woman and the girl like or dislike?

Monet, Claude (1840–1926). On the beach at Trouville, 1870–71. Canvas. Musée Marmottan–Claude Monet, Paris, France

Sur la plage à Trouville de Claude Monet

⑤ You haven't talked to your friend Hugo in a while. Write an e-mail in which you ask how he is doing, tell him about your classes, and invite him to do something with you this weekend. Suggest a second activity in case of bad weather, and a time and place to do each activity.

⑥ À ton tour

Ça te dit? Your French teacher wants you to work with a new student. Greet each other and exchange names. Discuss the sports and activities you each like to do at various times of the year and in different weather conditions. Invite the new student to do something with you and your friends after school.

Variations
littéraires

L'Île-de-France

 ## Le château de Versailles

Just outside of Paris, in Versailles, is one of the most famous palaces in France. It is where France's most famous artists worked and where angry mobs came to drag away Louis XVI and Marie-Antoinette during the early days of the French Revolution. While you read the guide that follows, decide which parts of Versailles you would like to visit.

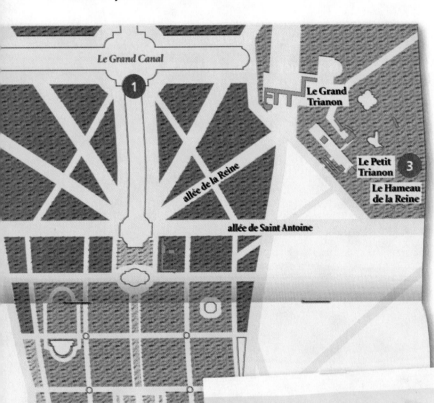

Le château de Versailles devient[1] la résidence royale de Louis XIV en 1682. Jusqu'à 20.000 courtisans[2] habitent au château. La château devient le centre du pouvoir[3] politique.

Quelques chiffres

Le château de Versailles a 700 pièces[4]. 800 personnes travaillent au château. 70 % des visiteurs sont des étrangers[5].

Louis XIV est surnommé[6] le Roi Soleil[7]. Le soleil est le motif principal de la décoration du château.

---

1. becomes 2. attendants at the royal court
3. power 4. rooms 5. foreigners 6. nicknamed
7. Sun King

Le Grand Canal ①

Il y a 50 bassins[1] : le plus grand est le Grand Canal. On compte 620 jets d'eau[2] et 35 km de canalisations.

L'Orangerie ②

André Le Nôtre et Jules Hardouin Mansart créent l'Orangerie, un jardin composé de 2.000 orangers.

Le Petit Trianon ③

En 1768, Louis XV fait construire[3] le « Petit Trianon » qui sert de[4] refuge contre les intrigues de la cour.

La galerie des Batailles[5] ④

Longue de 120 m, la galerie des Batailles est la plus vaste[6] salle du château. Il y a 33 tableaux de batailles victorieuses pour l'armée française dans cette salle.

HORAIRES
avril–octobre : 9h–18h30
novembre–mars : 9h–17h30

TARIFS
Visite du château
18 ans et plus : 7,50 euros
moins de 18 ans : gratuit[7]

INFORMATIONS (01.39.50.36.22)
http://www.chateauversailles.fr/

APRÈS ▶ la lecture

1. Who is the **Roi Soleil**?
2. What symbol was chosen as the main decorative motif?
3. Who was André Le Nôtre?
4. How many fountains are there at Versailles?
5. How much would a 16 year old pay to visit Versailles?

---

1. ornamental pools 2. fountains 3. orders the construction of 4. that is used as 5. battles 6. largest 7. free

L'Île-de-France

 ## Le Parc Astérix

Parc Astérix®, a theme park 30 kilometers north of Paris, is dedicated to Asterix the Gaul and his universe. This comic book hero was created in 1959 by René Goscinny and Albert Uderzo. Thanks to the magic potion brewed by the village druid, the villagers get supernatural strength and can overcome the Roman army.

STRATÉGIE

Cognates are words with the same meaning and similar spelling in both French and English. Recognizing them can help you better understand a text.

OBÉLIX

ASTÉRIX!

Astérix est le héros. C'est un guerrier[1] intelligent.

PANORAMIX

Obélix est le meilleur ami d'Astérix. Son plat préféré est le sanglier[2] rôti.

Panoramix le druide, prépare une potion magique qui rend[3] invincible.

LES SPECTACLES Les Gaulois, les gladiateurs et les Romains proposent de multiples spectacles toute la journée[4]. Au théâtre de Poséidon, les dauphins et les otaries[5] font un ballet aquatique. Dans la cité Médiévale, 18 rapaces[6] volent juste au-dessus de[7] vos têtes.

1. warrior 2. wild boar 3. makes 4. all day long 5. sea-lions 6. birds of prey 7. above

WEEEEE!

LES ATTRACTIONS 31 attractions sont proposées pour tous les âges : des montagnes russes[1], comme le « Tonnerre de Zeus » qui est la plus grande montagne russe en bois d'Europe, un train fantôme « Transdemonium » et des attractions aquatiques. « La forêt des druides », pleine d'arbres-toboggans[2] ou de champignons[3] géants, est pour les petits[4].

J'AI FAIM ! Dans les 15 restaurants du village, le hamburger au sanglier et la tarte romaine sont des spécialités.

HORAIRES
juillet–août,
de 9h30 à 19h

autres mois,
de 10h à 18h

Fermé[5] de
novembre à mars

PRIX
adulte 33€
enfant 23€

LES FASTES DE ROME

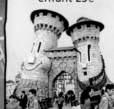

APRÈS ▶ **la lecture**

1. Who is **Astérix**?

2. What is the **Tonnerre de Zeus**?

3. What kind of shows can you see?

4. What can you eat at the park?

5. When is **Parc Astérix** open? When is it closed?

---

1. roller-coasters 2. tree-slides 3. mushrooms 4. young children 5. closed

La province de Québec

 ## Le Cirque du Soleil

You've probably heard of the *Cirque du Soleil.* You may have even seen one of its performances live or on television. This modern circus troupe, which performs regularly in cities around the world, is based in Quebec Province. While you read, decide in what ways the *Cirque du Soleil* is a traditional circus and in which respects it is a new kind of circus.

Créé en 1984, le *Cirque du Soleil* présente des spectacles[1] uniques et inoubliables[2]. On compte parmi[3] les artistes du *Cirque du Soleil* des jongleurs, des clowns, des mimes, des contorsionnistes, des acrobates, des danseurs et des chanteurs. Mais, contrairement aux cirques traditionnels, le *Cirque du Soleil* n'a pas d'animaux.

LE CIRQUE DU SOLEIL EN BREF
Siège social[4] international : Montréal

- 11 spectacles : *Varekai™, Quidam®, Alegría®, Saltimbanco®, « O® », Mystère®, Zumanity™, La Nouba™, Corteo™, Ka™*

- 3.000 employés, représentant 40 pays et parlant 25 langues

- 42 millions de spectateurs depuis 1984

---

1. shows   2. unforgettable   3. among
4. headquarters

« *O*® » est un spectacle aquatique. Un bassin d'eau[1] sert de scène[2]. Des acrobates survolent[3] l'eau sur des balançoires[4] en forme de bateaux[5] pendant que des équipes de natation synchronisée dansent sous l'eau.

Un Allemand nommé Otto Feick a inventé la *roue allemande*[6] en 1925. Les acrobates des spectacles « *Quidam*® » et « *La Nouba*™ » maîtrisent[7] l'art de cette roue géante.

Avec « *Alegría*® », les spectateurs peuvent[8] apprécier l'art de la contorsion. « *Varekai*™ » et « *Saltimbanco*® » sont des spectacles qui privilégient[9] l'acrobatie.

APRÈS ▷ la lecture

1. When did the *Cirque du Soleil* begin?

2. Name one thing that distinguishes the *Cirque du Soleil* from a traditional circus.

3. What type of stage do the artists perform on in "*O*®"?

4. Where are the *Cirque du Soleil's* world headquarters?

5. Which show would you like to see?

---

1. water **2.** stage **3.** fly over **4.** swings **5.** shaped like boats **6.** German wheel
7. master **8.** can **9.** focus

La province de Québec

 ## Les romans de Michel Tremblay

The following passage is from a book by Michel Tremblay, *Le Premier quartier de la lune*. The passage describes the way the students felt as they were about to take the geography final exam.

STRATÉGIE

One way to understand a story is to compare and contrast the experiences of the characters with your own. While you read the story on the next page, compare the experience of these students with your own.

Michel Tremblay est né[1] à Montréal en 1942. Il a passé son enfance dans le Plateau Mont-Royal, un quartier ouvrier[2] de Montréal. Dans ses écrits, il aime décrire la vie difficile de la classe ouvrière montréalaise pendant[3] les années 50. Il utilise aussi le joual, un dialecte québecois, dans ses romans. Il a aussi écrit, entre autres, *Bonbons assortis* (2002).

1. was born **2.** working-class neighborhood **3.** during

Le Premier quartier de la lune

Le Premier quartier de la lune est paru en 1999. L'histoire se passe dans le Montréal des années 50. Dans le livre, l'auteur nous fait partager¹ ses souvenirs d'école.

La géographie avait beau être plus facile que le français, une mauvaise note, surtout à la fin de l'année, était catastrophique. Tous, ils commencèrent mentalement à se réciter les dix capitales des dix provinces du Canada (ç'avait été la grande primeur² de l'année, avec les richesses naturelles de chacune des provinces, leur superficie³ et surtout, quelle horreur ! leur *emplacement* à l'intérieur du pays).

Des fronts se plissèrent, des sourcils se tricotèrent serré⁴… Des puzzles du Canada se formèrent, se déformèrent, prenant des allures bouffonnes frisant l'absurde⁵. Bon, c'est quoi la province en forme de poisson⁶ juste à côté du Québec ? Pis⁷ ensuite, là, les trois plates oùsque y'a rien⁸ que du Corn Flake qui pousse⁹ ? Pis celle à l'autre bout du monde avec des montagnes comme ça se peut pus ? La Colomb-Britannique¹⁰ ? Ceux qui trouvaient¹¹ avaient pendant un court instant le visage illuminé du thaumaturge¹² en plein miracle, les autres baissaient la tête¹³ et auraient donné cher¹⁴ pour avoir dans leur pupitre le manuel de géographie qu'ils avaient pourtant tellement haï¹⁵ durant toute l'année.

APRÈS > la lecture

1. When and where did Tremblay spend his childhood?

2. Students don't want to get a bad grade in geography at the end of the year. Why?

3. How do the students react to the questions on the geography exam?

4. What is the main subject of the geography exams?

5. What do you think school was like in the 50s?

---

1. share   2. the big new thing   3. area   4. Foreheads wrinkled, eyebrows knitted together   5. so grotesque as to be absurd   6. fish   7. Then (*Joual pronunciation of* **puis**)   8. where nothing (*Joual for* **plateaux où il n'y a rien**)   9. grows   10. British Columbia (*Joual pronunciation of* **Colombie-Britannique**)   11. The ones that found the answer   12. performer of miracles   13. lowered their heads   14. would have given everything   15. hated

L'Ouest de la France

 # Les légendes bretonnes

The region of Brittany has long been associated with romantic legends and folklore such as the legends of King Arthur, Merlin the Magician, and **Tristan et Iseult.** Many Breton legends go back to ancient times, when the Celts (a people that lived in the British Isles as well) inhabited the northwest region of France. The tale on these pages involves characters of traditional Breton legends: the **korrigans,** creatures that resemble elves.

STRATÉGIE

One of the ways that we understand a story is by anticipating what it might be about. The reader needs to think about what might happen next.

Les korrigans

Il existe dans les forêts de Bretagne un petit peuple[1] de la nuit, les korrigans. C'est un peuple du monde souterrain[2].

Odin, un des grands dieux[3] celtes, leur aurait ôté[4] leurs dons divins et magiques parce qu'il n'aimait pas du tout les nombreuses plaisanteries[5] que les korrigans faisaient aux humains. Malheureusement, ils continuèrent et continuent encore de nos jours à jouer des mauvais tours[6] aux gens qui habitent trop près[7] de leur territoire.

---

1. people **2.** underground world **3.** gods **4.** had taken away
5. jokes **6.** tricks **7.** live too close

N'avez-vous jamais remarqué[1] que des petits objets que vous adorez disparaissent par magie ?

C'est en fait l'œuvre[2] de l'un de ces petits korrigans qui se balladait[3] par là. Vous ayant entendu parler de cet objet préféré, il a décidé de vous l'emprunter[4] pour rigoler. Le problème, c'est que les korrigans sont assez distraits et bien souvent, ils oublient[5] à qui appartiennent[6] les choses qu'ils ont volées[7]. En conséquence, vous retrouvez rarement les objets chéris.

Mais il y a un moyen d'éviter[8] que les korrigans vous jouent l'un de leurs petits tours de mauvais goût[9]. Ils ont un autre grand défaut[10] : ils sont très curieux. Il vous suffit donc de verser[11] un sac de graines sur le seuil[12] de votre porte. Le pauvre korrigan sera tellement obsédé par son envie de connaître[13] le nombre de graines qu'il y passera toute la nuit, vous serez alors tranquille.

APRÈS ▶ la lecture

1. What very famous legends came from Brittany?

2. What is a **korrigan**?

3. Why did the **korrigans** lose their magic power?

4. What do **korrigans** like to do?

5. What is a **korrigan's** greatest weakness?

6. How can you trick a **korrigan**?

---

1. have you ever noticed **2.** It's the doing **3.** was wandering by **4.** borrow **5.** forget **6.** belong to **7.** stolen **8.** one way to avoid
9. poor taste **10.** weakness **11.** to pour **12.** threshold **13.** to know

Références

La France

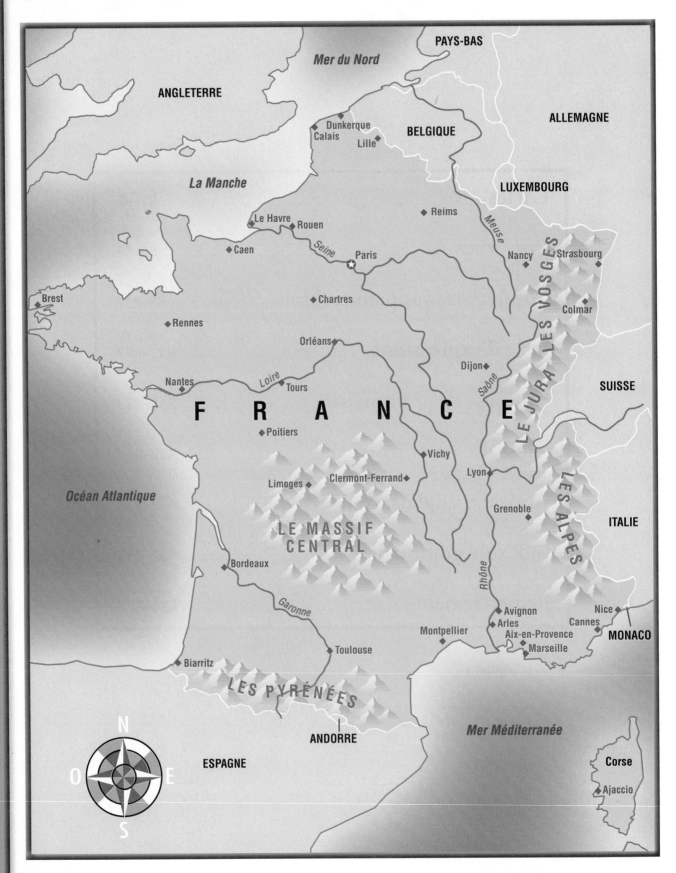

PAYS-BAS

Mer du Nord

ANGLETERRE

ALLEMAGNE

Dunkerque
Calais
Lille

BELGIQUE

La Manche

LUXEMBOURG

Reims

Le Havre
Rouen

Meuse

Caen

Seine

Nancy

Strasbourg

LES VOSGES

Paris

Colmar

Brest

Chartres

Rennes

Orléans

Dijon

Saône

LE JURA

SUISSE

Nantes

Loire

Tours

F R A N C E

Poitiers

Vichy

Lyon

Océan Atlantique

Limoges

Clermont-Ferrand

Grenoble

LES ALPES

ITALIE

LE MASSIF
CENTRAL

Rhône

Bordeaux

Garonne

Avignon
Arles
Aix-en-Provence

Nice
Cannes

MONACO

Montpellier

Marseille

Toulouse

Biarritz

LES PYRÉNÉES

Mer Méditerranée

N
O   E
S

ANDORRE

ESPAGNE

Corse

Ajaccio

L'Europe francophone

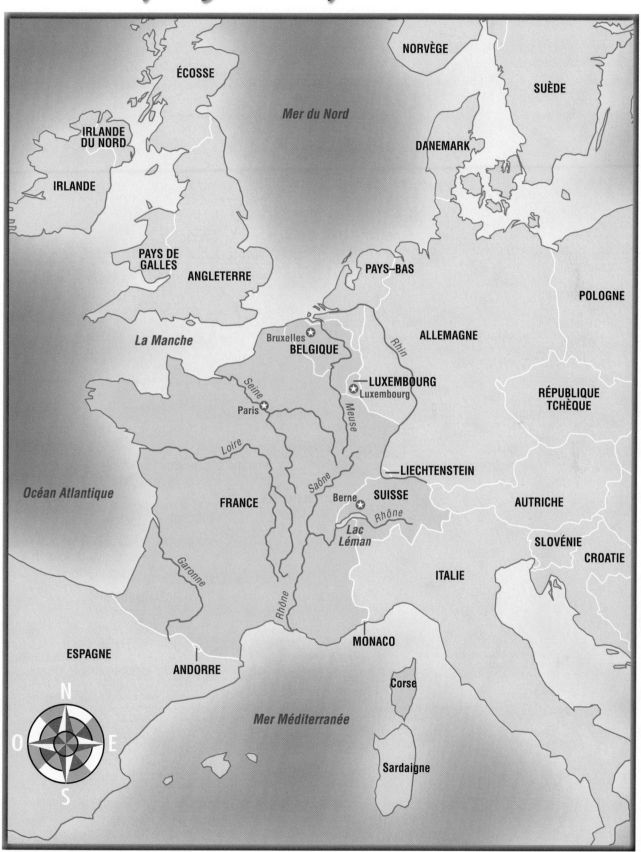

NORVÈGE

ÉCOSSE

SUÈDE

Mer du Nord

IRLANDE DU NORD

DANEMARK

IRLANDE

PAYS DE GALLES

PAYS-BAS

ANGLETERRE

POLOGNE

La Manche

Bruxelles ⭐

ALLEMAGNE

BELGIQUE

Rhin

Seine

LUXEMBOURG

⭐ Luxembourg

RÉPUBLIQUE TCHÈQUE

Paris ⭐

Meuse

Loire

LIECHTENSTEIN

Océan Atlantique

Saône

Berne ⭐

SUISSE

AUTRICHE

FRANCE

Rhône

Lac Léman

SLOVÉNIE

Garonne

CROATIE

ITALIE

Rhône

N

O   E

S

MONACO

ESPAGNE

ANDORRE

Corse

Mer Méditerranée

Sardaigne

L'Afrique francophone

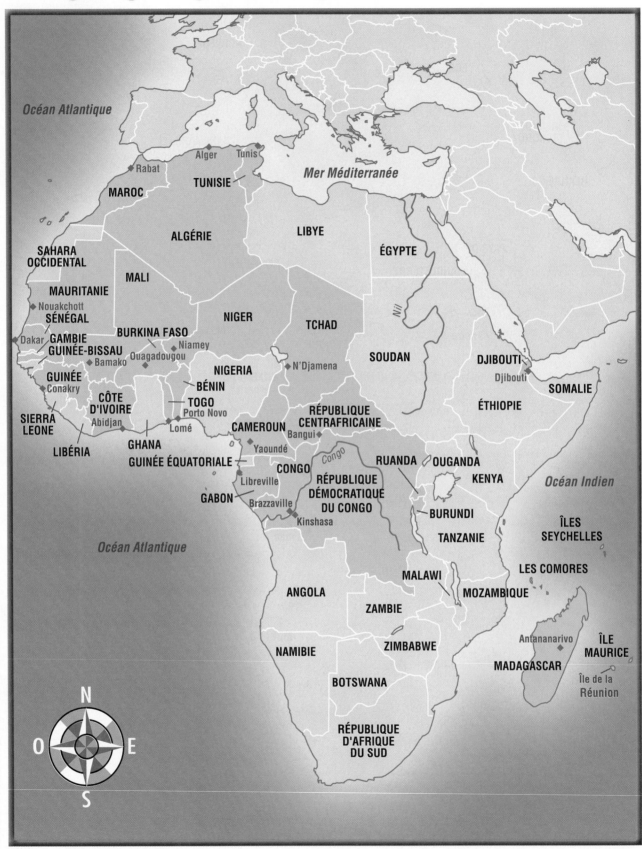

L'Amérique francophone

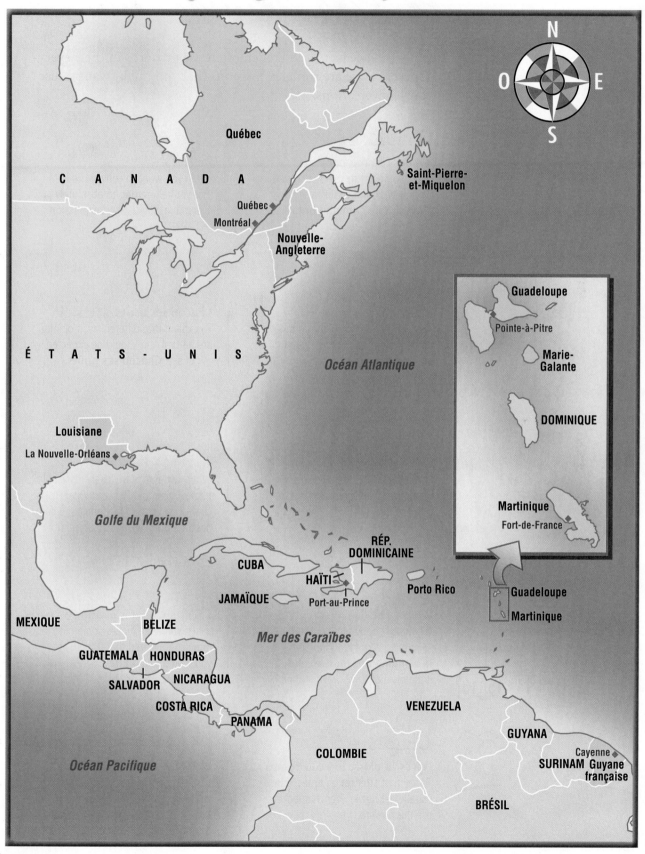

Québec

CANADA

Saint-Pierre-
et-Miquelon

Québec ◆
Montréal ◆

Nouvelle-
Angleterre

ÉTATS-UNIS

Océan Atlantique

Louisiane
La Nouvelle-Orléans ◆

Guadeloupe
Pointe-à-Pitre ◆

Marie-
Galante

DOMINIQUE

Golfe du Mexique

RÉP.
DOMINICAINE

Martinique
Fort-de-France ◆

CUBA

HAÏTI ◆
JAMAÏQUE   Port-au-Prince

Porto Rico

Guadeloupe

Martinique

MEXIQUE   BELIZE

Mer des Caraïbes

GUATEMALA   HONDURAS

SALVADOR   NICARAGUA

COSTA RICA

PANAMA

VENEZUELA

GUYANA

Cayenne ◆
SURINAM Guyane
française

COLOMBIE

Océan Pacifique

BRÉSIL

Proverbes
et expressions

Like English speakers, the French often use proverbs in their every-day speech. Here are some expressions that you might want to use in your conversations.

Chapitre 1

Simple comme bonjour
When you want to say that something is really easy, you could say:
C'est simple comme bonjour.

De A à Z
When you want to convey the idea that you're referring to absolutely everything, you use this expression.

Chapitre 2

Jouer cartes sur table
This expression means that one talks about or does something in an honest and straightforward manner.

Chacun ses goûts
To explain that differences in opinion are natural and should be expected, you might say: **Chacun ses goûts.**

Chapitre 3

Être comme chien et chat
This expression can be used to describe people who don't get along at all with one another.

Tel père, tel fils
When two relatives closely ressemble each other or share very similar characteristics and attitudes, you can describe them using this expression.

Chapitre 4

la semaine des quatre jeudis
When somebody tells you that something is going to happen **la semaine des quatre jeudis,** it means that it will *never* happen.

Chercher midi à quatorze heures
When someone makes something much more complicated that it needs to be, you would say: **Il/Elle cherche midi à quatorze heures.**

Chapitre 5

Après la pluie, le beau temps
To say that after rough times, things usually get better, French speakers use this proverb.

Une hirondelle ne fait pas le printemps
Use this expression to convey that you shouldn't jump to conclusions without having enough information.

Chapitre 6

Avoir une faim de loup
When you are really hungry, you could say: **J'ai une faim de loup.**

Compter pour du beurre
If you feel that you are being ignored, or that your opinion doesn't matter, you might say: **Je compte pour du beurre.**

Chapitre 7

Vider son sac
To describe someone who tells you everything that's in their heart, you may say: **Il/Elle vide son sac.**

Aller comme un gant
If an item of clothing, like a dress, fits someone perfectly, you could complement them by saying: **Elle te va comme un gant.**

Chapitre 8

Faire table rase
If you start something over from scratch, setting aside work already done, you can say: **Je fais table rase.**

Laver son linge sale en famille
This expression means to tackle a problem or an issue by discussing it only among the concerned parties and not involving others not related to it.

Chapitre 9

Jeter l'argent par les fenêtres
Use this expression to describe someone who spends money in a careless or wasteful manner.

Passer comme une lettre à la poste
If you're trying to do something that you think might be difficult and it turns out to be really easy, you can say **C'est passé comme une lettre à la poste.**

Chapitre 10

Prendre le train en marche
If you want to say that you started working on a project while it was already in progress, you can say **J'ai pris le train en marche.**

Attention, un train peut en cacher un autre
Use this expression when you want to say that something you perceive as a problem or a danger, can often hide something which could be far worse.

APRÈS ▶ la lecture

1. Can you think of English equivalents for some of these proverbs and expressions?

2. Pick a proverb that is not illustrated and work in groups of three to create an illustration to explain it.

3. Research the Internet or at the library to find additional proverbs that use vocabulary and themes you've learned.

4. Work in small groups to create a mini-skit in which you use one or more of these proverbs in context.

Vocabulaire supplémentaire

This list includes additional vocabulary that you may want to use to personalize activities. If you can't find a word you need here, try the French-English and English-French vocabulary sections, beginning on page R28.

Les animaux domestiques *(Pets)*

le cheval	*horse*
le cochon d'Inde	*guinea pig*
la grenouille	*frog*
le hamster	*hamster*
le lapin	*rabbit*
l'oiseau (m.)	*bird*
le serpent	*snake*
la souris	*mouse*
la tortue	*turtle*

Les commerces
(Stores and businesses)

la boulangerie	*bakery*
le disquaire	*music store*
l'épicerie (f.)	*grocery store*
le magasin de cadeaux	*gift store*
le magasin d'électronique	*electronics store*
le magasin de jouets	*toy store*
l'opticien (m.)	*optician*
le pressing/le teinturier	*dry cleaner*
la quincaillerie	*hardware store*
le rabais	*discount store*
le supermarché	*supermarket*

Le corps humain *(The human body)*

la bouche	*mouth*
le corps	*body*
le cou	*neck*
le coude	*elbow*
le doigt	*finger*
le dos	*back*
l'épaule (f.)	*shoulder*
l'estomac (m.)	*stomach*
le genou	*knee*
la jambe	*leg*
le menton	*chin*
le nez	*nose*
le pied	*foot*
le visage	*face*

Les corvées *(Chores)*

enlever à la pelle	*to shovel*
faire sécher	*to dry*
plier le linge	*to fold laundry*
repasser	*to iron*
ratisser	*to rake*

À l'école *(At school)*

le bureau du proviseur	*principal's office*
la cantine	*cafeteria*
le casier	*locker*
la cour de récréation	*recreation area*
la craie	*piece of chalk*
le foyer des élèves	*study room*
la salle des professeurs	*staff room*
le secrétariat	*secretary's office*
le tableau d'affichage	*bulletin board*

Les états (States)

l'Alabama (m.)	*Alabama*
l'Alaska (m.)	*Alaska*
l'Arizona (m.)	*Arizona*
l'Arkansas (m.)	*Arkansas*
la Californie	*California*
la Caroline du Nord/	*North/South*
du Sud	*Carolina*
le Colorado	*Colorado*

le district fédéral de Columbia	*Washington D.C.*
le Connecticut	*Connecticut*
le Dakota du Nord/ du Sud	*North/South Dakota*
le Delaware	*Delaware*
la Floride	*Florida*
la Géorgie	*Georgia*
l'île (f.) d'Hawaii	*Hawaii*
l'Idaho (m.)	*Idaho*
l'Illinois (m.)	*Illinois*
l'Indiana (m.)	*Indiana*
l'Iowa (m.)	*Iowa*
le Kansas	*Kansas*
le Kentucky	*Kentucky*
la Louisiane	*Louisiana*
le Maine	*Maine*
le Maryland	*Maryland*
le Massachusetts	*Massachussetts*
le Michigan	*Michigan*
le Minnesota	*Minnesota*
le Mississippi	*Mississippi*
le Missouri	*Missouri*
le Montana	*Montana*
le Nebraska	*Nebraska*
le Nevada	*Nevada*
le New Hampshire	*New Hampshire*
le New Jersey	*New Jersey*
le New York	*New York*
le Nouveau-Mexique	*New Mexico*
l'Ohio (m.)	*Ohio*

l'Oklahoma (m.)	*Oklahoma*
l'Oregon (m.)	*Oregon*
la Pennsylvanie	*Pennsylvania*
le Rhode Island	*Rhode Island*
le Tennessee	*Tennessee*
le Texas	*Texas*
l'Utah (m.)	*Utah*
le Vermont	*Vermont*
la Virginie (Occidentale)	*(West) Virginia*
le Washington	*Washington*
le Wisconsin	*Wisconsin*
le Wyoming	*Wyoming*

La famille *(Family)*

adopté(e)	*adopted*
l'arrière-grand-mère (f.)	*great grandmother*
l'arrière-grand-père (m.)	*great grandfather*
l'arrière-petite-fille (f.)	*great granddaughter*
l'arrière-petit-fils (m.)	*great grandson*
le beau-frère	*brother-in-law*
le beau-père	*father-in-law*
la belle-mère	*mother-in-law*
la belle-sœur	*sister-in-law*
célibataire	*single*
le fiancé/la fiancée	*fiancé(e)*
la marraine	*godmother*
le parrain	*godfather*
veuf	*widower*
veuve	*widow*

Les fournitures scolaires
(School supplies)

l'agrafe (f.)	*staple*
l'agrafeuse (f.)	*stapler*
le calendrier	*calendar*
les ciseaux (m.)	*scissors*
la colle	*glue*
l'élastique (m.)	*rubber band*
le feutre	*marker*
le liquide correcteur	*correction fluid*
le ruban adhésif	*transparent tape*
la tenue de gymnastique	*gym uniform*

Les fruits et les légumes
(Fruits and vegetables)

l'ananas (m.)	*pineapple*
l'asperge (f.)	*asparagus*
l'aubergine (f.)	*eggplant*
l'avocat (m.)	*avocado*
le céleri	*celery*
la cerise	*cherries*
le champignon	*mushroom*
le chou	*cabbage*
le chou-fleur	*cauliflower*
le concombre	*cucumber*
la courgette	*zucchini*
épicé(e)	*spicy*
les épinards (m.)	*spinach*
fade	*bland*
les haricots verts (m.)	*green beans*
la laitue	*lettuce*
la mangue	*mango*
la papaye	*papaya*
la pastèque	*watermelon*
la patate douce	*sweet potato*
la pêche	*peach*
les petits pois (m.)	*peas*
le piment	*hot pepper*
la poire	*pear*
le poivron	*bell pepper*
la prune	*plum*

Les instruments de musique
(Musical instruments)

l'accordéon (m.)	*accordion*
la basse	*bass guitar*
la clarinette	*clarinet*
la flûte	*flute*
la harpe	*harp*
l'orgue (m.)	*organ*
le saxophone	*saxophone*
le synthétiseur	*synthesizer*
la trompette	*trumpet*
le violon	*violin*
le violoncelle	*cello*

À la maison (At home)

la baignoire	*bathtub*
la cave	*basement*
la cheminée	*fireplace*
le congélateur	*freezer*
la cuisinière	*stove*
la douche	*shower*
l'évier (m.)	*kitchen sink*
le four	*oven*
le four à mirco-ondes	*microwave oven*
le grenier	*attic*
le lavabo	*bathroom sink*
le lave-linge	*clothes washer*
le réfrigérateur	*fridge*
le sèche-linge	*clothes dryer*
la terrasse	*patio*

Les matières à l'école
(School subjects)

l'algèbre (f.)	*algebra*
l'arabe (m.)	*Arabic*
l'art (m.) dramatique	*drama*
l'audiovisuel (m.)	*audiovisual*
le chinois	*Chinese*
la comptabilité	*accounting*
la géométrie	*geometry*
l'histoire (f.) de l'art	*art history*
le japonais	*Japanese*
le latin	*Latin*
la littérature	*literature*
le russe	*Russian*

La météorologie (The weather)

l'arc-en-ciel (m.)	*rainbow*
l'averse (f.)	*shower*
le brouillard	*fog*
bruiner	*to drizzle*
la brume	*mist*
la canicule	*heat wave*
le cyclone	*cyclone*

l'éclair (m.)	lightning
grêler	to hail
Il fait frais.	It is cool.
l'incendie de forêt (f.)	forest fire
le nuage	cloud
l'ouragan (m.)	hurricane
la tempête (neige)	(snow)storm
la tornade	tornado
le verglas	ice (on the road)
le tonnerre	thunder

Les motifs (Patterns)

à carreaux	checked
à fleurs	flowered
à motifs	patterned
à rayures	striped
à pois	polka-dotted

Les mots descriptifs
(Descriptive words)

aimable	likeable
la barbe	beard
bavard(e)	talkative
bien élevé(e)	well-mannered
le bouc	goatee
branché(e)	in, with 'it'
chauve	bald
la cicatrice	scar
débrouillard(e)	resourceful
égoïste	selfish
des lentilles (f.) de contact	contact lenses
des lunettes (f.) de vue	eyeglasses
mal élevé(e)	ill-mannered
la moustache	mustache
des pattes (f.)	sideburns
des piercings (m.)	piercings
sage	well-behaved
des taches (f.) de rousseur	freckles
têtu(e)	stubborn
travailleur/travailleuse	hard-working

La nourriture (Food)

l'agneau (m.)	lamb
le canard	duck
la côte	chop
la dinde	turkey
les œufs (m.) brouillés	scrambled eggs
les œufs (m.) sur le plat	fried eggs
les épices (f.)	spices
la margarine	margarine
la mayonnaise	mayonnaise
le miel	honey
la moutarde	mustard
le rôti	roast
la saucisse	sausage
le saumon	salmon
le sirop d'érable	maple syrup
la soupe	soup
le sucre	sugar
le thon	tuna
végétarien(ne)	vegetarian
la viande (hâchée)	(ground) meat
le vinaigre	vinegar

Les pays (Countries)

l'Algérie (f.)	Algeria
l'Argentine (f.)	Argentina
l'Autriche (f.)	Austria
la Belgique	Belgium
la Colombie	Columbia
l'Écosse (f.)	Scotland
la Grèce	Greece
l'Inde (f.)	India
l'Irlande (f.)	Ireland
l'état (m.) d'Israël	Israel
l'Italie (f.)	Italy
la Jamaïque	Jamaica
le Japon	Japan
le Liban	Lebanon
le Luxembourg	Luxembourg
Monaco	Monaco
les Pays-Bas (m.)	Netherlands
le Pérou	Peru
la Pologne	Poland
la (République de) Côte d'Ivoire	Ivory Coast
la Suisse	Switzerland
la Thaïlande	Thailand
le Viêtnam	Vietnam

Vocabulaire supplémentaire

Les sports et les passe-temps
(Sports and leisure activities)

l'alpinisme (m.)	*mountain climbing*
les arts (m.) martiaux	*martial arts*
l'astronomie (f.)	*astronomy*
le babyfoot	*foosball*
le billard	*pool, billiards*
la boxe	*boxing*
les fléchettes (f.)	*darts*
l'haltérophilie (f.)	*weightlifting*
le jeu de société	*board game*
jouer dans un groupe	*to play in a band*
la menuiserie	*woodworking*
la motoneige	*snowmobile*
le patinage artistique	*figure skating*
peindre	*to paint*
la plongée sous-marine	*scuba diving*
le plongeon	*diving*
le roller	*roller blading*
le scooter des mers	*jet ski*
la spéléologie	*spelunking*
le surf des neiges	*snowboarding*
le tennis de table	*table tennis*

Les vacances en plein air
(Vacationing outdoors)

le bois	*woods*
la chute d'eau	*waterfall*
le circuit	*tour*
la colline	*hill*
le désert	*desert*
la falaise	*cliff*
le fleuve	*river*
le parc national	*national park*
la source	*spring*
les vacances (f.) vertes	*ecotourism*
la vallée	*valley*
le volcan	*volcano*

Les vêtements et les accessoires
(Clothing and accessories)

le chandail	*sweater*
les espadrilles (f.)	*sandals*
la manche	*sleeve*
les mocassins (m.)	*loafers*
les mules (f.)	*mules*
les pantoufles (f.)	*slippers*
le peignoir	*bathrobe*
le pyjama	*pajamas*
les tongs (f.)	*flip-flops*
le velours	*velvet*
le gilet	*vest*

En ville *(In town)*

l'arrondissement (m.)	*district*
la banlieue	*suburb*
la caserne de pompiers	*fire station*
le commissariat	*police station*
le gratte-ciel	*skyscraper*
l'hôtel de ville (m.)	*city hall*
la mosquée	*mosque*
le palais de justice	*courthouse*
le palais des congrès	*convention center*
le passage pour piétons	*pedestrian crossing*
le quartier des affaires	*business district*
la salle de spectacles	*concert hall*
la station-service	*gas station*
la synagogue	*synagogue*
le trottoir	*sidewalk*

Les villes *(Cities)*

Alger	*Algiers*
Amsterdam	*Amsterdam*
Beijing	*Beijing*
Berlin	*Berlin*
Bruxelles	*Brussels*
Genève	*Geneva*
Lisbonne	*Lisbon*
Londres	*London*
Montréal	*Montreal*
Moscou	*Moscow*
La Nouvelle-Orléans	*New Orleans*
Québec	*Quebec City*
Tanger	*Tangier*
Venise	*Venice*
Vienne	*Vienna*

Vocabulaire supplémentaire

Liste d'expressions

Functions are the ways in which you use a language for particular purposes. In specific situations, such as in a restaurant, in a grocery store, or at school, you will want to communicate with those around you. In order to do that, you have to "function" in French: you place an order, make a purchase, or talk about your class schedule.

Here is a list of the functions presented in this book along with the French expressions you'll need to communicate in a wide range of situations. Following each function is the chapter and page number from the book where it is introduced.

Commands

Giving classroom commands
Ch.1, p. 20
> Asseyez-vous!
> Silence!
> Écoutez!
> Répétez!
> Allez au tableau!
> Regardez (la carte)!
> Retournez à vos places!
> Ouvrez vos livres à la page…
> Fermez vos cahiers.

Exchanging Information

Asking and giving names
Ch. 1, p. 6
> Comment tu t'appelles?
> Je m'appelle…
> Comment il/elle s'appelle?
> Il/Elle s'appelle…

Asking about things in a classroom
Ch. 1, p. 18
> Il y a… dans la salle de classe?
> Oui, il y a…
> Non, il n'y a pas de…
> Il n'y en a pas.
> Combien d'élèves il y a dans la classe?
> Il y en a…

Asking the teacher something
Ch.1, p. 20
> Monsieur/Madame/Mademoiselle,…
> Je ne comprends pas.
> Répétez, s'il vous plaît?
> Comment dit-on… en français?
> Qu'est-ce que ça veut dire… ?

Asking how words are spelled
Ch. 1, p. 22
> Comment ça s'écrit,…
> Comment tu épelles…
> Ça s'écrit…

Giving e-mail addresses
Ch. 1, p. 22
> Quelle est ton adresse e-mail?
> C'est… arobase… point…

Asking and saying how often
Ch. 2, p. 53
> Tu aimes… régulièrement?
> Oui, souvent.
> De temps en temps.
> Non, rarement.
> Non, jamais.

Describing people
Ch. 3, p. 79
> Comment est… ?
> Il/Elle est comment,… ?
> Il/Elle est très…
> Il/Elle n'est ni… ni…
> Mon ami(e) est…
> Il/Elle a les cheveux…
> Il/Elle a les yeux…
> Comment sont… ?
> Ils/Elles sont comment,… ?
> Ils/Elles sont assez…

Identifying family members
Ch. 3, p. 91
> Qui c'est, ça?
> Ça, c'est…
> Ça, ce sont…

Asking and telling about someone's family
Ch. 3, p. 93

Tu as des frères et des soeurs?

J'ai… et…

Non, je suis fils/fille unique.

Je n'ai pas de… mais…

Tu as combien de… ?

J'en ai…

Vous êtes combien dans ta famille?

Nous sommes…

Talking about classes
Ch. 4, p. 113

Quel jour est-ce que tu as… ?

J'ai… lundi.

Quand est-ce que tu as… ?

… le lundi, le mercredi et le vendredi.

À quelle heure tu as… ?

Tu as quel cours… ?

J'ai… à…

Quelle heure est-il?

Il est…

Asking others what they need and telling what you need
Ch. 4, p. 125

De quoi tu as besoin?

J'ai besoin de…

Qu'est-ce qu'il te faut pour… ?

Il me faut…

Tu pourrais me prêter… ?

Tiens.

Tu as… à me prêter?

Voilà.

Inquiring about and buying something
Ch. 4, p. 126

Je cherche…

De quelle couleur?

…, c'est combien?

C'est…

Merci,…

À votre service.

Je vous en prie.

Talking about one's interests
Ch. 5, p. 151

Qu'est-ce que tu fais comme sport?

Je joue…

Qu'est-ce que tu fais pour t'amuser?

Je fais…

Est-ce que tu fais du sport?

Non, je ne fais pas de sport.

Est-ce que tu joues… ?

Non, je ne joue pas…

Qu'est-ce que tu fais… ?

Je ne fais rien.

En hiver j'aime…

Au printemps, j'aime…

En été, nous aimons…

En automne, j'aime…

Telling when and how often
Ch. 5, p. 153

Quand est-ce que… ?

En quelle saison… ?

… pendant quels mois?

… en…

… régulièrement… ?

… rarement…

Making plans
Ch. 5, p. 165

Qu'est-ce que tu vas faire s'il… ?

Je vais…

Avec qui… ?

Avec…

Où ça?/Où est-ce qu'on se retrouve?

À la/Au/À l'…

Qu'est-ce qu'on fait… ?

On pourrait…

Tu vas faire quoi… ?

Pas grand-chose.

Rien de spécial.

Offering, accepting and refusing food
Ch. 6, p. 185

Qu'est-ce que tu veux manger/boire?

J'aimerais…

Tu veux/Vous voulez… ?

Oui, je veux bien.

Encore/Tu reprends… ?

Oui, s'il te/vous plaît.

Non, merci./Non, ça va.

Non, je n'ai plus faim/soif.

Inquiring about food and ordering
Ch. 6, p. 197

La carte s'il vous plaît!
Un moment, s'il vous plaît.
Qu'est-ce que vous me conseillez?
Je vous recommande…
Qu'est-ce que vous avez comme boissons?
On a…
Je voudrais/vais prendre…
Donnez-moi…
Vous avez choisi?
Vous désirez autre chose?

Asking how much and paying the check
Ch. 6, p. 198

C'est combien,… ?
C'est…
Ça fait combien?
Ça fait…
L'addition, s'il vous plaît.
Oui, tout de suite.
Le service est compris?
Oui, bien entendu.

Inquiring about prices
Ch. 7, p. 235

Il/Elle coûte combien,… ?
Il/Elle coûte…
… en solde,… ?
… ils/elles sont soldé(e)s à…
Ça fait combien en tout?
Alors,… ça fait…

Making a decision
Ch. 7, p. 237

Vous avez décidé?
Je ne sais pas quoi choisir.
Je n'arrive pas à me décider.
Je peux vous montrer… ?
… un peu trop…
… bon marché!
… c'est une bonne affaire!

Asking for permission
Ch. 8, p. 257

Tu es d'accord si… ?
D'accord, si tu…
Est-ce que je peux… ?
Bien sûr, mais il faut d'abord…
Pas question!
Non, tu dois…

Telling how often you do things
Ch. 8, p. 259

… tous les…
D'habitude,…
C'est toujours… qui…
… fois par…
… ne… jamais…

Describing a house
Ch. 8, p. 269

J'habite dans une maison/un appartement.
C'est un immeuble de…
Il y a…
Là, c'est…
Dans… , il y a…

Asking where something is
Ch. 8, p. 271

Où se trouve… ?
… au premier/deuxième/troisième étage.
… en bas/en haut.
… à gauche/à droite de…
… au fond du/de la…
… en face de…
Où est… ?
… sur/sous…
… à côté de…

Planning your day
Ch. 9, p. 295

D'abord,…
Ensuite,…
Après/Et puis,…
Finalement,…
Et je dois aussi passer…

Asking for and giving directions
Ch. 9, p. 297

Excusez-moi… , je cherche…
Est-ce que vous pouvez me dire où il y a… ?
C'est tout de suite sur votre…
Continuez/Allez tout droit jusqu'à…
Pardon… , savez-vous où est… ?
Prenez…
Tournez… prochain…
Traversez…

Asking for information
Ch. 9, p. 307

À quelle heure ouvre/ferme… ?
Savez-vous… ?
Est-ce que vous pouvez me dire… ?
Dites-moi,…
C'est combien pour… ?

Expressing needs

> Avez-vous de la monnaie sur… ?
>
> Oui, bien sûr.
>
> Non, je regrette.
>
> Je voudrais retirer/déposer/changer…
>
> Pour prendre de l'argent, s'il vous plaît?
>
> Adressez-vous…

Getting information about hotel reservations

> … disponible pour… ?
>
> … c'est complet.
>
> Je voudrais réserver une chambre du… au…
>
> À quel nom?
>
> Est-ce que vous faites pension complète?
>
> Nous ne faisons que demi-pension.
>
> Jusqu'à quelle heure… ?
>
> Toute la nuit.

Asking for information about travel

> Où est-ce qu'on peut composter les billets?
>
> Avez-vous les horaires… entre… et… ?
>
> Est-ce que je dois enregistrer… ?
>
> Quand part… à destination de… ?
>
> À quelle heure arrive… en provenance de… ?
>
> Est-ce qu'il y a un vol direct pour… ?
>
> Est-ce que l'avion fait escale à… ?

Buying tickets and making a transaction

> … un aller simple/aller-retour pour… ?
>
> … tarif réduit,…
>
> … changer… en… ?
>
> … payer par chèque/avec une carte/en liquide?

Expressing Attitudes and Opinions

Talking about likes and dislikes

> Tu aimes… ?
>
> Oui, j'aime…
>
> Non, je n'aime pas/Je déteste…
>
> J'aime mieux/Je préfère…
>
> Qu'est-ce que tu aimes faire?
>
> J'aime bien/J'adore…

Agreeing and disagreeing

> Moi, j'aime… Et toi?
>
> Moi aussi.
>
> Pas moi.
>
> Moi, je n'aime pas…
>
> Moi, si.
>
> Moi non plus.

Telling how well you do something

> Tu… bien… ?
>
> Oui, je… assez bien/bien/très bien…
>
> Non, je… mal/très mal…

Talking about preferences

> Tu préfères… ou… ?
>
> … mais…
>
> Quelles sont tes activités préférées?
>
> … et…

Giving an opinion

> Comment tu trouves… ?
>
> Je le/la trouve…
>
> Qu'est-ce que tu penses de/d'… ?
>
> À mon avis,…
>
> Comment c'est,… ?
>
> D'après moi, c'est…

Giving an opinion about classes

> Comment est ton cours de…?
>
> … difficile/facile.
>
> Comment c'est,… ?
>
> C'est intéressant/fascinant/ennuyeux.
>
> D'après moi, c'est…
>
> Ça te plaît,… ?
>
> Je trouve ça…

Commenting on food

> Il/Elle est bon(ne),… ?
>
> … il/elle est vraiment mauvais(e).
>
> … délicieux/délicieuse!
>
> Il/Elle est comment,… ?
>
> Excellent(e)!/Pas mauvais(e).
>
> Comment tu trouves… ?
>
> Pas bon/bonne du tout!

Giving opinions about clothing
Ch. 7, p. 224

Qu'est-ce que tu penses de… ?
C'est tout à fait toi!
Il/Elle est joli(e)/élégant(e)/horrible.
Il/Elle te plaît,… ?
Franchement, il/elle est un peu tape-à-l'œil.
Il/Elle me va,… ?
… il/elle te va très bien.
… il/elle ne te vas pas du tout.

Persuading

Offering and asking for help in a store
Ch. 7, p. 223

Je peux vous aider?
Je voudrais quelque chose pour…
Je cherche… pour mettre avec…
Je peux essayer… ?
Vous avez… en… ?
Non, merci, je regarde.
Quelle taille/pointure faites-vous?
Je fais du…

Giving advice
Ch. 10, p. 329

N'oublie pas…
Tu ne peux pas partir sans…
Tu devrais/Vous devriez…
Je te conseille de…
Tu as intérêt à…

Socializing

Greeting someone
Ch.1, p. 6

Salut!
Bonjour, Monsieur/Madame/Mademoiselle…
Bonsoir.

To say goodbye
Ch.1, p. 6

À bientôt./À demain.
À plus tard./À tout à l'heure.
Au revoir.

Asking how someone is
Ch. 1, p. 8

Ça va?/Comment ça va?
Comment allez-vous?
Et toi?
Et vous?
Oui, ça va. Merci.
Bien./Très bien.
Pas mal./Plus ou moins.
Non, pas très bien.

Introducing someone
Ch. 1, p. 11

Je te/vous présente…
Ça, c'est… . C'est un ami/une amie.
Bonjour./Salut!
Enchanté(e)!

Asking and saying how old someone is
Ch. 1, p. 11

Tu as quel âge?
J'ai… ans.
Il/Elle a quel âge?
Il/Elle a… ans.

Extending, accepting and refusing an invitation
Ch. 5 p. 163

On fait… ?
D'accord./Bonne idée!/Pourquoi pas?
On va… ?
Si tu veux/vous voulez.
Tu as envie de… ?
Ça te/vous dit de… ?
… ça ne me dit rien.
Tu viens… ?
Désolé(e), je n'ai pas le temps.
J'ai trop de choses à faire.
Je suis très occupé(e).

Synthèse de grammaire

ADJECTIVES

Adjective Agreement

Adjectives are words that describe nouns. They agree in gender (masculine or feminine) and number (singular or plural) with the nouns they modify. Adjectives that end in an unaccented -e, only change to agree in number. To make most adjectives plural, add an -s to the singular form, unless it already ends in an -s or -x.

		MASCULINE	FEMININE
Regular adjectives	SINGULAR PLURAL	intelligent intelligents	intelligente intelligentes
Adjectives ending in unaccented -e	SINGULAR PLURAL	jeune jeunes	jeune jeunes
Adjectives ending in -s	SINGULAR PLURAL	gris gris	grise grises

Adjectives ending in *-eux*

If the masculine singular form of the adjective ends in **-eux**, change the **-x** to **-se** to make it feminine.

heureux → heureuse

Adjectives ending in *-if*

If the masculine singular form of the adjective ends in **-if**, change the **-f** to **-ve** to create the feminine form.

sportif → sportive

Adjectives with Irregular Feminine Forms

MASCULINE	FEMININE		MASCULINE	FEMININE
blanc	blanche		gros	grosse
bon	bonne		mignon	mignonne
gentil	gentille		long	longue

Some adjectives, like **cool, chic, orange,** and **marron,** are invariable

Solange a acheté des calculatrices **orange.**

Position of Adjectives

Most adjectives in French follow the noun. Some adjectives, like **bon, grand, petit,** and **jeune,** always come before the noun. The article **des** becomes **de** when it is used with adjectives that come before the noun.

Michèle est une fille **intelligente.**   Il y a **de jeunes** professeurs dans mon école.

The Adjectives *beau, nouveau,* and *vieux*

The adjectives **beau** (*beautiful*), **nouveau** (*new*), and **vieux** (*old*) have special forms and they come before the nouns they describe.

MASCULINE SINGULAR (before a consonant)	MASCULINE SINGULAR (before a vowel)	MASCULINE PLURAL	FEMININE SINGULAR	FEMININE PLURAL
beau	bel	beaux	belle	belles
nouveau	nouvel	nouveaux	nouvelle	nouvelles
vieux	vieil	vieux	vieille	vieilles

Demonstrative Adjectives

	MASCULINE		FEMININE
SINGULAR	ce pull *(starting with a consonant)*		cette chemise
	cet imperméable *(starting with a vowel)*		
PLURAL	ces pulls		ces chemises
	ces imperméables		

To distinguish *this* from *that* and *these* from *those,* add **-ci** and **-là** to the end of the noun.

> J'aime **ces** bottes-**ci,** mais je n'aime pas **ces** bottes-**là.**
> *I like **these** boots, but I don't like **those** boots.*

Possessive Adjectives

These words also modify nouns and show ownership. In French, the possessive adjective agrees in number and gender with the object possessed and not the owner.

	MASCULINE SINGULAR	FEMININE SINGULAR (beginning with a consonant)	FEMININE SINGULAR (beginning with a vowel)	MASCULINE AND FEMININE PLURAL
my	**mon** père	**ma** mère	**mon** école	**mes** amies
your (tu)	**ton** livre	**ta** famille	**ton** amie	**tes** cours
his/her/its	**son** chat	**sa** cousine	**son** écharpe	**ses** cahiers
our	**notre** frère	**notre** maison	**notre** idée	**nos** professeurs
your (vous)	**votre** chien	**votre** ordinateur	**votre** eau minérale	**vos** étudiants
their	**leur** ami	**leur** classe	**leur** omelette	**leurs** devoirs

In English, possession can be shown by using **'s**. In French, the preposition **de/d'** is used to show possession.

> Le livre **de** Marie est sur la commode.

ADVERBS

Formation of Adverbs

Adverbs modify a verb, an adjective, or another adverb. To form most adverbs in French, take the feminine form of the adjective and add -**ment**.

heureux → heureuse → **heureusement**

The following are two irregular adverbs.

bon → **bien** (*well*)   mauvais → **mal** (*badly*)

Some common adverbs of frequency are: **souvent, de temps en temps, rarement,** and **régulièrement.**

Placement of Adverbs

While adverbs are generally placed near their verbs, they can take other positions in the sentence. Here is a general overview that might help when deciding where to place French adverbs.

TYPE OF ADVERB	EXAMPLES	PLACEMENT IN THE SENTENCE
how much, how often, or how well something is done	rarement, souvent, bien, mal	after the verb
adverbs of time	hier, maintenant, demain	the beginning or the end of the sentence

INTERROGATIVES

There are several ways to ask yes-no questions. One way is to raise the pitch of your voice. Another way is to add **Est-ce que** before a statement and raise your voice at the very end.

Tu aimes sortir?   **Est-ce qu'**ils aiment nager?
You like to go out?   *Do they like to swim?*

Inversion

Another way to ask yes-no questions is to use inversion. Reverse the subject pronoun and verb and add a hyphen between them. If the subject pronoun is **il, elle,** or **on** and the verb ends in a vowel, add -**t**- between the subject and verb. If the verb is in the **passé composé,** reverse the subject and helping verb.

Vous faites du ski.   →   **Faites-vous** du ski?

Elle a deux sœurs.   →   **A-t-elle** deux sœurs?

Il y a des stylos dans le sac.   →   **Y a-t-il** des stylos dans le sac?

Tu as trouvé un plan de la ville.   →   **As-tu** trouvé un plan de la ville?

Question Words

To ask for information, use a question word followed by either **est-ce que** plus a subject and verb or an inverted subject and verb.

Quand?	*When?*	**Comment?**	*How?*
Pourquoi?	*Why?*	**Qui?***	*Who?*
Que (Qu')?	*What?*	**Avec qui?**	*With whom?*
Où?	*Where?*		

Quand est-ce qu'il arrive?   **Comment fait-on** du ski?

Don't use **est-ce que** or inversion with question words followed by **être**.

Où est ton frère?   *Where is your brother?*

*****Qui** is usually the subject of a sentence, so it's often followed by a verb.

Qui joue de la guitare?   *Who plays the guitar?*

Interrogative Adjectives

Quel means *which* or *what*. It has four forms.

	MASCULINE	FEMININE
SINGULAR	**Quel** chemisier?	**Quelle** jupe?
PLURAL	**Quels** chemisiers?	**Quelles** jupes?

Quel can also be used as an exclamation.

Quel joli pull!   *What a pretty pullover!*

NEGATIVE EXPRESSIONS

Negative Expressions

To make a sentence negative in the present tense, add **ne... pas** around the verb. In the **passé composé**, add **ne... pas** around the helping verb.

Ça **ne** va **pas**.   Anne **n'**a **pas** fait ses devoirs.

NEGATIVE EXPRESSION		EXAMPLE
ne... pas encore	*not yet*	Ils n'ont **pas encore** finis leurs devoirs.
ne... plus	*no longer*	Elle **ne** travaille **plus** au café Magnolia.
ne... ni... ni	*neither nor*	Je n'aime **ni** les bananes **ni** les pommes.
ne... jamais	*never*	Tu **ne** viens **jamais** au parc avec nous.
ne... personne	*no one*	Danièle n'entend **personne** au téléphone.
ne... rien	*nothing*	Nous **ne** faisons **rien** ce soir.
ne... que	*only*	Je n'aime **que** le chocolat suisse.

If **rien** and **personne** are subjects, put **ne** directly before the conjugated verb.

Personne n'a téléphoné.   **Rien n'**est facile.

NOUNS AND ARTICLES

Nouns

In French, all nouns have a gender: masculine or feminine. You must learn a noun's gender when you learn its meaning.

FORMATION OF PLURAL NOUNS

	Add **-s** to most nouns	No change to nouns that end in **-s** or **-x**	No change to nouns that are abbreviations	Add **-x** to nouns that end in **-eau** or **-eu**	Replace **-al** with **-aux** in nouns that end in **-al**
SINGULAR	magazine	bus fax	DVD	tableau jeu	journal
PLURAL	magazines	bus fax	DVD	tableaux jeux	journaux

Indefinite Articles

Indefinite articles are used with nouns to signal their gender and number. In French, there are three indefinite articles: **un, une,** (*a* or *an*) and **des** (*some*).

	MASCULINE	**FEMININE**
SINGULAR	**un** livre	**une** fenêtre
PLURAL	**des** livres	**des** fenêtres

Definite Articles

Definite articles also signal gender and number. There are four in French, **le, la, l',** and **les** (*the*).

	MASCULINE (beginning with a consonant)	**FEMININE (beginning with a consonant)**	**MASCULINE OR FEMININE (beginning with a vowel)**
SINGULAR	**le** livre	**la** fenêtre	**l'**ami / **l'**école
PLURAL	**les** livres	**les** fenêtres	**les** amis / **les** écoles

Use **le** before a day of the week to say you do something regularly on that particular day.

J'ai anglais **le** vendredi. *I have English class on Fridays.*

Partitive Articles

To say that you want *part* or *some of* an item, use a partitive article.

MASCULINE SINGULAR	FEMININE SINGULAR	SINGULAR NOUN (beginning with a vowel)	PLURAL
du beurre	de la confiture	de l'omelette	des céréales

Tu veux **du** bacon?   *Do you want some bacon?*

To say that you want a whole item (or several whole items), use the indefinite articles **un, une,** and **des.**

Je veux **un** croissant et **des** œufs.   *I want a croissant and eggs.*

Negation and the Articles

Indefinite and partitive articles change to **de** or **d'** in a negative sentence. Definite articles remain the same.

Il y a **une** carte dans la classe. → Il n'y a pas **de** carte dans la classe.

Il y a **des** fenêtres. → Il n'y a pas **de** fenêtre.

Je veux **du** bacon. → Je ne veux pas **de** bacon.

PREPOSITIONS

Contractions with *à* and *de*

The preposition **à** usually means *to* or *at.* The preposition **de** usually means *from* or *of.* It can also be used to show possession: **J'aime bien le frère d'André** (*I like André's brother.*) When **à** and **de** are used with the definite articles **le** and **les,** they form contractions.

à + le = au	à + la = à la	à + l' = à l'	à + les = aux
de + le = du	de + la = de la	de + l' = de l'	de + les = des

Prepositions with Countries and Cities

To say that you are *in* or going *to* a country or city, use a form of the preposition **à** or the preposition **en.** To say that you are *from* or coming *from* a country or city, use a form of the preposition **de.**

CITIES	MASCULINE COUNTRIES	FEMININE COUNTRIES OR MASCULINE COUNTRIES BEGINNING WITH A VOWEL	PLURAL COUNTRIES
à Paris	au Sénégal	en France en Egypte	aux États-Unis
de Paris	du Sénégal	de France d'Egypte	des États-Unis

PRONOUNS

Subject Pronouns

je (j')	*I*	nous	*we*
tu	*you (familiar)*	vous	*you (plural or formal)*
il	*he / it*	ils	*they*
elle	*she / it*	elles	*they*
on	*they (people in general)*		

C'est versus *Il/Elle est*

C'est	Il/Elle est
with a person's name **C'est Norbert.**	with an adjective by itself **Elle est blonde.**
with an article plus a noun **C'est une élève.** **C'est mon père.**	
with an article, plus a noun, plus an adjective **C'est un homme intelligent.**	

VERBS

Present Tense of Regular Verbs

In French, we use a formula to conjugate regular verbs. The endings change in each person, but the stem of the verb remains the same.

INFINITIVE		aimer	attendre	finir
PRESENT	je/j'	aim**e**	attend**s**	fin**is**
	tu	aim**es**	attend**s**	fin**is**
	il/elle/on	aim**e**	attend	fin**it**
	nous	aim**ons**	attend**ons**	fin**issons**
	vous	aim**ez**	attend**ez**	fin**issez**
	ils/elles	aim**ent**	attend**ent**	fin**issent**

The Verbs *dormir, sortir,* and *partir*

INFINITIVE		dormir	sortir	partir
PRESENT	je/j'	dor**s**	sor**s**	par**s**
	tu	dor**s**	sor**s**	par**s**
	il/elle/on	dor**t**	sor**t**	par**t**
	nous	dorm**ons**	sort**ons**	part**ons**
	vous	dorm**ez**	sort**ez**	part**ez**
	ils/elles	dorm**ent**	sort**ent**	part**ent**

Synthèse de grammaire

Verbs with Stem and Spelling Changes

These verbs are not irregular, but they do have stem and spelling changes.

INFINITIVE		manger	commencer	préférer	acheter	appeler	nettoyer
PRESENT	je (j')	mange	commence	préfère	achète	appelle	nettoie
	tu	manges	commences	préfères	achètes	appelles	nettoies
	il/elle/on	mange	commence	préfère	achète	appelle	nettoie
	nous	mangeons	commençons	préférons	achetons	appelons	nettoyons
	vous	mangez	commencez	préférez	achetez	appelez	nettoyez
	ils/elles	mangent	commencent	préfèrent	achètent	appellent	nettoient

Verbs like **manger**: changer, échanger, corriger, déranger, encourager, voyager.

Verbs like **commencer**: placer, prononcer, remplacer, avancer, lancer.

Verbs like **préférer**: espérer, répéter.

Verbs like **acheter**: amener, emmener, lever, promener.

Verbs like **appeler**: épeler, jeter, rappeler.

Verbs like **nettoyer**: balayer, envoyer, essayer, payer.

Verbs with Irregular Forms

INFINITIVE		aller	avoir	être	faire
PRESENT	je/j'	vais	ai	suis	fais
	tu	vas	as	es	fais
	il/elle/on	va	a	est	fait
	nous	allons	avons	sommes	faisons
	vous	allez	avez	êtes	faîtes
	ils/elles	vont	ont	sont	font

INFINITIVE		devoir	pouvoir	vouloir	venir
PRESENT	je/j'	dois	peux	veux	viens
	tu	dois	peux	veux	viens
	il/elle/on	doit	peut	veut	vient
	nous	devons	pouvons	voulons	venons
	vous	devez	pouvez	voulez	venez
	ils/elles	doivent	peuvent	veulent	viennent

INFINITIVE		prendre	voir	boire	mettre
PRESENT	je/j'	prends	vois	bois	mets
	tu	prends	vois	bois	mets
	il/elle/on	prend	voit	boit	met
	nous	prenons	voyons	buvons	mettons
	vous	prenez	voyez	buvez	mettez
	ils/elles	prennent	voient	boivent	mettent

Verbs like **prendre**: apprendre, comprendre, reprendre.

Savoir and connaître

Savoir and **connaître** both mean *to know*. **Savoir** means to know information or how to do something. **Connaître** means to know or be familiar with a person, place, etc.

INFINITIVE		savoir	connaître
PRESENT	je/j'	sais	connais
	tu	sais	connais
	il/elle/on	sait	connaît
	nous	savons	connaissons
	vous	savez	connaissez
	ils/elles	savent	connaissent

Nous **connaissons** le père de Julie.

Je ne **sais** pas jouer au hockey.

The *futur proche*

You can use a form of **aller** plus an infinitive to talk about something that is going to happen in the near future.

Nous **allons étudier** le géo.   *We're going to study geography.*

The *passé récent*

You can use a form of **venir** plus **de** and an infinitive to talk about something that just happened.

Je **viens de téléphoner** à Ali.   *I just phoned Ali.*

The Imperative

To form the imperative, or commands, use the **tu, vous,** or **nous** form of the present tense of the verb, without the subject. For -er verbs and **aller,** drop the final -s in the **tu** form.

écouter	finir	attendre	faire	aller
Écoute!	Finis!	Attends!	Fais!	Va!
Écoutez!	Finnissez!	Attendez!	Faîtes…!	Allez!
Écoutons!	Finnissons!	Attendons!	Faisons…!	Allons!

To make a command negative, put **ne** before the verb and **pas** after it.

N'allez **pas** au cinéma demain!

N'attendons **pas** le bus!

The *passé composé* with *avoir*

The passé composé of most verbs consists of two parts: a form of the helping verb **avoir** and a past participle.

INFINITIVE	chercher		choisir		perdre	
PAST PARTICIPLE	cherché		choisi		perdu	
je/j'	ai		ai		ai	
tu	as		as		as	
il/elle/on	a	cherché	a	choisi	a	perdu
nous	avons		avons		avons	
vous	avez		avez		avez	
ils/elles	ont		ont		ont	

To say what didn't happen, place **ne... pas** around the helping verb.

> Je **n'**ai **pas** trouvé de chemise à ma taille.
> *I didn't find a shirt in my size.*

The following verbs use **avoir** as the helping verb in the **passé composé,** but have irregular past participles.

avoir	→	**eu**	être	→	**été**	pouvoir	→ **pu**
boire	→	**bu**	faire	→	**fait**	prendre	→ **pris**
connaître	→	**connu**	lire	→	**lu**	savoir	→ **su**
devoir	→	**dû**	mettre	→	**mis**	voir	→ **vu**
dire	→	**dit**	pleuvoir	→	**plu**	vouloir	→ **voulu**
écrire	→	**écrit**					

The *passé composé* with *être*

Some verbs, mainly verbs of motion like **aller,** use **être** instead of **avoir** as the helping verb in the **passé composé.** For these verbs, the past participle agrees with the subject.

aller			
je	suis **allé(e)**	nous	sommes **allé(e)s**
tu	es **allé(e)**	vous	êtes **allé(e)(s)**
il	est **allé**	ils	sont **allés**
elle	est **allée**	elles	sont **allées**
on	est **allé(e)(s)**		

The following are verbs conjugated with **être** in the **passé composé.**

arriver	→	**arrivé**	partir	→	**parti**
descendre	→	**descendu**	rester	→	**resté**
devenir	→	**devenu**	retourner	→	**retourné**
(r)entrer	→	**(r)entré**	revenir	→	**revenu**
monter	→	**monté**	sortir	→	**sorti**
mourir	→	**mort**	tomber	→	**tombé**
naître	→	**né**	venir	→	**venu**

Glossaire français–anglais

This vocabulary includes almost all of the words presented in the textbook, both active (for production) and passive (for recognition only). An entry in **boldface** type indicates that the word or phrase is active. Active words and phrases are practiced in the chapter and are listed in the **Résumé** pages at the end of each chapter. You are expected to know and be able to use active vocabulary.

All other words are for recognition only. These words are found in activities, in optional and visual material, in the **Géoculture, Comparaisons, Lecture et écriture, Télé-roman,** and **Variations littéraires.** Many words have more than one definition; the definitions given here correspond to the way the words are used in *Bien dit!*

The number after each entry refers to the chapter or the page number of the section where the word or phrase first appears or becomes active vocabulary.

à *to, at,* 2; *to/at + city,* 10
À bientôt. *See you soon.,* 1
à côté de *next to,* 8
À demain. *See you tomorrow.,* 1
à destination de *heading for,* 10
à droite de *to the right of,* 8
a fait connaître *made known,* 7
à gauche de *to the left of,* 8
à haute voix *aloud,* 9
à la carte *individually,* 5
à la fin *at the end,* 369
à la main *by hand,* 9
à la réflexion *if you really think about it,* 4
à l'avance *in advance,* 381
à l'heure *on time,* 10
à mon avis *in my opinion,* 3
à partir de *from (a certain time),* 6
à pied *by foot,* 9
À plus tard. *See you later.,* 1
à point *medium,* 6
à propos de *about,* 9
À quel nom? *Under what name?,* 9
à quelle heure *at what time,* 4
À quelle heure tu as...? *At what time do you have...?,* 4
À saisir! *Great deal!,* 8
À table! *Dinner is served!,* 6
À toute à l'heure. *See you later.,* 1
à vélo *by bicycle,* 9
À votre service. *You're welcome.,* 4
l' abbaye (f.) *monastery,* 5

l' abécédaire (m.) *a reader for small children,* 379
abondant(e) *plentiful,* 376
abriter *to shelter,* 5
l' absence (f.) *absence,* 377
Absolument. *Absolutely.,* 9
absurde *absurd,* 369
l' accès handicapé (m.) *handicapped access,* 10
les accessoires (m.) *accessories,* 7
accompagné de *accompanied by,* 6
accorder *to grant,* 6
accueillir *to welcome,* 381
acheter *to buy,* 4, 9
l' acrobate (m./f.) *acrobat,* 366
l' acrobatie (f.) *acrobatics,* 367
l' activité (f.) *activity,* 2
actuel(le) *of the present time,* 375
l' adaptateur (m.) *adapter,* 10
adapter *to adapt,* 375
l' addition (f.) *bill,* 6
admirable *admirable,* 379
adorer *to love, to adore,* 2
les ados (m./f.) *teens,* 2
l' adresse e-mail (f.) *e-mail address,* 1
s' adresser *to address,* 9
Adressez-vous... *Ask...,* 9
l' adversaire (m.) *adversary,* 7
l' aérobic (f.) *aerobics,* 5
l' aéroport (m.) *airport,* 10
africain(e) *African,* 8
l' âge (m.) *age,* 1
âgé(e) *elderly,* 3
l' agence (f.) immobilière *real estate agency,* 8

agréable *pleasant,* 8
aider *to help,* 7
aimer *to like, to love,* 2; **aimer bien** *to quite like,* 2; **aimer mieux** *to like better, to prefer,* 2
ainsi *thus,* 10
ainsi que *as well as,* 9
ajouter *to add,* 373
l' alerte (f.) *alarm,* 6
allemand *German,* 4
l' Allemangne (m.) *Germany,* 10
aller *to go,* 2
l' aller simple (m.) *one way,* 10
l' aller-retour (m.) *round-trip,* 10
Allez au tableau! *Go to the board!,* 1
Allez tout droit jusqu'à... *Go straight until...,* 9
l' allure *shape,* 369
alors *so, well,* 7
Alors,... ça fait... *Let's see,... your total is...,* 7
l' alpinisme (m.) *mountain climbing,* 5
les amandes (f.) *almonds,* 6
ambulant *traveling, wandering,* 374
amener *to bring someone/a pet along,* 4
américain *American,* 6
l' ami(e) *friend,* 1
l' ampleur (f.) *abundance,* 375
amuser (s') *to have fun,* 5
ancien(ne) *old,* 8
anglais *English,* 2
l' Angleterre (m.) *England,* 10

l' **animal/les animaux** (m.) *animal(s)*, 2
l' **animal domestique** *pet*, 3
l' **année** (f.) *year*, 7
annuler *to cancel*, 10
l' **anorak** (m.) *winter jacket*, 7
l' Antiquité *ancient times*, 380
l' **août** (m.) *August*, 5
l' **appareil** (m.) *appliance*, 10
l' **appareil photo (numérique)** (m.) *(digital) camera*, 5
l' **appartement** (m.) *apartment*, 8
appartenir *to belong to*, 371
appeler *to call*, 10
appeler (s') *to be named*, 1
apprécié(e) *valued*, 5
apprécier *to appreciate*, 370
apprendre *to learn*, 6
apprendre (quelque chose) à quelqu'un *to teach*, 379
approuver *to approve*, 380
l' aqueduc (m.) *aqueduct*, 9
l' arbre-toboggan (m.) *tree-slide*, 365
après *after*, 9
l' **après-midi** (m.) *afternoon*, 4
les arachides (f.) *peanuts*, 7
l' arbre (m.) frutier *fruit tree*, 8
l' **argent** (m.) *silver*, 7; *money*, 9
l' **armée** (f.) *army*, 1
l' **armoire** (f.) *wardrobe*, 8
l' **arrêt (de bus)** (m.) *(bus) stop*, 9
l' **arrivée** (f.) *arrival*, 10
arrondir *to make round*, 379
arroser *to water*, 8
artisanal(e) *crafting*, 7
l' artiste (m./f.) *artist*, 7
les **arts** (m.) **plastiques** *visual arts*, 4
l' **ascenseur** (m.) *elevator*, 10
l' aspect (m.) *aspect*, 9
l' **aspirateur** (m.) *vacuum cleaner*, 8
l' aspirine (f.) *aspirin*, 9
asseoir (s') *to sit down*, 376
Asseyez-vous! *Sit down!*, 1
assez *quite*, 3
assez bien *pretty well*, 2
assiéger *to lay siege to*, 6
l' **assiette** (f.) *plate*, 2
assis(e) *seated*, 379
associer *to associate*, 7
les astuces (f.) *tips*, 373
l' atelier (m.) *workshop*, 1
l' **athlétisme** (m.) *track and field*, 5
atteindre *to reach, to attain*, 5
attendre *to wait*, 4
attirer *to attract*, 9
attraper *to catch*, 3
au *to /at the*, 2; *to / at + masculine country*, 10
au début *at the beginning*, 6
au-dessus de *above*, 9
au fond de *at the end of*, 8

au moins *at least*, 373
Au revoir. *Goodbye.*, 1
au sud de *to the south of*, 8
audacieux (-ieuse) *daring*, 380
aujourd'hui *today*, 4
auraient donné *(they) would have given*, 369
auraient ôté *had taken away*, 370
aurait reçu *would have received*, 6
les aurores (f.) boréales *Northern Lights*, 3
aussi *also*, 1, 2
l' **Australie** (f.) *Australia*, 10
autre *other*, 369
autrefois *formerly*, 372
autant *as much*, 2
l' **automne** (m.) *fall*, 5
aux *to/at the*, 2
avaient *(they) had*, 369
avaient haï *(they) had hated*, 369
avait beau être *was in vain*, 369
avait-il affaire à *was he dealing with*, 10
avant *before*, 1
avant J.-C. *B.C.*, 5
avec *with*, 2
avec qui *with whom*, 5
avec vue *with a view*, 10
Avez-vous de la monnaie? *Do you have change?*, 9
l' **avion** (m.) *plane*, 10
avoir *to have*, 1
avoir besoin de *to need*, 4
avoir chaud *to be hot*, 5
avoir envie de *to feel like*, 5
avoir faim *to be hungry*, 5
avoir froid *to be cold*, 5
avoir intérêt à *to be in one's best interest*, 10
avoir le temps de *to have time to*, 5
avoir les cheveux... *to have... hair*, 3
avoir les yeux... *to have... eyes*, 3
avoir lieu *to take place*, 5
avoir mal à *to hurt*, 9
avoir soif *to be thirsty*, 5
avoir sommeil *to be sleepy*, 5
l' **avril** *April*, 5

le **bacon** *bacon*, 6
les **bagages** (m.) **(à main)** *(carry-on) luggage*, 10
la **bague** *ring*, 7
la **baguette** *loaf of French bread*, 6; *teacher's stick*, 379

la **baie** *bay*, 5
la **baignoire** *bath tub*, 8
baisser *to lower*, 369
se **balader** *to wander by*, 371
le **baladeur (MP3)** *walkman (MP3 player)*, 2
le balafon *traditional Senegalese musical instrument*, 7
balançait sa tête de droite et de gauche *shaking his head from left to right*, 10
la balançoire *swing*, 367
balayer *to sweep*, 8
le **balcon** *balcony*, 8
la **balle** *ball*, 2
le **ballet** *ballet*, 9
le **ballon** *(inflatable) ball*, 2
bambou *bamboo*, 379
la **banane** *banana*, 6
la **bande dessinée (BD)** *comic strip*, 2
la **banque** *bank*, 9
le baobab *tree found in Africa*, 7
bas *low*, 8
le **bas** *stocking*, 10
le **base-ball** *baseball*, 2
le **basket(ball)** *basketball*, 5
les **baskets** (f.) *tennis shoes*, 4
le bassin *ornamental pool*, 363
la bataille *battle*, 5
le bateau *boat*, 367
le **batik** *batik (technique used to create patterns on fabric using hot wax and dyes)*, 7
la **batte** *bat*, 2
la **batterie** *drums*, 5
beau/belle *handsome, beautiful*, 3
beaucoup *a lot*, 4
le **beau-père** *step-father*, 3
les **beaux-arts** (m.) *fine arts*, 1
les **beaux-parents** (m.) *inlaws*, 376
la **belle-mère** *step mother*, 3
la bête *beast, animal*, 9
le **beurre** *butter*, 6
la **bibliothèque** *library*, 2
bien *well*, 1
la **bien-aimée** *beloved*, 376
bien cuit *well-done*, 6
bien entendu *of course*, 6
bien sûr *of course*, 9
Bien sûr, mais il faut d'abord... *Of course, but first you must...*, 8
la **bijouterie** *jewelry*, 7
le **billet** *bill (money), ticket*, 9
le **billet d'avion** *plane ticket*, 10
le **billet de train** *train ticket*, 10
blanc(he) *white*, 3
le blason familial *coat-of-arms*, 3
bleu(e) *blue*, 3
blond(e) *blond(e)*, 3
bloqué(e) *stuck*, 9
le **bodyboard** *bodyboard*, 5

Glossaire français–anglais

le **chèque de voyage**
traveler's check, 10
cher/chère *expensive,* 7
chercher *to look for,* 4
chéri(e) *beloved,* 371
le **cheval** *horse,* 9
les **cheveux** (m.) *hair,* 3
chez moi *at (my) home,* 8
le **chien** *dog,* 3
les chiens (m.) de traîneaux
dog-sledding, 5
la **chimie** *chemistry,* 4
le chimpanzé *chimpanzee,* 7
la **Chine** *China,* 10
le **chocolat** *chocolate,* 2
le **chocolat chaud** *hot chocolate,* 6
la chose *thing,* 371
choisir *to choose,* 6
le choix *choice,* 7
la **chose** *thing,* 6
le cimetière *cemetery,* 5
le cinéaste (la cinéaste)
film-maker, 378
le **cinéma** *movie theatre,* 2
cinq *five,* 1
cinquante *fifty,* 4
la cipâte de bleuets *special blueberry
pie made in Quebec,* 3
circulaire *circular,* 8
le cirque *circus,* 366
la cité *city, ancient center of town,* 9
le citron *lemon,* 7
clair *light (color),* 4
la **classe** *class, classroom,* 1
le **classeur** *binder,* 4
classique *classical,* 2
la **clé** *key,* 9
la **climatisation** *air conditioning,* 10
climatisé(e) *air-conditioned,* 8
le clown *clown,* 366
le **club (de tennis, de foot)**
(sports) club, 5
le **coca** *soda,* 6
le cochonnet *wooden ball used
in pétanque,* 5
le **code postal** *zip code,* 9
la **coiffure** *hairdo,* 9
le coin *corner,* 377
le **colis** *package,* 9
le **collier** *necklace,* 7
la colline *hill,* 380
la colonie de vacances
summer camp, 5
coloré(e) *brightly colored,* 7
combien *how much, how many,* 1
**Combien d'élèves il y a dans la
classe?** *How many students are
there in the class?,* 1
la comité *committee,* 381
comme *as, like,* 4
commencer *to begin,* 4

comment *how,* 1
Comment allez-vous? *How are
you? (formal),* 1
Comment ça s'écrit? *How do you
write that?,* 1
Comment ça va? *How are you?
(informal),* 1
Comment c'est,...? *How is…?,* 3
Comment dit-on... en français?
How do you say… in French?, 1
Comment est...? *How is…?,* 3
Comment est ton cours de...?
How is your… class?, 4
Comment il / elle s'appelle? *What's
his / her name?,* 1
Comment sont...? *How are…?,* 3
Comment tu épelles...? *How do
you spell…?,* 1
Comment tu t'appelles? *What is
your name?,* 1
Comment tu trouves...? *What do
you think of…?,* 3
les commerces (f.) *businesses,* 8
la **commode** *chest of drawers,* 8
le **compartiment** *compartment,* 10
complet *booked, full,* 10
complètement *completely,* 9
composé(e) *composed,* 5
composter *to punch (a ticket),* 10
la composition *composition,* 375
comprendre *to understand,* 1
le **comprimé** *pill,* 9
compter *to count,* 1
concerner *to relate to,* 376
le concert *concert,* 9
conduire *to drive,* 381
confisqué(s) à *confiscated from,* 6
la **confiture** *jam,* 6
confortable *comfortable,* 376
conjuguer *to conjugate,* 4
connaître *to know,* 9
connu(e) *well-known,* 6
le conseil de classe *student council,* 4
conseiller *to advise,* 6
la **consigne** *baggage locker,* 10
consister *to consist,* 6
le consommateur *consumer,* 2
la construction *construction,* 8
construire *to construct, build,* 5
le conte *story,* 5
contenir *to contain,* 10
le continent *continent,* 7
continuer *to continue,* 9
Continuez jusqu'à... *Continue
until…,* 9
le contorsionniste (la contorsionniste)
contortionist, 366
contrairement *in opposition,* 366
contre *against,* 1
le **contrôleur** *ticket collector,* 10
le coquillage *shellfish,* 5

le **copain** *friend,* 2
la **cora** *traditional Senegalese musical
instrument,* 374
la **correspondance** *connecting flight,
connection,* 10
correspondre *to correspond,
to communicate,* 1
corriger *to correct,* 4
la **corvée** *chore,* 8
le **costume** *suit,* 7
la côte *coast,* 5
le **coton** *cotton,* 7
la **couchette** *sleeping car,* 10
la **couleur** *color,* 4
le **coupe-vent** *windbreaker,* 7
couper la parole *to leave
speechless,* 379
la **cour** *(royal) court,* 1; *courtyard,* 9
le **courage** *courage,* 6
courir *to run,* 377
le **courrier** *mail,* 1
le **cours** *class(es),* 4;
flow (of water), 380
la course *race,* 5
court(e) *short (length),* 3
le courtisan *person who is part
of the royal court,* 362
le **cousin/la cousine** *cousin,* 3
le **couteau** *knife,* 6
coûter *to cost,* 7
la coutume *custom,* 376
le couturier *fashion designer,* 7
le **couvert** *table setting,* 6
la couverture *cloak,* 10
le crabe *crab,* 5
crachoter *to crackle,* 9
la **cravate** *tie,* 7
le **crayon** *pencil,* 4; **le crayon
de couleur** *colored pencil,* 2
créatif(-ive) *creative,* 3
la crèche *manger,* 10
créer *to create,* 9
la crème *cream,* 9
la crème Chantilly *whipped
cream,* 373
la crêpe *thin, light pancake,* 372
la crêperie *restaurant that serves
crêpes,* 372
creusant *digging,* 6
la crevette *shrimp,* 5
crier *to shout,* 379
croire *to think, believe,* 7
la croisière *cruise,* 381
le **croissant** *croissant,* 6
le croissant de lune *crescent moon,* 6
le **croque-monsieur** *toasted ham and
cheese sandwich,* 6
le crustacé *Crustacean,* 5
cubain(e) *Cuban,* 374
la **cuillère** *spoon,* 6
le **cuir** *leather,* 7

cuire *to cook,* 372
la cuisine *cooking, kitchen,* 8
le cuisinier/la cuisinère *cook,* 10
la cuisson *cooking,* 373
cuit(e) *cooked,* 7
cuit(e) au four *baked,* 6
cultiver *to cultivate,* 5
le curé *parish priest,* 378
curieux(-euse) *curious,* 371
le cybercafé *Internet café,* 5

d'abord *first,* 9
D'accord. *Okay.,* 5
D'accord, si tu... *It's okay
if you...,* 8
d'ailleurs *moreover,* 10
dans *in,* 1
danser *to dance,* 2
le danseur/la danseuse *dancer,* 366
d'après moi *according to me,* 3
le dauphin *dolphin,* 2
de *of/from + city, feminine
country,* 10
de l' *of the,* 6; **de la** *of the,* 6
De quelle couleur? *In what
color?,* 4
de nos jours *these days,* 370
De quoi tu as besoin? *What do
you need?,* 4
de récupération *salvaged,* 7
de temps en temps *from time
to time,* 2
le débarquement *landing,* 5
débarrasser (la table) *to clear
(the table),* 8
le début *debut,* 375
décembre *December,* 5
décider *to decide,* 6
déconseillé(e) *advised against,* 381
la décoration *decoration,* 6
décoratif(-ve) *decorative,* 5
décorer *decorate,* 10
découvert(e) *discovered,* 5
la découverte *discovery,* 381
décrire *to describe,* 9
dedans *inside,* 10
le défaut *character flaw,* 371
défensif(-ve) *defensive,* 5
le défilé *parade,* 9
se déformer *to lose shape,* 369
le déjeuner *lunch,* 6
le délégué de classe *student
representative,* 4
Délicieux!/Délicieuse!
Delicious!, 6

le deltaplane *hang-gliding,* 5
demain *tomorrow,* 4
demander *to ask, demand,* 4
demi(e) *half,* 4
le demi-frère *half-brother,* 3
la demi-pension *half-board,* 10
la demi-sœur *half-sister,* 3
le départ *departure,* 10
les dépendances (f.) *out-buildings,* 8
déposer *to deposit,* 9
depuis *since,* 5
déranger *to disturb,* 4
dernier(-ère) *last,* 7
se dérouler *to take place,* 9
derrière *behind,* 9
des *some,* 1; *of the,* 6
descendre *to come down,* 8
désigner *to name, to designate,* 375
le désinfectant *disinfectant,* 9
désirer *to want,* 6
désolé(e) *sorry,* 5
Désolé(e), je n'ai pas le temps.
Sorry, I don't have the time., 5
le dessert *dessert,* 6
le dessin *drawing,* 2
le dessinateur *drawer,* 9
dessiner *to draw,* 2
la destination *destination,* 10
détacher *to detach,* 373
détester *to hate,* 2
deux *two,* 1
deux cent un *two hundred
and one,* 4
deux cents *two hundred,* 4
deuxième *second,* 10
la deuxième classe *second class,* 10
devant *in front (of),* 9
développer *to develop,* 380
devenir *to become,* 8
deviner *to guess,* 6
devoir *to have to,* 8
le devoir *homework,* 4; *to have to,* 8
d'habitude *usually,* 8
le diamètre *diameter,* 7
le dictionnaire *dictionary,* 4
les dieux (m.) *gods,* 370
difficile *difficult,* 4
la difficulté *difficulty,* 379
le dimanche *Sunday,* 4
le dîner *diner,* 6
discret (discrète) *discrete,* 8
dire *to say,* 1; *to tell,* 9; **Dites-
moi...** *Tell me...,* 9; se dit-il
he says to himself, 10
diriger vers *to aim at,* 379
discuter (avec des amis) *to talk
(with friends),* 2
disparaître *disappear,* 370
disponible (pour) *available
(for),* 10
se distinguer *to gain
distinction,* 375

distrait *absent-minded,* 371
le distributeur d'argent *cash
machine,* 9
le distributeur de billets *ticket
machine,* 10
divin(e) *divine,* 370
divorcer *to divorce,* 3
dix *ten,* 1
dix-huit *eighteen,* 1
dix-neuf *nineteen,* 1
dix-sept *seventeen,* 1
le djembé *traditional Senegalese
musical instrument,* 374
le doigt *finger,* 379
doit *owes,* 7
le domaine *domain,* 9
le don *talent,* 370
donc *then,* 371
donner *to give,* 6
Donnez-moi... *Give me...,* 6
dont *of which,* 10
dormir *to sleep,* 2
le dos *back,* 7
la douche *shower,* 8
douze *twelve,* 1
le dramaturge *playwright,* 378
dresser *to erect,* 5
la droite *right,* 8
le druide *druid,* 2
du *of the,* 6
du... au *from the... to the...,* 10
durable *durable,* 9
durant *during,* 369
durer *to last,* 5
le DVD *DVD,* 1

l' **eau** (f.) **minérale** *mineral water,* 6
l' **écharpe** (f.) *winter scarf,* 7
les **échecs** (m.) *chess,* 2
l' **éclair** *French pastry,* 1
les **écluses** (f.) *(canal) locks,* 380
l' **école** (f.) *school,* 2
écouter *to listen,* 1
écouter de la musique *to listen to
music,* 2; **Écoutez!** *Listen!,* 1
les **écouteurs** (m.) *headphones,* 2
s'**écrier** *to exclaim,* 379
écrire *to write,* 1
les **écrits** (m.) *writings,* 368
l' **écrivain** (m.) *writer, author,* 9
l' **édition** (f.) *edit (computer),* 1
l' **éducation** (f.) **musicale** *music
education,* 4
également *also,* 381
l' **église** (f.) *church,* 9

l' Égypte (m.) *Egypt*, 10
électrique *electrical*, 10
l' élégance (f.) *elegance*, 7
élégant(e) *elegant*, 7
l' élément (m.) *element*, 5
l' **élève (m./f.)** *student*, 1
élevé(e) *high, elevated*, 7
élever *to raise*, 5
elle *she*, 1
Elle est comment,...?
How is…?, 6
Elle est forte, celle-là!
It's a bummer!, 10
Elle s'appelle... *Her name is…*, 1
elles *they (female)*, 1
l' **e-mail** (m.) *e-mail*, 1
embarrassé(e) *embarrassed*, 377
embêtant(e) *annoying*, 3
l' emblème (m.) *emblem, symbol*, 7
l' emplacement (m.) *place, location*, 369
l' **employé(e)** *employee*, 9
emporter *to take something (with)*, 10
emprunter *to borrow*, 371
en *to/at (a feminine country)*, 10;
en argent *(of) silver*, 7
en avance *early*, 10
en bas *downstairs*, 8
en bois *wooden*, 2
en bref *in a few words*, 366
en bus *by bus*, 9
en conséquence *accordingly*, 371
en coton *cotton*, 7
en courant *running*, 377
en diamant *made of diamond*, 7
en face de *across from*, 8
en fait *in fact*, 371
en forme de *in the shape of*, 6
en général *in general*, 376
en haut *upstairs*, 8
en incorporant *adding*, 373
en jean *denim*, 7
en laine *woollen* 7
en lin *linen*, 7
en métro *by subway*, 9
ennuyeuse, ennuyeux *boring*, 4
en or *(of) gold*, 7
en osier *of willow, wicker*, 7
en pleine nature *in the great outdoors*, 5
en possession de *in possession of*, 381
en provenance de *from*, 10
En quelle saison...? *In which season…?*, 5
en récompense de *as a reward for*, 6
en retard *late*, 10
en route *on the way*, 10

en soie *silk*, 7
en solde *on sale*, 7
en solitaire *solo*, 5
en taxi *by taxi*, 9
en tenant *while holding*, 372
en vogue *in style*, 375
en voiture *by car*, 9
Enchanté(e)! *Delighted!*, 1
encore *more*, 6; *still*, 7; *yet, again*, 8
encourager *to encourage*, 4
l' **endroit** (m.) *place*, 9
l' endurance (f.) *endurance*, 5
l' enfance (f.) *childhood*, 368
l' **enfant** (m./f.) *child*, 3
enfilé(e) par la tête *slipped on over the head*, 7
enfin *finally*, 379
l' ennemi(e) *enemy*, 6
ennuyeux *boring*, 4
énorme *enormous*, 7
enregistrer *to check in*, 10
ensemble *together*, 2
ensuite *then, next*, 9
entendre *to hear*, 4
s'entêter *to persist*, 9
entier(-ère) *entire*, 5
entièrement *completely*, 8
entre *between*, 10
entre-coupé *interspersed with*, 375
l' entrée (f.) *appetizer*, 6; *entry-way*, 8
entrer *to enter*, 8
envahir *to invade*, 375
l' **enveloppe** (f.) *envelope*, 9
l' envie (f.) *desire*, 371
l' environnement (m.) *environment*, 7
envoyer (des e-mails) *to send (e-mails)*, 2
s'envoyer *to send each other*, 2
l' épaule (f.) *shoulder*, 7
épeler *to spell*, 10
l' épicerie (f.) *grocery store*, 9
les épices (f.) *spices*, 9
l' épisode (m.) *episode*, 379
l' **EPS (éducation** (f.) **physique et sportive)** *Physical education (P.E.)*, 4
l' équipe (f.) *team*, 367
équipé(e) *equipped*, 8
l' équitation (f.) *horseback riding*, 5
l' équivalent (m.) *equivalent*, 9
l' escalade (f.) *rock-climbing*, 5
l' **escale** (f.) *stopover, layover*, 10
l' **escalier** (m.) *staircase*, 8
les escargots (m.) *snails*, 1
l' espace (m.) *space*, 1
l' **Espagne** (f.) *Spain*, 10
l' **espagnol** (m.) *Spanish*, 4

espérer *to hope*, 4
l' esprit (m.) *mind*, 10
essayer *to try on*, 7; *to try*, 8
l' est (m.) *east*, 5
Est-ce que je peux...? *Can I…?*, 8
Est-ce que tu aimes... régulièrement? *Do you like… regularly?*, 2
Est-ce que tu fais du sport? *Do you play sports?*, 5
Est-ce que tu joues à...? *Do you play…?*, 5
Est-ce que vous faites pension complète? *Are all meals included with the room?*, 10
Est-ce que vous pouvez me dire...? *Can you tell me…?*, 9
et *and*, 2
les **États-Unis** (m.) *United States*, 10
Et toi? *How about you? (informal)*, 1
Et vous? *How about you? (formal)*, 1
l' **étage** (m.) *floor*, 8
l' **étagère** (f.) *bookshelf*, 8
était *was*, 10
étaler *to spread*, 373
l' étape *stage (of a trip or race)*, 381
l' état (m.) *condition*, 8
l' **été** (m.) *summer*, 5
l' été (m.) des indiens *Indian summer*, 3
ethnique *ethnic*, 7
étonnant(e) *surprising*, 380
l' étranger(-ère) *foreigner*, 376
être *to be*, 3
être dans les nuages *to daydream*, 4
être en train de *to be in the process of (doing something)*, 7
étroit(e) *tight*, 7
étudier *to study*, 2
eut *had (literary form of* **avoir**), 379
éviter *to avoid*, 371
l' évolution (f.) *evolution*, 375
exact(e) *exact, correct*, 4
Excellent(e)! *Excellent!*, 6
exceptionnel(le) *exceptional*, 8
excessivement *excessively*, 4
s'excuser (auprès de) *to excuse one's self*, 376; *to apologize*, 377
Excusez-moi, je cherche... *Excuse-me, I am looking for…*, 9
l' exemple (m.) *example*, 9
exercer *to practice (profession)*, 379
exister *to exist*, 370
exotique *exotic*, 8
expliquer *to explain*, 6
l' extérieur (m.) *outside of*, 8
l' extinction (f.) *extinction*, 7

F

la fabrication *manufacture*, 10
fabriquer *to make*, 7
face à *(when) faced with*, 376
facile *easy*, 4
faciliter *to facilitate*, 380
le facteur *mail carrier*, 9
faire *to do, to make*, 2; se fait remarquer *make him/herself noticed*, 379; se font *are made*, 6
faire (la France) *to visit (France)*, 10
faire du sport *to play sports*, 2
faire escale à *to make a stopover, layover*, 10
faire la cuisine *to cook*, 8
faire la fête *to party*, 2
faire la gymnastique *to do gymnastics*, 3
faire la lessive *to do the laundry*, 8
faire la queue *to stand in line*, 10
faire la vaisselle *to do the dishes*, 8
faire le tour *to look around*, 381
faire les magasins *to go shopping*, 2
faire les valises *to pack the bags*, 10
faire partie de *to be a member of, to be part of*, 1
faire sauter *to flip*, 372
faire son lit *to make one's bed*, 8
faire sur mesure *to custom fit*, 7
faire un pique-nique *to go on a picnic*, 2
faire un voyage *to take a trip*, 10
fait construire *orders the construction of*, 1
la famille *family*, 3
la famille d'accueil *host family*, 8
le far breton *traditional Breton cake*, 5
la farine *flour*, 373
fascinant *fascinating*, 4
le fauteuil *armchair*, 8
faux/fausse *false*, 4
les favoris (m.) *favorites (computer)*, 1
la femme *wife*, 3; *woman*, 7
la fenêtre *window*, 1
la ferme *farm*, 8
fermer *to close*, 1
Fermez vos cahiers. *Close your notebooks.*, 1
le festival *festival*, 3
la fête *party*, 2
le feu *traffic light*, 9
la feuille de papier *sheet of paper*, 4
février *February*, 5
la fierté *pride*, 379
la figurine *figurine*, 9
la fille *girl*, 1; *daughter*, 3

la fille unique *only daughter*, 3
le film *film, movie*, 2
le fils *son*, 3
le fils unique *only son*, 3
la fin *end*, 369
finalement *finally*, 9
finir *to finish*, 6
le flamant rose *flamingo*, 9
fleuri(e) *flowered*, 8
le fleuriste *flower shop*, 9
le fleuve *river*, 7
la fois *time*, 8
fois par... *times per...*, 8
foncé(e) *dark*, 4
fond en larmes *burst into tears*, 377
fondre *to melt*, 373
la fontaine *fountain*, 1
le football *soccer*, 2; **le football américain** *American football*, 2
la forêt *forest*, 2
la forme *shape*, 6
se former *to take shape*, 369
la formule *schedule*, 5
fort(e) *stout, strong*, 3
fortement *strongly*, 381
fortifié(e) *fortified*, 5
la fortune *fortune*, 380
le fou *madman*, 10
le foulard *scarf*, 7
la fourchette *fork*, 6
les fournitures (f.) scolaires *school supplies*, 4
le français *French*, 2
franchement *honestly*, 7
Franchement, il/elle est un peu tape-à-l'œil. *Honestly, it's a bit gaudy.*, 7
frapper *to hit*, 379
la fraternité *brotherhood*, 375
le frère *brother*, 3
friser *to border on*, 369
les frites (f.) *fries*, 2
le froid *cold*, 5
le fromage *cheese*, 6
le fromager (la fromagère) *cheese maker*, 10
le front *forehead*, 369
les fruits (m.) de mer *seafood*, 5
fulminant(e) *bursting with*, 378

G

le gadget *gadget*, 2
gagner *to win*, 7
la galerie *gallery*, 1
la galette *cake*, 372
le gamin *kid*, 379
les gants (m.) *gloves*, 7

le garage *garage*, 8
garantir *to guarantee*, 372
le garçon *boy*, 1
la garde-robe *wardrobe*, 10
garder *to keep*, 377
le gardien *door-keeper*, 8
la gare *train station*, 10
la garniture *filling*, 6
la gastronomie *culinary custom or style*, 1
le gâteau *cake*, 9
la gauche *left*, 8
la gaufre *waffle*, 372
le gaz *gas*, 8
géant(e) *gigantic*, 2
gêné *embarrassed*, 377
général *general*, 8
généreux(-euse) *generous*, 3
génial(e) *great*, 3
le genre *kind, sort*, 7
les gens (m.) *people*, 370
gentil(-le) *sweet*, 3
gentiment *nicely*, 376
la géographie *geography*, 4
le geste *gesture*, 1
le gestionnaire *managing company*, 381
la glace *ice cream*, 2; *mirror*, 1
la glacière *ice cooler*, 7
le gladiateur *gladiator*, 2
la gloire *glory, pride*, 378
le golf *golf*, 5
la gomme *eraser*, 4
la gorge *throat*, 9; *gorge*, 9
goudronné(e) *paved*, 381
gourmand(e) *greedy*, 376
goût *taste*, 371
le goûter *afternoon snack*, 6
goûter *to taste*, 376
la goutte *drop*, 376
grâce à *thanks to*, 375
la graine *seed*, 371
grand(e) *big, tall*, 3
la grande surface *superstore*, 7
grandir *to grow (up)*, 6
la grand-mère *grandmother*, 3
le grand-parent *grandparent*, 3
le grand-père *grandfather*, 3
le granit *granite*, 5
gratuit(e) *free*, 1
la grenadine *pomegranate drink*, 6
grillé(e) *grilled*, 7
les griots (m.) *traveling poets/singers (Senegal)*, 374
gris(e) *gray*, 4
gros(se) *fat*, 3
grossir *to gain weight*, 6
la guerre *war*, 5
le guerrier *warrior*, 2
le guichet *window, counter, ticket office*, 9
la guitare *guitar*, 5

habiller (s') *to dress,* 7
habitable *habitable,* 381
les habitant(e)s *inhabitants,* 5
l' habitation (f.) *residence, dwelling,* 8
habiter *to live,* 8
l' habitude (f.) *habits, customs,* 2
haïr *to hate,* 369
le hall (m.) *lobby,* 10
haut *high,* 8
hein *(at beginning of sentence) hey, what?,* 4
le héros *hero,* 6
l' heure (f.) *hour,* 4
heureusement *fortunately,* 5
heureux (-euse) *happy,* 5
hier *yesterday,* 7
l' histoire (f.) *history,* 4; *story,* 10
l' historien (m.) *historian,* 378
historique *historical,* 7
l' hiver (m.) *winter,* 5
le hockey *hockey,* 5
l' homme (m.) *man,* 7
l' homme (m.) d'affaires *businessman,* 378
homogène *homogeneous,* 373
l' hôpital (m.) *hospital,* 9
hoqueter *to hiccough,* 9
l' horaire (m.) *schedule,* 10
l' horreur (f.) *horror,* 369
horrible *horrible,* 7
les hors d'œuvre (m.) *dishes served at beginning of meal,* 6
hors-saison *off-season,* 5
l' hôte (m.) *steward,* 10
l' hôtel (m.) *hotel,* 10
l' hôtesse (f.) *stewardess,* 10
huit *eight,* 1
les humains (m.) *humans,* 370
l' hymne (f.) *hymn,* 375

ici *here,* 5
l' idée (f.) *idea,* 6
l' idéologie (f.) *ideology,* 375
il *he,* 1; **Il/Elle coûte combien,...?** *How much does... cost?,* 7; **Il/Elle coûte...** *It costs...,* 7; **Il/Elle est brun(e)** *He/She has brown hair.,* 3; **Il/Elle est comment...?** *How is...?,* 3; **Il/Elle est horrible.** *It's horrible.,* 7; **Il/Elle est très...** *He/She is very...,* 3; **Il/Elle me**

va,...? *How does... fit me?,* 7; **Il/Elle n'est ni... ni...** *He/She is neither... nor...,* 3; **Il/Elle s'appelle...** *His/Her name is...,* 1; **Il /Elle te plaît,...?** *Do you like...?,* 7
Il est bon/Elle est bonne,...? *Is the... good?,* 6
Il est deux heures dix. *It is ten past two.,* 4; **Il est deux heures et demie.** *It is two thirty.,* 4; **Il est deux heures et quart.** *It is a quarter past two.,* 4; **Il est deux heures.** *It is two o'clock.,* 4; **Il est midi.** *It is noon.,* 4; **Il est minuit.** *It is midnight.,* 4; **Il est trois heures moins le quart.** *It is quarter till three.,* 4; **Il est trois heures moins vingt.** *It is twenty till three.,* 4; **Il est une heure.** *It is one o'clock.,* 4
Il fait beau. *It's nice outside.,* 5
Il fait chaud. *It's hot.,* 5
Il fait froid. *It's cold.,* 5
Il fait mauvais. *It's bad weather.,* 5
il faut *it is necessary,* 8
Il me faut... *I need...,* 4
il fit *he made,* 10
Il ne put. *He couldn't.,* 10
Il neige. *It's snowing.,* 5
Il n'y en a pas. *There aren't any.,* 1
Il pleut. *It's raining.,* 5
il suffit de *it is enough to,* 371
il vaut mieux *it is better,* 381
il y a *there is/are,* 6
Il y a des nuages. *It's cloudy.,* 5
Il y a du soleil. *It's sunny.,* 5
Il y a du vent. *It's windy.,* 5
Il y a... dans la salle de classe? *Is there... in the classroom?,* 1
Il y en a... *There are... of them.,* 1
Il/Elle ne te va pas du tout. *It doesn't suit you at all.,* 7
l' île (f.) *island,* 1
illuminé(e) *illuminated,* 369
ils *they (masc.),* 1
Ils/Elles sont comment,...? *What are... like?,* 3
Ils/elles sont soldé(e)s à... *They are on sale for...,* 7
l' image (f.) *picture,* 9
l' immeuble (m.) *apartment complex,* 8
l' imperméable (m.) *raincoat,* 7
important(e) *important,* 7
importer *to import,* 9
imprimer *to print,* 1
inattentif(-tive) *inattentive,* 379
inconsciemment *unconsciously,* 10
incorporer *to incorporate, to add,* 373
incroyable *incredible,* 8

l' indépendance (f.) *independence,* 5
indiquer *to point out,* 8
l' ingénierie (f.) *engineering,* 380
l' ingénieur (m.) *engineer,* 380
l' ingrédient (m.) *ingredient,* 373
l' instituteur (-trice) *teacher,* 378
l' instrument (m.) *instrument,* 7
l' industrie (f.) alimentaire *food industry,* 10
l' informatique (f.) *computer science,* 4
inonder *to soak,* 377
inoubliable *unforgettable,* 366
insister *to insist,* 376
insolite *novel, unusual,* 366
inspirer *to inspire,* 5
l' instant (m.) *moment,* 10
intégrer *to integrate,* 375
intelligent(e) *intelligent, smart,* 3
intéressant(e) *interesting,* 4
l' intérêt (m.) *interest,* 10
l' intérieur (m.) *interior,* 369
international(e) *international,* 3
l' Internet (m.) *Internet,* 2
l' intrigue (f.) *intrigue,* 1
intrigué(e) *intrigued,* 6
l' introduction (f.) *introduction,* 375
introduit(e) *introduced,* 6
l' invasion *invasion,* 5
inventer *to invent,* 9
l' inventeur (-trice) *inventor,* 378
investir *to invest,* 380
invincible *invincible,* 2
invité(e) *invited,* 6
l' Italie (f.) *Italy,* 10

J'adore... *I love...,* 2
J'aime bien... *I like...,* 2
J'aime mieux... *I like... better.,* 2
J'ai besoin de... *I need...,* 4
J'ai... ans. *I am... years old.,* 1
J'ai... et... *I have... and...,* 3
J'aimerais... *I would like...,* 6
jamais *never,* 2
le jambon *ham,* 6
janvier *January,* 5
le Japon (m.) *Japan,* 10
le jardin *yard, garden,* 8
le jardin à la française *classic French-style garden characterized by flowerbeds in geometric patterns,* 5
jaune *yellow,* 4
le jazz *jazz,* 3
je *I,* 1
Je cherche... *I'm looking for...,* 4

malheureusement *unfortunately*, 370
la **malle** *trunk*, 10
le mandat *money order*, 9
manger *to eat*, 2
la mangrove *swamp*, 7
manquer *to miss*, 10
le manteau *coat*, 7
le manuel *textbook*, 369
le marchand *merchant*, 372
la marchandise *merchandise*, 380
le marché *open air market*, 9
marcher *to walk*, 10
le mardi *Tuesday*, 4
les marées (f.) *tides*, 5
le mari *husband*, 3
marin(e) *marine*, 5
mariné(e) *marinated*, 7
le Maroc (m.) *Morocco*, 10
la maroquinerie *leather goods*, 7
marrant(e) *funny*, 3
marron *brown(-eyed)*, 3
mars *March*, 5
le masque de plongée *diving mask*, 7
le match *game*, 1
le matériel *material*, 8
les mathématiques (maths) (f.) *mathematics (math)*, 2
la matière *school subject*, 4
le matin *morning*, 4
mauvais *bad*, 5
le mauvais goût *bad taste*, 371
les mauvais tours (m.) *bad tricks*, 370
le mbalax *style of Senegalese music*, 374
méchant(e) *mean*, 3
mécontent(e) *displeased*, 4
le médicament *medicine*, 9
médecine *medicine*, 9
médiéval(e) *Medieval*, 9
meilleur(e) *better*, 7; *best*, 9
mélanger *to mix, blend*, 7
mêler *to mix*, 376
même *even*, 9
menacé(e) *threatened*, 7
mentalement *mentally*, 369
la menthe *mint*, 6
mentionné(e) *mentioned*, 9
le menu à prix fixe *fixed-price menu*, 6
la mer *sea*, 5
Merci. *Thank you.*, 1
le mercredi *Wednesday*, 4
la mère *mother*, 3
mes *my*, 3
le métier *trade, profession*, 10
le métro *subway*, 9
mettre *to set*, 6; *to put (on), to wear*, 7
mettre la table *to set the table*, 8
mettre le couvert *to set the table*, 6

meublé(e) *furnished*, 8
le micro-organisme *micro-organism*, 7
midi *noon*, 4
mignon(ne) *cute*, 3
la migration *migration*, 7
le mille-feuille *layered French pastry*, 1
le millimètre *millimeter*, 9
le mime *mime*, 366
mince *thin*, 3
minuit *midnight*, 4
le miracle *miracle*, 369
mis par dessus *worn over*, 7
le mobile *cell phone*, 4
la mode *fashion*, 7
moderne *modern*, 2
modeste *modest*, 10
moi *me*, 2
Moi aussi. *Me, too.*, 2
Moi non plus. *Me neither.*, 2
Moi si. *I do.*, 2
Moi, j'aime... Et toi? *I like... And you?*, 2
Moi, je n'aime pas... *I don't like...*, 2
le moine *monk*, 10
moins *minus*, 4
le mois *month*, 5; **le mois dernier** *last month*, 7
mon *my*, 3
le monde *world*, 10
la monnaie *change (coins)*, 9
monsieur (m.) *Mr.*, 1
la montagne *mountain(s)*, 5
la montagne russe *roller coaster*, 2
monter *to go up*, 8
la montgolfière *hot air balloon*, 3
la montre *watch*, 7
montrer *to point to*, 379
le morceau *piece*, 7
la mort *death*, 376
mort(e) *died*, 378
la mosquée *mosque*, 7
le mot *word*, 10
le motif *theme*, 1
la moto *motor bike*, 7
mourir *to die*, 8
le moussor *traditional scarf worn on the head in Africa*, 7
le mouvement *movement*, 375
le moyen *means, way*, 371
le Moyen Âge *Middle Ages*, 5
le MP3 *MP3*, 2
municipal *municipal, of the local government*, 1
murmurer *to murmur, whisper*, 10
le musée *museum*, 5
la musique *music*, 2
mystérieux (-se) *mysterious*, 5

nager *to swim*, 2
naître *to be born*, 8
la nappe *table cloth*, 6
le narrateur *narrator*, 9
la natation synchronisée *synchronized swimming*, 367
national(e) *national*, 7
nature *natural, plain*, 6
né(e) *born*, 6
ne... jamais *never*, 8
ne... pas *not*, 1
ne... pas encore *not yet*, 8
ne... personne *no one*, 8
ne... plus *no longer*, 8
ne... que *only*, 8, 10
ne... rien *nothing*, 8
négociable *negotiable*, 8
la neige *snow*, 5
neiger *to snow*, 5
nettoyer *to clean*, 8
neuf *nine*, 1; *new*, 8
le neveu *nephew*, 3
le nez *nose*, 3
la nièce *niece*, 3
la noix de beurre *pat of butter*, 373
le Noël *Christmas*, 10
noir(e) *black*, 3
le nom *name*, 7
nombreux (nombreuse) *numerous*, 7
non *no*, 2
Non, ça ne me dit rien. *No, I don't feel like it.*, 5
Non, ça va. *No, I am fine.*, 6
Non, il est mauvais. *No, it's bad.*, 6
Non, il n'y a pas de... *No, there is no...*, 1
Non, je déteste... *No, I hate...*, 2
Non, je n'ai plus faim/soif. *No, I'm not hungry/thirsty any more.*, 6
Non, je n'aime pas... *No, I don't like...*, 2
Non, je ne fais pas de sport. *No, I don't play sports.*, 5
Non, je regrette. *No, I'm sorry.*, 9
Non, je suis fils/fille unique. *No, I'm an only child.*, 3
Non, merci, je regarde. *No thank you, I'm just looking.*, 7
Non, merci. *No, thank you.*, 6
Non, pas très bien. *No, not too well.*, 1
Non, tu dois... *No, you have to...*, 8
non-fumeur *non-smoking*, 10
le nord *North*, 3
normand(e) *from Normandy*, 5
nos *our*, 3

Glossaire français–anglais

la note *grade*, 369
notre *our*, 3
N'oublie pas... *Don't forget...,* 10
la nourriture *food*, 376
nous *we*, 1
Nous sommes... *There are... of
us.*, 3; *Today is...,* 4
nouveau/nouvelle *new*, 3
novembre *November*, 5
le nuage *cloud*, 5
la nuit *night*, 10
le numéro *number*, 4
le numéro de téléphone
phone number, 4

l' objet (m.) *object*, 7
obsédé(e) *obsessed*, 371
obtenir *to obtain*, 7
occidental(e) *western*, 7
octobre *October*, 5
l' **œuf** (m.) *egg*, 6
l' œuf (m.) (sur le plat) *fried
egg*, 373
l' **œuvre** (m.) *(artist's) work*, 9
offrir *to offer*, 5
l' oignon (m.) *onion*, 6
l' oiseau (m.) *bird*, 5
l' **omelette** (f.) *omelet*, 6
on *one/we*, 1
On a... *We have...,* 6
On fait...? *Shall we do...?,* 5
On pourrait... *We could...,* 5
On va...? *How about going to...?,* 5
l' **oncle** (m.) *uncle*, 3
l' onomatopée (f.) *onomatopoeia*, 9
onze *eleven*, 1
l' **opéra** (m.) *opera*, 5
l' **or** (m.) *gold*, 7
orale *oral*, 374
orange *orange*, 4
l' **orange** (f.) *orange*, 6
l' oranger (m.) *orange tree*, 1
l' **ordinateur** (m.) *computer*, 1
l' **oreille** (f.) *ear*, 3
organiser *to organize*, 5
l' origine (f.) *origin*, 6
ornithologique *ornithological*, 7
l' **osier** (m.) *willow, wicker*, 7
ôter *to remove, take away*, 370
l' otarie (f.) *sea-lion*, 2
ou *or*, 2
où *where*, 5
Où ça? *Where?,* 5
Où est...? *Where is...?,* 8
Où se trouve...? *Where is...?,* 8
oublier *to forget*, 10

l' ouest *west*, 7
oui *yes*, 1
Oui, ça va. Merci. *Yes, fine.
Thank you.,* 1
Oui, il/elle te va très bien.
Yes, it fits you very well., 7
Oui, il y a... *Yes, there is/are...,* 1
Oui, j'aime... *Yes, I like...,* 2
Oui, je veux bien. *Yes, I would
indeed.,* 6
Oui, s'il te plaît. *Yes, please.,* 6
Oui, s'il vous plaît. *Yes, please.,* 6
les outils (m.) *tools (computer)*, 1
Ouvrez vos livres à la page...
Open your books to page..., 1
ouvert(e) *open*, 5
ouvrier(-ière) *working (class)*, 368
ouvrir *to open*, 1

la **page** *page*, 1
le pagne *traditional African cloth
worn as a garment*, 7
la paille *straw*, 8
le **pain** *bread*, 6
les pains (m.) du singe *fruit of the
baobab tree*, 7
le palais *palace*, 9
les **palmes** (f.) *flippers*, 7
le **pamplemousse** *grapefruit*, 6
paniquer *to panic*, 373
le **pansement** *bandage*, 9
le **pantalon** *pair of pants*, 7
la panthère *panther*, 7
le pape *Pope*, 9
la **papeterie** *stationary store*, 9
le **papier** *paper*, 4
par *by*, 10
le parachutisme *parachuting*, 5
le parapente *paragliding*, 5
le **parapluie** *umbrella*, 7
le **parc** *park*, 2
le parcours *route, journey*, 381
par-dessus *over*, 7
pardon *excuse-me*, 9
Pardon, savez-vous où est...?
*Excuse-me, do you know
where... is?,* 9
le pare-chocs *bumper*, 9
le **parent** *parent*, 3
paresseux(-euse) *lazy*, 3
parfait(e) *perfect*, 8
la parfumerie *perfumery*, 9
le **parking** *parking*, 10
parler *to speak*, 2
parmi *among*, 9
la parole *words, lyrics*, 9

partager *to share*, 8
participer *to participate*, 7
le particulier *owner*, 8
particulier (-ière) *special*, 380
la **partie** *part*, 380
partir *to leave*, 8
partir à pied *to go for a walk*, 3
partout *everywhere*, 9
paru *appeared*, 369
Pas bon(ne) du tout ! *Not good
at all!,* 6
pas du tout *not at all*, 7
pas encore *not yet*, 8
Pas grand-chose. *Not much.,* 5
Pas mal. *Not bad.,* 1
Pas mauvais. *Not bad.,* 6
Pas moi. *Not me., I don't.,* 2
Pas question! *Out of the
question!,* 8
pas tant de manières *don't put
on airs*, 4
le passager *passenger*, 10
le passeport *passport*, 10
passer (à un endroit) *to stop by,
to pass*, 9; *to spend (time)*, 368
passer l'aspirateur *to vacuum*, 8
se passer *to take place*, 369
le passe-temps *pastime*, 5
la **pâte** *crust*, 6; *dough*, 373
paternel(le) *paternal, fatherly*, 379
les **pâtes** (f.) *pasta*, 6
le patin à glace *ice-skating*, 5
la patinoire *ice-skating rink*, 5
les pâtisseries (f.) *pastries*, 1
pauvre *poor*, 371
pauvre ami(e) *poor thing*, 4
payer *to pay*, 8
payer avec une carte *to pay with
a credit card*, 10
payer en liquide *to pay cash*, 10
payer par chèque *to pay
by check*, 10
le pays *country*, 375
les **Pays-Bas** (m.) *Netherlands*, 10
le paysage *landscape, scenery*, 5
la **pêche** *fishing*, 7
la pêche blanche *Inuit/Amerindian
sport of fishing on frozen rivers
and lakes*, 3
le pêcheur *fisherman*, 7
pédestre *on foot*, 5
peint *painted*, 9
le peintre *painter*, 9
la peinture *painting*, 7
le pèlerin *pilgrim*, 7
la **pelouse** *lawn*, 8
pendant *during*, 2
pénible *tiresome, difficult*, 3
la péniche *barge*, 381
penser *to think*, 3
la **pension complète** *full-board*, 10
perdre *to lose*, 4
le père *father*, 3

Glossaire français–anglais

que *what*, 5
quel(le) *which*, 4. 7
Quel jour sommes-nous?
  What day is today?, 4
Quel temps fait-il? *What is the*
  weather like?, 5
Quelle est ton adresse (e-mail)
  mail? *What is your (e-mail)*
  address?, 1
Quelle heure est-il? *What time*
  is it?, 4
Quelle horreur!
  What horror!, 369
Quelle pointure faites-vous?
  What shoe size do you wear?, 7
Quelle taille faites-vous? *What size*
  do you wear?, 7
Quelles sont tes activités
  préférées? *What are you favorite*
  activities?, 2
quelque *some, a few*, 376
Qu'est-ce que tu aimes faire?
  What do you like to do?, 2
Qu'est-ce que tu fais comme sport?
  What sports do you play?, 5
Qu'est-ce que tu fais...? *What are*
  you doing on…?, 5
Qu'est-ce que tu penses de...?
  What do you think of…?, 7
Qu'est-ce que vous me conseillez?
  What do you recommend?, 6
Qu'est-ce que ça veut dire...?
  What does…mean?, 1
Qu'est-ce que tu fais pour
  t'amuser? *What do you do*
  for fun?, 5
Qu'est-ce que tu penses de...?
  What do you think of…?, 3
Qu'est-ce que tu vas faire
  s'il...? *What are you going to do*
  if…?, 5
Qu'est-ce que tu veux...? *What do*
  you want…?, 6
Qu'est-ce que vous avez comme...
  What type of… do you have?, 6
Qu'est-ce qui se passe? *What's*
  happening?, 4
Qu'est-ce qu'il te faut pour...?
  What do you need for…?, 4
Qu'est-ce qu'on fait...? *What are*
  we doing…?, 5
la question *question*, 4
la queue *line*, 10
qui *who*, 3
Qui c'est, ça? *Who is that?*, 3
la quiche *quiche*, 6
quinze *fifteen*, 1
quitter *to leave*, 10
quotidien(-ne) *daily*, 7
Quoi? *What?*, 4

raconter *to tell*, 6
la radio *radio*, 2
la raffinerie *refinery*, 7
le rafting *rafting*, 5
le raisin sec *raisin*, 5
la raison *reason*, 5
la randonnée *hike*, 7
le rang *row*, 379
  ranger *to put away, to tidy*, 8
  ranger sa chambre *to pick up*
    one's bedroom, 8
le rapace *bird of prey*, 2
  râpé *grated*, 373
  rappeler *to remember*, 10
la raptitude *ideology of Senegalese*
    rap music, 375
la raquette *racket*, 5
les raquettes (f.) à neige
    snow-shoeing, 5
rare *uncommon, exceptional*, 8
rarement *rarely*, 2
la ratatouille *typical dish of the south*
    of France, 9
rater *to miss*, 10
le rayon *department*, 7
le rayon bijouterie *jewelry*
    department, 7
le rayon maroquinerie *leather*
    department, 7
le rayon plein air *outdoor goods*
    department, 7
rebaptisé *renamed*, 380
récemment *recently*, 9
recenser *to count*
    (to inventory), 375
la réception *reception*, 10
  réceptionniste *receptionist*, 10
recevoir *to receive*, 9
rechercher *search (computer)*, 1
se réciter *to recite*
    to themselves, 369
recommander *to recommend*, 6
récompensé(e) *awarded*, 9
la récréation *break*, 4
reçu *received*, 6
refléter *to reflect*, 5
le refuge *refuge*, 1
refuser *to refuse*, 376
regarder *to look at*, 1; *to watch*, 2
regarder la télé *to watch TV*, 2
Regardez (la carte)! *Look (at*
    the map)!, 1
la région *region*, 7
la règle *ruler*, 4
regretter *to be sorry*, 9
régulièrement *regularly*, 5

rejoignit *rejoins*, 10
les relations *connections*, 376
relier *to connect*, 7
religieux(-se) *religious*, 7
remarier *to remarry*, 3
remarquer *to notice*, 370
remercier *to thank*, 6
remis(e) *presented*, 9
remonter *to date back to*, 372
les remparts (m.) *ramparts*, 5
remplacer *to replace*, 4
rendre *to give back*, 4;
    to make, 2
les renseignements (m.)
    information, 5
renverser *to spill*, 377
répartir *to distribute*, 373
la répartiteur *spreader*, 373
le repas *meal*, 6
  répéter (se) *to repeat (itself)*, 1;
    to rehearse, 375
Répétez! *Repeat!*, 1
Répétez, s'il vous plaît?
    Could you please repeat that?, 1
la répétition *rehearsal*, 1
replacer *to put back*, 376
répondre (à) *to answer*, 4
reposer *to rest, to sit*, 373
  reprendre *to take/have more*, 6;
    to take up again, 376
représenter *to represent*, 10
repris(e) *taken up again*, 7
réputé(e) *well-known*, 9
la réservation *reservation*, 10
la réserve naturelle
    game preserve, 5
  réserver *to reserve*, 10
la résidence *residence*, 362
résidenciel *residential*, 375
la ressource *resource*, 7
restaurer *to restore*, 9
rester *to stay*, 8
retirer *to withdraw*, 9
le retour *return*, 377
  retourner *to return*, 1;
    to turn over, 373
retourner (se) *to turn*
    around, 379
  Retournez à vos places! *Go back*
    to your seats!, 1
retrouver (se) *to get together* 2
retrouver *find again*, 371
réussir (à) *to pass, to succeed*, 6
réveiller (se) *to wake up*, 3
la révolution *revolution*, 1
le rez-de-chaussée *first floor*, 8
le rhume *cold*, 9
la richesse *wealth*, 369
les richesses (f.) naturelles
    natural resources, 369

Glossaire français–anglais

rien *nothing*, 5
Rien de spécial. *Nothing special.*, 5
rigoler *to have fun*, 371
le riz *rice*, 6
la robe *dress*, 7
le rocher *rock*, 3
le roi *king*, 1
le rôle *role*, 9
le roller *roller-blading*, 5
le roman *novel*, 2
le romancier (-ière) *novelist*, 378
rose *pink*, 4
rôti *roasted*, 2
rouge *red*, 4
roux/rousse *red-head(ed)*, 3
royal(e) *royal*, 362
la rue *street*, 9
ruiné(e) *ruined*, 380
la Russie *Russia*, 10
le rythme *rhythm*, 7

sa *his/her*, 3
le sabar *traditional Senegalese musical instrument*, 374
le sac *bag*, 6
le sac (à dos) *backpack*, 4
le sac (à main) *purse*, 7
le sac de voyage *traveling bag*, 10
sage *well-behaved*, 379
saignant *rare*, 6
saisir *seize*, 8
la saison *season*, 5
la salade *salad*, 6
salé *salty*, 372
la salle *room*, 8
la salle à manger *dining room*, 8
la salle de bain *bathroom*, 8
la salle de classe *classroom*, 1
la salle d'eau *showers*, 8
le salon *living room*, 8
Salut. *Hi., Goodbye.*, 1
le samedi *Saturday*, 4
les sandales (f.) *sandals*, 7
le sandwich *sandwich*, 6
le sanglier *wild boar*, 364
sans *without*, 10
sans doute *without a doubt*, 374
le santon *small clay statues that decorate nativity scenes*, 10
le saucisson *salami*, 6
sauf *except (for)*, 6
sauté *sauteed*, 373
sauter *jump, flip*, 372

sauvage *wild*, 9
sauver *to save*, 6
Savais-tu que...? *Did you know...?*, 1
Savez-vous...? *Do you know...?*, 9
savoir *to know (facts), to know how*, 9
la scène *scene*, 7; *stage*, 367
scolaire *scholastic*, 4
se dit-il *he says to himself*, 10
se fait remarquer *make him/herself noticed*, 379
se font *are made*, 6
le sèche-cheveux *hair-dryer*, 10
le secret *secret*, 378
seize *sixteen*, 1
le séjour *stay*, 5; *lounge*, 8
le sel *salt*, 6
selon *according to*, 372
la semaine *week*, 4
la semaine dernière *last week*, 7
le sentiment *feeling*, 9
sentir (se) *to feel*, 10
séparé(e) *separated*, 8
sept *seven*, 1
septembre *September*, 5
sera (il/elle/on) *will be*, 371
serez (vous) *will be*, 371
la série *series*, 378
sérieux(-euse) *serious*, 3
serré(e) *tight*, 7
sert *serves*, 8
le service *service*, 6; Le service est compris? *Is the tip included?*, 6
la serviette *napkin*, 6
servir *to serve*, 6
ses *his/her*, 3
le seuil *threshold*, 371
seul(e) *only one*, 6
seulement *only*, 6
le short *a pair of shorts*, 4
si l'on en croit *if one believes*, 6
Si tu veux. *If you want.*, 5
Si vous voulez. *If you want.*, 5
le siècle *century*, 10
le siège *siege*, 6
le siège social international *headquarters*, 366
s'il te plaît *please*, 6
s'il vous plaît *please*, 1, 6
Silence! *Quiet!*, 1
simple *simple*, 6
le sirop *syrup*, 6
le sirop d'érable *maple syrup*, 3
le sirop de menthe *mint syrup*, 6
situé(e) *situated*, 8
six *six*, 1
le skate(board) *skateboarding*, 5
le ski/les skis *skiing, skis*, 5

le ski de randonnée *cross-country skiing*, 5
le SMS *instant message*, 2
le snowboard *snowboarding*, 5
la sœur *sister*, 3
le sofa *couch*, 8
la soie *silk*, 7
soigneusement *carefully*, 10
le soir *evening*, 4
soixante *sixty*, 4
soixante et onze *seventy-one*, 4
soixante-dix *seventy*, 4
soixante-douze *seventy-two*, 4
le solde *sale*, 7
le soleil *sun*, 5
la solidarité *solidarity*, 375
son *his/her*, 3
la sortie *dismissal*, 4
sortir *to go out*, 2; **sortir la poubelle** *to take out the trash*, 8
soudain *suddenly*, 379
souhaiter *to wish*, 5
le soupir *sigh, gasp*, 377
le sourcil *eyebrow*, 369
sous *under*, 8
sous-terre *underground*, 6
le souterrain *underground passage*, 6
souterrain(e) *underground*, 370
le souvenir *memory*, 369
souvent *often*, 2
les souwères *Senegalese paintings under glass*, 7
la spatule *spatula*, 373
spécialisé *specialized*, 372
le spectacle *performance*, 9
le spectateur *spectator*, 366
le sport *sports*, 2
sportif(-ive) *athletic*, 3
le stade *stadium*, 2
le stage *camp*, 5
la station de métro *subway station*, 9
la station touristique *tourist resort*, 8
la statuette *small statue*, 10
le steak *steak*, 6
stopper *to stop*, 9
stupéfait *stunned*, 379
le styliste *stylist, designer*, 7
le stylo *pen*, 4
su *knew (past participle of **savoir**)*, 379
le sucre *sugar*, 373
le sucre en poudre *powdered sugar*, 373
sucré(e) *sweet*, 373
le sud *south*, 7
Suffit. *Enough.*, 4
suivant *forward (computer)*, 1
suivi *followed*, 375
la superficie *surface area*, 369

le supermarché *supermarket*, 9
la superstition *superstition*, 372
sur *on*, 8
le surf *snowboarding, surfing*, 5
la surface habitable *living space*, 8
surfer *to surf*, 2
surfer sur Internet *surf the Net*, 2
surnommé(e) *nicknamed*, 1
supris(e) *surprised*, 377
sursautant *starting, jumping*, 4
surtout *above all*, 6
survoler *to fly over*, 367
le sweat-shirt *sweat-shirt*, 4
le symbole *symbol*, 6
sympathique *nice*, 3
le système *system*, 10

ta *your (informal)*, 3
la table *table*, 1
la table basse *coffee table*, 8
la table de nuit *night stand*, 8
le tableau *board*, 1; *painting*, 8
le tableau d'affichage *information board*, 10
le tableau noir *blackboard*, 379
la taille *clothing size*, 7
le taille-crayon *pencil sharpener*, 4
le tailleur *woman's suit, tailor*, 7
tandis que *while*, 379
la tante *aunt*, 3
tape-à-l'œil *gaudy*, 7
le tapis *rug*, 8
la tapisserie *tapestry*, 5
le tarif *fee*, 10
le tarif réduit *reduced rate, discount*, 10
la tarte *pie*, 6
la tarte aux fruits *fruit tart/pie*, 6
la tarte tatin *upside-down apple tart*, 6
la tarte tropézienne *cream cake from Saint-Tropez*, 6
la tartine *bread with butter or jam*, 6
la tasse *cup*, 6
le taureau *bull*, 9
le taxi *taxi*, 9
le technicien *technician*, 9
la technique *technique*, 7
la technologie *technology*, 2
le tee-shirt *T-shirt*, 4
la télé(vision) *television*, 1
le téléphone *telephone*, 4
téléphoner (à des amis) *to call (friends)*, 2; téléphoner (se) *to call each other*, 2
tellement *so (much)*, 369
le temps *time*, 5; *weather*, 5

le temps libre *free time*, 5
tenir *to hold*, 372
le tennis *tennis*, 5
la tente *tent*, 7
tenir *to hold*, 379
le terminal *terminal*, 10
terminer (se) *to end*, 5
le terrain de jeux *playing field*, 7
la terrasse *terrace*, 8
la terre *earth, land*, 5; *ground*, 7
la terre cuite *clay*, 10
le territoire *territory*, 370
tes *your (informal)*, 3
la tête *head*, 3
têtu(e) *stubborn*, 9
le texto *instant message*, 2
le thaumaturge *worker of miracles*, 369
le théâtre *drama*, 5; *theater*, 5
le thème *theme*, 376
le ticket *ticket*, 9
la tieboudienne *traditional dish of Senegal*, 7
Tiens. *Here.*, 4
le timbre *stamp*, 9
timide *shy*, 3
la tintamarre *racket, noise*, 9
le tissu *fabric*, 7
le titre *title*, 6
le toast *toast*, 6
toi *you*, 2
les toilettes (f.) *restroom*, 8
le toit *roof*, 8
la tomate *tomato*, 373
tomber *to fall*, 8
ton *your (informal)*, 3
tondre (la pelouse) *to mow (the lawn)*, 8
la tonnerre *thunder*, 2
la tortue *tortoise*, 9
toucher *to touch*, 7
toujours *always*, 7
la tour *tower*, 1
le tour *trick*, 371
le tour du monde *around the world*, 10
le tourisme *tourism*, 381
le touriste (la touriste) *tourist*, 9
tourner *to turn*, 9
Tournez au/à la prochain(e)... *Turn at the next...*, 9
le tournoi *tournament*, 1
la tourtière *minced meat pie that is a Quebec specialty*, 3
tous les jours *every day*, 8
toussoter *cough*, 9
tout(e) *all, whole*, 3
tout à fait *totally, absolutely*, 7
tout de suite *right away*, 6
tout droit *straight ahead*, 9
tout le monde *everyone*, 4
toute la journée *all day*, 2
toute la nuit *all night*, 10

la toute-puissance *omnipotence*, 379
la toux *cough*, 9
la tradition *tradition*, 374
traditionnel(le) *traditional*, 7
le train *train*, 10
le train fantôme *ghost train*, 2
le traîneaux à chiens *dog-sledding*, 3
tranquille *quiet, tranquil*, 10
transformé(e) *transformed*, 381
le transformateur *transformer*, 10
transmettre *to transmit*, 374
travailler *to work*, 2
traverser *to cross*, 9
Traversez... *Cross...*, 9
treize *thirteen*, 1
trente *thirty*, 1
trente et un *thirty-one*, 4
très *very*, 1
Très bien. *Very well.*, 1
très mal *very badly*, 2
tricoter *to knit*, 369; se tricotèrent serré *to knit together*, 369
trois *three*, 1
troisième *third (largest)*, 7
le tronc *trunk*, 7
trop *too*, 370
troublé(e) *troubled*, 10
la trousse *pencil case*, 4
la trousse de toilette *vanity case*, 10
trouver *to find, to think*, 3
trouver (se) *to be located*, 8
le truc *thing*, 1; *trick*, 373
tu *you*, 1
Tu aimes...? *Do you like...?*, 2
Tu as combien de...? *How many... do you have?*, 3
Tu as des frères et des sœurs? *Do you have brothers and sisters?*, 3
Tu as envie de...? *Do you feel like...?*, 5
Tu as intérêt à... *You'd better...*, 10
Tu as quel âge ? *How old are you?*, 1
Tu as quel cours...? *What class do you have...?*, 4
Tu as... à me prêter? *Do you have... to lend me?*, 4
Tu... bien? *Do you... well?*, 2
Tu devrais... *You should...*, 10
Tu es d'accord si...? *Is it all right with you if...?*, 8
Tu ne peux pas partir sans... *You can't leave without...*, 10
la Tunisie *Tunisia*, 10
Tu pourrais me prêter...? *Could you lend me...?*, 4
Tu préfères... ou...? *Do you prefer... or...?*, 2
Tu reprends...? *Do you want more...?*, 6
Tu vas faire quoi...? *What are you going to do...?*, 5

Tu veux...? *Do you want to...?*, 5; *Do you want...?*, 6
Tu viens...? *Do you want to come to...?*, 5
le tuba *snorkel*, 7
la tunique *tunic*, 7
le turc *Turk*, 6
typique *typical*, 7
typiquement *typically*, 6

un/une *one*, 1
un peu trop... *a little bit too...*, 7
unique *only*, 3; *unique*, 5
l' ustensil (m.) *utensil*, 373
utiliser *to use*, 8

les vacances (f.) *vacation*, 2
la vache *cow*, 5
vaincu(e)(s) *defeated*, 6
valeureux *brave, valiant*, 6
la vaisselle *dishes*, 8
la valise *suitcase*, 10
la vallée *valley*, 5
valoir mieux *to be better*, 381
la vannerie *artistic technique using wicker*, 7
la variante *variant*, 6
la variété *variety*, 5
vaste *large*, 1
vaut mieux *is better*, 381
véhiculé *carried*, 374
le vélo *biking, bike*, 5
le vélo de course *racing bike*, 381
le vélo tout terrain (VTT) *mountain bike*, 7
vendre *to sell*, 4
le vendredi *Friday*, 4
venir *to come*, 5
venir de *to have just done something*, 5
le vent *wind*, 5

le verbe *verb*, 4
le verre *glass*, 6
vers *towards*, 377
verser *to pour*, 371
vert(e) *green*, 3
la veste *jacket*, 7
les vêtements (m.) *clothes*, 7
le viaduc *viaduct*, 9
victorieux(-se) *victorious*, 1
la vidéo amateur *amateur film-making*, 5
vider (le lave-vaisselle) *to empty (the dish-washer)*, 8
la vie *life*, 7
viennois(e) *from Vienna*, 6
vieux/vieille *old*, 3
le village *village*, 8
le village perché *perched village, village set on a hill*, 9
les villageois(-oises) *villagers*, 376
la ville *city*, 9
vingt *twenty*, 1
vingt et un/vingt et une *twenty-one*, 1
vingt-cinq *twenty-five*, 1
vingt-deux *twenty-two*, 1
vingt-huit *twenty-eight*, 1
vingt-neuf *twenty-nine*, 1
vingt-quatre *twenty-four*, 1
vingt-sept *twenty-seven*, 1
vingt-six *twenty-six*, 1
vingt-trois *twenty-three*, 1
violet(te) *purple*, 4
le visa *visa*, 10
le visage *face*, 369
vite *quickly*, 1
la vitesse *speed*, 5
Vive...! *Long live...!*, 5
vivre *to live*, 7
la voie *track*, 10
voilà *here is...*, 3; *Here.*, 4
la voile *sailing*, 5
le voilier *sailboat*, 5
voir *to see*, 9
la voiture (de sport) *(sports) car*, 2
la voix *voice*, 9
le vol *flight*, 10
voler *to fly*, 2; *to steal*, 371
le volet *shutter*, 3
le volley *volleyball*, 5
vos *your*, 3
votre *your*, 3
vouloir *to want*, 6
vouloir dire *to mean*, 10

vous *you*, 1
Vous avez décidé? *Have you decided?*, 7
Vous avez... en...? *Do you have... in...?*, 7
Vous désirez autre chose? *Would you like anything else?*, 6
Vous devriez... *You should...*, 10
Vous êtes combien dans ta famille? *How many are you in your family?*, 3
vous n'y êtes pas *you aren't serious*, 4
Vous voulez...? *Do you want...?*, 6
le voyage *trip*, 10
voyager *to travel*, 4
vrai(e) *true*, 4
la vue *view*, 10

le wagon *car (in a train)*, 10
le wagon-restaurant *buffet car*, 10
le week-end *weekend*, 4
le wolof *Wolof (language spoken in Senegal)*, 7

y *there*, 6; **Il y a** *There is/There are*, **Il n'y a pas de** *There is not a/ aren't any...*, 1; **Il y en a...** *There are...of them*, 1; **Il n'y en a pas.** *There aren't any (of them).*, 1
les yeux (m.) *eyes*, 3

zéro *zero*, 1
le zoo *zoo*, 5

Glossaire anglais–français

This vocabulary includes all of the words presented into the **Vocabulaire** sections of the chapters. These words are considered active—you are expected to know them and be able to use them. French nouns are listed with the definite article and the plural forms if it is irregular, Expressions are listed under the English word you would most likely to look up. The number after each entry refers to the chapter in which the word or phrase is introduced.

To be sure you are using French words and phrases in their correct context, refer to the chapters listed. You may also want to look up French phrases in the Liste d'expressions, pages R13–R17.

a *un, une,* 1
about; how about you *Et, toi? Et, vous?,* 1
a little bit too… *un peu trop…,* 7
a lot *beaucoup,* 4; **I like it a lot** *Ça me plaît beaucoup.,* 4
access *l'accès* (m.), 10
accessory *l'accessoire* (m.), 7
according to me *d'après moi,* 3
across from *en face de,* 8
activity *l'activité* (f.), 2
to **address** *s'adresser,* 9
to **advise** *conseiller,* 6; **I advise you to…** *Je te conseille de…,* 10
aerobics *l'aérobic* (f.), 5
after *après,* 9
afternoon *l'après-midi* (m.), 4
age *l'âge* (m.), 1
air conditioning *la climatisation,* 10
airport *l'aéroport* (m.), 10
all night *toute la nuit,* 10
always *toujours,* 8
amateur film-making *la vidéo amateur,* 5
American *américain,* 6
and *et,* 2
animal(s) *l'animal, les animaux* (m.), 2
to **answer** *répondre (à),* 4
apartment *l'appartement* (m.), 8;
apple *la pomme,* 6; **apple juice** *le jus de pomme,* 6
April *avril* (m.), 5
armchair *le fauteuil,* 8
arrival *l'arrivée* (f.), 10
to **ask (for)** *demander,* 1; **Ask…** *Adressez-vous…,* 9

athletic *sportif, sportive,* 3
ATM *le distributeur d'argent/ de billets,* 9
August *août* (m.), 5
aunt *la tante,* 3
available (for) *disponible (pour),* 10

backpack *le sac (à dos),* 4
bacon *le bacon,* 6
bad *mauvais, mauvaise,* 5; **badly** *mal,* 2
baggage locker *la consigne,* 10
balcony *le balcon,* 8
ball *la balle,* 2; **ball (inflatable)** *le ballon,* 2
banana *la banane,* 6
bandage *le pansement,* 9
bank *la banque,* 9
bank card *la carte bancaire,* 9
baseball *le base-ball,* 2
basketball *le basket(ball),* 5
bat *la batte,* 2
bathroom *la salle de bain,* 8
to **be** *être,* 3; **be able** *pouvoir,* 8; **be born** *naître,* 8; **be cold** *avoir froid,* 5; **be hot** *avoir chaud,* 5; **be hungry** *avoir faim,* 5; **be in one's best interest** *avoir intérêt à,* 10; **be located** *trouver (se),* 8; **be named** *appeler (s'),* 1; **be sorry** *regretter,* 9; **be thirsty** *avoir soif,* 5
beach *la plage,* 5
beautiful *beau, belle,* 3
because *parce que,* 4

to **become** *devenir,* 8
bed *le lit,* 8; **single bed** *le lit simple,* 10; **double bed** *le lit double,* 10
bedroom *la chambre,* 8
to **begin** *commencer,* 4
behind *derrière,* 9
belt *la ceinture,* 7
between *entre,* 9;
big *grand, grande,* 3
bike *le vélo,* 5; **by bicycle** *à vélo,* 9
bill *l'addition* (f.), 6; **bill (money)** *le billet,* 9
binder *le classeur,* 4
binoculars *les jumelles* (f.), 7
black *noir, noire,* 3
blond *blond, blonde,* 3
blue *bleu, bleue,* 3
board *le tableau,* 1
boarding gate *la porte d'embarquement,* 10; **boarding pass** *la carte d'embarquement,* 10
book *le livre,* 1; **bookshelf** *l'étagère* (f.), 8; **bookstore** *la librairie,* 9
booked, *complet,* 10
boots *bottes,* 7
boring *ennuyeux, ennuyeuse,* 4
bowl *le bol,* 6
boy *le garçon,* 1
bouquet *le bouquet,* 9
bracelet *le bracelet,* 7
bread *le pain,* 6; **bread with butter and jam** *la tartine,* 6
break *la récréation,* 4
breakfast *le petit-déjeuner,* 6
bridge *le pont,* 9
to **bring someone along** *amener,* 4
brother *le frère,* 3; **step brother** *le demi-frère,* 3; **half brother** *le demi-frère,* 3

brown(-eyed) *marron*, 3;
brown(-haired) *brun, brune*, 3;
light brown(-haired)
châtain(s), 3
buffet car *le wagon-restaurant*, 10
building *l'immeuble (m.)*, 8
bus *le bus*, 9; **bus stop** *l'arrêt de
bus (m.)*, 9; **by bus** *en bus*, 9
busy *occupé(e)*, 5; **I'm too busy.**
Je suis trop occupé(e), 5
but *mais*, 2
butter *le beurre*, 6
to **buy** *acheter*, 4
by *par*, 9

cabinet *le placard*, 8
café *le café*, 2
calculator *la calculatrice*, 4
to **call (oneself)** *appeler (s')*, 10
to **call (friends)** *téléphoner (à des
amis)*, 2; **calling card** *la carte
téléphonique*, 9
camera (digital) *l'appareil photo
(numérique) (m.)*, 5
can, be able to *pouvoir*, 8; **Can
I…?** *Est-ce que je peux…?*, 8; **Can
you tell me…?** *Est-ce que vous
pouvez me dire…?*, 9
to **cancel** *annuler*, 10
cap *la casquette*, 7
car *la voiture*, 2; **sports car**
la voiture de sport, 2; **by car**
en voiture, 2
car (in a train) *le wagon*, 10
card(s) *la carte*, 2; **credit card**
la carte de crédit, 9
cash *le liquide*, 10; **cash machine**
le distributeur d'argent, 9
cat *le chat*, 3
CD *le CD*, 1; **CD player** *le lecteur
de CD*, 1
cell phone *le mobile, le portable*, 4
cereal *les céréales*, 6
chain *la chaîne*, 7
chair *la chaise*, 1
to **change** *changer*, 4; *changer de
l'argent*, 9; **to change (in)**
changer (en), 10
change (coins) *la monnaie*, 9;
change purse *le porte-
monnaie*, 7; **Do you have
change?** *Avez-vous de la
monnaie?*, 9
check *le chèque*, 10; **traveler's
checks** *les chèques de voyage*, 10
to **check in** *enregistrer*, 10

cheese *le fromage*, 6
chemistry *la chimie*, 4
chess *les échecs*, 2
chest of drawers *la commode*, 8
chicken *le poulet*, 6
child *l'enfant (m.)*, 3
chocolate *le chocolat*, 2; **hot
chocolate** *le chocolat chaud*, 6
to **choose** *choisir*, 6; **I don't know
what to choose.** *Je ne sais pas
quoi choisir.*, 7
chore *la corvée*, 8
church *l'église (m.)*, 9
city *la ville*, 9
class, classroom *la classe, la salle de
classe*, 1; **class** *le cours*, 4; **What
class do you have…?** *Tu as quel
cours…?*, 4
classical *classique*, 2
to **clean** *nettoyer*, 8
to **clear the table** *débarrasser
la table*, 8
to **close** *fermer*, 1; **Close your
notebooks.** *Fermez vos
cahiers.*, 1
closet *le placard*, 8
clothes *les vêtements*, 7
clothing size *la taille*, 7
cloud *le nuage*, 5; **It's cloudy.**
Il y a des nuages., 5
club *le club (de tennis, de foot)*, 5
coat *le manteau*, 7
coffee *le café*, 6; **coffeehouse**
le café, 2; **coffee table** *la table
basse*, 8; **coffee with milk** *le café
au lait*, 6
coin *la pièce*, 9
cold *froid*, 5; *le rhume*, 9; **to be
cold** *avoir froid*, 5; **It's cold.**
Il fait froid. 5; **to have a cold**
avoir un rhume, 5
color *la couleur*, 4
to **come** *venir*, 5; **to come down,
to go down** *descendre*, 8
comic strip *la bande dessinée
(BD)*, 2
compartment *le compartiment*, 10
computer *l'ordinateur (m.)*, 1
computer science
l'informatique (m.), 4
connecting flight, connection
la correspondance, 10
to **continue** *continuer*, 9
Continue until… *Continuez
jusqu'à…*, 9
to **cook** *faire la cuisine*, 8
to **correct** *corriger*, 4
to **cost** *coûter*, 7
cotton *le coton*, 7
couch *le sofa*, 8
cough *la toux*, 9
counter *le guichet*, 9

countryside *la campagne*, 5
cousin *le cousin, la cousine*, 3
creative *créatif, créative*, 3
croissant *le croissant*, 6
to **cross** *traverser*, 9;
Cross… *Traversez…*, 9
cup *la tasse*, 6
currency exchange office *bureau
de change*, 10
cute *mignon, mignonne*, 3

to **dance** *danser*, 2
dark *foncé, foncée*, 4
daughter *la fille*, 3; **only
daughter** *la fille unique*, 3;
granddaughter *la petite-fille*, 3
day *le jour*, 4; **What day is today?**
Quel jour sommes-nous?, 4
to **decide** *to decide*, 7; **Have you
decided?** *Vous avez choisi?/
Vous avez décidé?*, 6, 7; **I can't
decide.** *Je n'arrive pas à me
décider.*, 7
December *décembre*, 5
delicious *Délicieux!, Délicieuse!*, 6
Delighted! *Enchanté(e)!,
Enchantée!*, 1
denim *en jean*, 7
department *le rayon*, 7
departure *le départ*, 10
to **deposit** *déposer*, 9
desk *le bureau*, 1
destination *la destination*, 10
diamond *le diamant*, 8; **out of
diamond** *en diamant*, 8
dictionary *le dictionnaire*, 4
to **die** *mourir*, 8
difficult *difficile*, 4
dining room *la salle à manger*, 8
dishes *la vaisselle*, 8
dishwasher *le lave-vaisselle*, 8
dismissal *la sortie*, 4
to **disturb** *déranger*, 4
diving mask *le masque de
plongée*, 7
to **divorce** *divorcer*, 3
to **do, to make** *faire*, 2; **to do the
dishes** *faire la vaisselle*, 8; **to do
the laundry** *faire la lessive*, 8;
I'm not doing anything.
Je ne fais rien., 5; **What are
we doing…?** *Qu'est-ce qu'on
fait…?* 5; **What are you going to
do if…?** *Qu'est-ce que tu vas faire
s'il…?*, 5; **What are you going to
do…?** *Tu vas faire quoi…?*, 5;

What do you do for fun? *Qu'est-ce que tu fais pour t'amuser?*, 5
dog *le chien*, 3
door *la porte*, 1
double bed *le lit double*, 10
downstairs *en bas*, 8
downtown *le centre-ville*, 9
drama *le théâtre*, 5
to **draw** *dessiner*, 2
drawing *le dessin*, 2
dress *la robe*, 7
to **drink** *boire*, 6; **drink** *la boisson*, 6
drums *la batterie*, 5; **to play drums** *jouer de la batterie*, 5;
DVD *le DVD*, 1; **DVD player** *le lecteur de DVD*, 1

ear *l'oreille* (f.), 3
early *en avance*, 10
earrings *les boucles d'oreilles*, 7
easy *facile*, 4
to **eat** *manger*, 2
egg *l'œuf* (m.), 6
eight *huit*, 1
eighteen *dix-huit*, 1
eighty *quatre-vingts*, 4; **eighty-one** *quatre-vingt-un*, 4
elderly *âgé(e)*, 3
elegant *élégant, élégante*, 7
elevator *l'ascenseur* (m.), 10
eleven *onze* (m.), 1
e-mail *l'e-mail* (m.), 1; **e-mail address** *l'adresse e-mail* (f.), 1; **What is your e-mail address?** *Quelle est ton addresse e-mail?*, 1; **It's...@...** *C'est...arobase... point...*, 1
employee *l'employé* (m.), *l'employée* (f.), 9
to **empty** *vider*, 8; **to empty the dishwasher** *vider le lave-vaisselle*, 8
to **encourage** *encourager*, 4
end *la fin*, 8; **at the end of** *au fond de*, 8
to **enter** *entrer*, 8
English *l'anglais*, 2
Enjoy your meal *Bon appétit!*, 6
envelope *l'enveloppe* (f.), 9
eraser *la gomme*, 4
evening *le soir*, 4
every day *tous les jours*, 8
Excellent! *Excellent(e)!*, 6
excuse-me *pardon*, 9; **Excuse-me, do you know where... is?** *Pardon, savez-vous où est...?*, 9; **Excuse-me, I am looking for...** *Excusez-moi, je cherche...*, 9

expensive *cher, chère*, 7
eyes *les yeux*, 3

fall *l'automne* (m.), 5
to **fall** *tomber*, 8
family *la famille*, 3
far from *loin de*, 9
fascinating *fascinant, fascinante*, 4; **It's fascinating.** *C'est fascinant.*, 4
fat *gros, grosse*, 3
father *le père*, 3
favorite *préféré, préférée*, 2
February *février*, 5
fee *le tarif*, 10
to **feel like** *avoir envie de*, 5; **Do you feel like...?** *Ça te/vous dit de...?*, 5; **Do you feel like...?** *Tu as envie de...?*, 5
fifteen *quinze*, 1
fifty *cinquante*, 4
film, movie *le film*, 2
finally *finalement*, 9
to **find, to think** *trouver*, 3
to **finish** *finir*, 6
first *d'abord*, 9; **first** *premier, première*, 10; **first class** *la première classe*, 10; **first floor** *le rez-de-chaussée*, 8
fish *le poisson*, 6; **fishing pole** *la canne à pêche*, 7
five *cinq*, 1
flight *le vol*, 10
flight attendant *l'hôte* (m.), *l'hôtesse* (f.), 10
flippers *les palmes*, 7
floor *l'étage* (m.), 8
flower *la fleur*, 9;
flower vendor *le fleuriste, la fleuriste*, 9
foot *le pied*, 9; **by foot** *à pied*, 9
to **forget** *oublier*, 10; **Don't forget...** *N'oublie pas...*, 10
fork *la fourchette*, 6
fortunately *heureusement*, 5
forty *quarante*, 4
four *quatre*, 1
fourteen *quatorze*, 1
free *libre*, 5; **free time** *le temps libre*, 5
French *le français*, 2
Friday *vendredi*, 4
friend *l'ami* (m.), *l'amie* (f.), 1; *le copain, la copine*, 2; **He, She is a friend.** *C'est un ami, une amie.*, 1
fries *les frites*, 2
from *en provenance de*, 10;

from the... to the... *du... au*, 10
from time to time *de temps en temps*, 2
funny *marrant, marrante*, 3

to **gain weight** *grossir*, 6
game *le jeu*, 2
garage *le garage*, 8
gaudy *tape-à-l'œil*, 7
generous *généreux, généreuse*, 3
geography *la géographie*, 4
German *l'allemand*, 4
girl *la fille*, 1
to **give** *donner*, 6; **to give back** *rendre*, 4; **Give me...** *Donnez-moi...*, 6
glass *le verre*, 6
glasses *les lunettes*, 7
gloves *les gants*, 7
to **go** *aller*, 2; **Go back to your seats!** *Retournez à vos places!*, 1; **to go down** *descendre*, 8; **to go forward** *avancer*, 4; **to go on a picnic** *faire un pique-nique*, 2; **to go out** *sortir*, 2, 8; **to go shopping** *faire les magasins*, 2; **Go straight until...** *Allez tout droit jusqu'à...*, 9; **Go to the board!** *Allez au tableau!*, 1; **to go up** *monter*, 8
gold *or*, **out of gold** *en or*, 7
good *bon, bonne*, 3; **Good idea!** *Bonne idée!*, 5
Goodbye. *Au revoir./Salut.*, 1
grandchild *le petit-enfant*, 3; **granddaughter** *la petite-fille*, 3; **grandfather** *le grand-père*, 3; **grandmother** *la grand-mère*, 3; **grandparent** *le grand-parent*, 3; **grandson** *le petit-fils*, 3
grapefruit *le pamplemousse*, 6
gray *gris, grise*, 4
great *génial, géniale*, 3
green *vert, verte*, 3
to **grow (up)** *grandir*, 6
guitar *la guitare*, 5; **to play the guitar** *jouer de la guitare*, 5

hair *les cheveux*, 3; **He, She has brown hair.** *Il, Elle est brun(e).*, 3
hair salon *le salon de coiffure*, 9

half *demi, demie,* 4; **half-brother** *le demi-frère,* 3; **half-sister** *la demi-sœur,* 3

ham *le jambon,* 6

handicapped access *l'accès handicapé* (m.), 10

handsome *beau, belle,* 3

happy *heureux, heureuse,* 5

hat *le chapeau,* 7

to hate *détester,* 2

to have *avoir,* 1; **to have dinner** *dîner,* 6; **have… eyes** *avoir les yeux…,* 3; **to have fun** *s'amuser,* 5; **to have… hair** *avoir les cheveux…,* 3; **to have just…** *venir de…,* 5; **to have more** *reprendre,* 6; **to have time** *avoir le temps de,* 5

he *il,* 1

head *la tête,* 3

headphones *les écouteurs,* 2

heading for *à destination de,* 10

to hear *entendre,* 4

Hello (in the evening) *Bonsoir.,* 1; (in the morning) *Bonjour.,* 1

helmet *le casque,* 5

to help *aider,* 7; **May I help you?** *Je peux vous aider?,* 7

Here it is. *Voilà/Tiens.* 3, 4; **Here is…** *Là, c'est…,* 8; **here** *là,* 8

Hi. *Salut.,* 1

high *haut,* 8

high school *le lycée,* 2

hike *la randonnée,* 7; **hiking shoes** *les chaussures de randonnée,* 7

his, her *son, sa, ses* 3

history *l'histoire* (f.), 4

hockey *le hockey,* 5

home *la maison,* 8; **at (my) home** *chez moi,* 8

homework *les devoirs,* 4

honestly *franchement,* 7; **Honestly, it's a bit gaudy.** *Franchement, il/elle est un peu tape-à-l'œil.,* 7

to hope *espérer,* 4

horrible *horrible,* 7; **It's horrible.** *Il/Elle est horrible.,* 7

hospital *l'hôpital* (m.), 9

hot *chaud,* 5; **be hot,** *avoir chaud,* 5; **hot chocolate** *le chocolat chaud,* 6; **It's hot.** *Il fait chaud.,* 5

hotel *l'hôtel* (m.), 10

hour *l'heure* (f.), 4

house *la maison,* 8

how *comment, combien* 1; **How is…?** *Comment c'est,…? Comment est…?,* **How are** *Comment sont…?,* 3; **How about going to…?** *On va…?,* 5; **How about you?** *Et vous?* (formal), *Et toi?* (informal), 1; **How are you?**

How are you? *Comment allez-vous?* (formal), *Ça va? Comment ça va?* (informal), 1; **How do you say… in French?** *Comment dit-on… en français?,* 1; **How do you spell…?** *Comment tu épelles…?,* 1; **How do you write that?** *Comment ça s'écrit?,* 1; **How does… fit me?** *Il/Elle me va…?,* 7; **How is your… class?** *Comment est ton cours de…?,* 4; **How many are you in your family?** *Vous êtes combien dans ta famille?,* 3; **How many students are there in the class?** *Combien d'élèves il y a dans la classe?,* 1; **How many… do you have?** *Tu as combien de…?,* 3; **How much does… cost?** *Il/Elle coûte combien,…?,* 7; **How much is it total?** *Ça fait combien en tout?,* 7; **How much is it?** *Ça fait combien?,* 6; **How much is…?** *C'est combien pour…?,* 9; **How old are you?** *Tu as quel âge?,* 1

hurt *avoir mal à,* 9

husband *le mari,* 3

I *je,* 1

ice cooler *la glacière,* 7

ice cream *la glace,* 2

ice-skating *le patin à glace,* 5; **ice-skating rink** *la patinoire,* 5

in *dans, en* 8

in front (of) *devant,* 9

in my opinion *à mon avis,* 3

In what color? *De quelle couleur?,* 4

In which season…? *En quelle saison…?,* 5

In…, there is… *Dans…, il y a…,* 8

inexpensive *bon marché, bon marchée,* 7

information board *le tableau d'affichage,* 10

intelligent, smart *intelligent, intelligente,* 3

interest *l'intérêt* (m.), 10; **interesting** *intéressant, intéressante,* 4; **It's interesting.** *C'est intéressant.,* 4

Internet *Internet,* 2; **Internet café** *le cybercafé,* 5

intersection *le carrefour,* 9

to introduce *présenter,* 1; **Let me introduce you to…** *Je te/vous présente…,* 1

jacket *la veste,* 7

jam *la confiture,* 6

January *janvier,* 5

jeans *le jean,* 7

jewelry *la bijouterie,* 7; **jewelery department** *le rayon bijouterie,* 7;

jogging *le jogging,* 5

juice *le jus,* 6

July *juillet,* 5

June *juin,* 5

kitchen *la cuisine,* 8

kite *le cerf-volant,* 7

knife *le couteau,* 6

to know *connaître/savoir,* 9

L

lake *le lac,* 5

lamp *la lampe,* 8

laptop *le portable,* 4

last *dernier, dernière,* 7

late *en retard,* 10

laundry *la lessive,* 8

lawn *la pelouse,* 8

layover *l'escale* (f.), 10; **to have a layover at** *faire escale à,* 10

lazy *paresseux, paresseuse,* 3

to learn *apprendre,* 6

leather *le cuir,* 7; **leather department** *le rayon maroquinerie,* 7; **leather goods** *la maroquinerie,* 7

to leave *partir,* 8

left *gauche,* 8

lemon-lime soda *la limonade,* 6

to lend *prêter,* 4; **Could you lend me…?** *Tu pourrais me prêter…?,* 4; **Do you have… to lend me?** *Tu as… à me prêter?,* 4

letter *la lettre,* 9

library *la bibliothèque,* 2

light *clair,* 4

to like *aimer,* 2; **I like…better.** *J'aime mieux…,* 4; **I really like it.** *Ça me plaît beaucoup.,* 4; **Do you like…?** *Il, Elle te plaît,…?,* 7

line *la queue,* 10

linen *le lin;* **out of linen** *en lin,* 7

to listen *écouter*, 1; **Listen!** *Écoutez!*, 1

to live *habiter*, 8

living room *le salon*, 8

loaf of French bread *la baguette*, 6

long *long, longue*, 3

to look at *regarder*, 1; **Look (at the map)!** *Regardez (la carte)!*, 1; **No thank you, I'm just looking.** *Non, merci, je regarde.*, 7; **to look for** *chercher*, 4

loose *large*, 7

to lose *perdre*, 4; **to lose weight** *maigrir*, 6

to love *aimer, adorer*, 2

low *bas*, 8

luggage (carry-on) *les bagages (à main)*, 10; **luggage carrier, rack** *le porte-bagage*, 10

lunch *le déjeuner*, 6

magazine *le magazine*, 2

mail *le courrier*, 9

mail carrier *le facteur*, 9

to make *faire*, 2; **to make one's bed** *faire son lit*, 8

mall *le centre commercial*, 2

man's shirt *la chemise*, 7

map *la carte*, 1; **map** *le plan*, 9

March *mars*, 5

mathematics *les mathématiques (maths)*, 2

May *mai*, 5

me *moi*, 2; **Me neither.** *Moi non plus.* 2; **Me, too.** *Moi aussi.* 2

meal *le repas*, 6; **Are all meals included with the room?** *Est-ce que vous faites pension complète?*, 10

mean *méchant, méchante*, 3

medicine *le médicament*, 9

medium *à point*, 6

menu *la carte*, 6

message *le message*, 2; **instant text message** *le SMS, le texto*, 2

midnight *minuit*, 4

milk *le lait*, 6

mint *la menthe*, 6; **mint syrup** *le sirop de menthe*, 6

minus *moins*, 4

Miss *mademoiselle*, 1

to miss *manquer/rater*, 10

modern *moderne*, 2

Monday *lundi*, 4

money *l'argent* (m.), 9

month *le mois*, 5; **which month** *pendant quel mois*, 5

more *encore*, 6; **more or less** *plus ou moins*, 1

morning *le matin*, 4

mother *la mère*, 3

mountain *la montagne*, 5; **mountain bike** *le vélo tout terrain, le VTT*, 7

mouth *la bouche*, 3

movie theatre *le cinéma*, 2

to mow *tondre*, 8; **mow the lawn** *tondre la pelouse*, 8

MP3 *le MP3*, 2

Mr. *monsieur*, 1

Mrs. *madame*, 1

museum *le musée*, 5

music *la musique*, 2; **music class** *l'éducation musicale* (f.), 4

my *ma, mon, mes*, 3

name *le nom*, 10; **What is your name?** *Comment tu t'appelles?*, 1; **My name is…** *Je m'appelle…*, 1; **His, Her name is…** *Il/Elle s'appelle…*, 1; **Under what name?** *À quel nom?*, 9

napkin *la serviette*, 6

near *près de*, 9

necklace *le collier*, 7

to need *avoir besoin de*, 4; **What do you need for…?** *Qu'est-ce qu'il te faut pour…?*, 4; **What do you need?** *De quoi tu as besoin?*, 4; **I need…** *J'ai besoin de…*, 4; **I need…** *Il me faut…*, 4 **He, She is neither… nor…** *Il, Elle n'est ni… ni…*, 3

nephew *le neveu*, 3

never *jamais*, 2; *ne... jamais*, 8

new *nouveau, nouvelle*, 3

newspaper *le journal*, 2

next *prochain, prochaine*, 9; **next to** *à côté de*, 8; *près de*, 9

nice *sympathique*, 3

niece *la nièce*, 3

night *la nuit*, 10; **night stand** *la table de nuit*, 8

nine *neuf*, 1

nineteen *dix-neuf*, 1

ninety *quatre-vingt-dix*, 4; **ninety-one** *quatre-vingt-onze*, 4

no *non*, 2; **no longer** *ne... plus*, 8; **no one** *ne... personne, personne*, 8

non-smoking *non-fumeur*, 10

noon *midi*, 4

nose *le nez*, 3

not *ne... pas*, 1; **not at all** *pas du tout*, 7; **Not bad.** *Pas mal.*, 1; *Pas mauvais.*, 6; **Not good at all!** *Pas bon du tout!*, 6; **Not me.** *Pas moi.*, 2; **Not much.** *Pas grand-chose.*, 5; **not yet** *ne... pas encore*, 8

notebook *le cahier*, 1

nothing *rien*, 5; *ne... rien*, 8; **Nothing special.** *Rien de spécial.*, 5

novel *le roman*, 2

November *novembre*, 5

now *maintenant*, 4

number *le numéro*, 4

October *octobre*, 5

of, from + city, feminine country *de*, 10

of course *bien entendu*, 6, *bien sûr*, 9; **Of course, but first you must…** *Bien sûr, mais il faut d'abord…*, 8

of the *de l', de la, des, du*, 6

often *souvent*, 2

Okay. *D'accord.*, 5

old *vieux, vieille*, 3; **I am…years old.** *J'ai… ans.*, 1

omelet *l'omelette* (f.), 6

on *sur*, 8; **on sale** *en solde*, 7; **on time** *à l'heure*, 10

one *un, une*, 1 **one hundred** *cent*, 4; **one hundred and one** *cent un*, 4; **one way** *aller simple*, 10; **one (we)** *on*, 1

only *unique*, 3

open *ouvrir*, 1; **Open your books to page…** *Ouvrez vos livres à la page…*, 1; **open air, outdoors** *plein air*, 7; **open air market** *le marché*, 9

opera *l'opéra* (m.), 5

or *ou*, 2

orange *orange (fruit)*, 6; *orange color*, 4; **orange juice** *jus d'orange*, 6

our *nos; notre*, 3

Out of the question! *Pas question!*, 8

outdoor goods department *le rayon plein air*, 7

P

pack the bags *faire les valises*, 10
package *le colis*, 9
page *la page*, 1
painting *le tableau*, 8
pants *le pantalon*, 7
paper *le papier*, 4
parent *le parent*, 3
park *le parc*, 2
parking *le parking*, 10
to party *faire la fête*, 2; party *la fête*, 2
to pass *réussir (à)*, 6; to pass by *passer (à un endroit)*, 9
passenger *le passager*, 10
passport *le passeport*, 10
pasta *les pâtes*, 6
to pay *payer*, 8; to pay by check *payer par chèque*, 10; to pay cash *payer en liquide*, 10; to pay with a credit card *payer avec une carte*, 10
pen *le stylo*, 4
pencil *le crayon*, 4; (colored) pencil *le crayon (de couleur)*, 2; pencil case *la trousse*, 4; pencil sharpener *le taille-crayon*, 4
pepper *le poivre*, 6
pharmacist *le pharmacien, la pharmacienne*, 9
pharmacy *la pharmacie*, 9
phone number *le numéro de téléphone*, 4
photo *la photo*, 5
Physical education (P.E.) *l'EPS (éducation physique et sportive)* (f.), 4
physics *la physique*, 4
piano *le piano*, 5; to play the piano *jouer du piano*, 5;
to pick up one's bedroom *ranger sa chambre*, 8
picnic *le pique-nique*, 2
pie *la tarte*, 6
piece of paper *la feuille de papier*, 4
pilot *le pilote*, 10
pill *le comprimé*, 9
pink *rose*, 4
pizza *la pizza*, 6
to place *placer*, 4
plane *l'avion* (m.), 10; plane ticket *le billet d'avion*, 10
plant *la plante*, 8
plate *l'assiette* (f.), 6
platform *le quai*, 10
to play *jouer*, 2; to play baseball *jouer au base-ball*, 2; to play cards *jouer aux cartes*, 2; to play chess *jouer aux échecs*, 2; to play

soccer *jouer au football*, 2; to play sports *faire du sport*, 2; to play video games *jouer à des jeux vidéo*, 5; Do you play sports? *Est-ce que tu fais du sport?*, 5; Do you play…? *Est-ce que tu joues...?*, 5
please *s'il te plaît, s'il vous plaît*, 1
pomegranate drink *la grenadine*, 6
pool *la piscine*, 2
pork *le porc*, 6
post card *la carte postale*, 9; post office *la poste*, 9
poster *le poster*, 1
to prefer *préférer*, 2
pretty *joli(e)*, 7
pretty well *assez bien*, 2
to pronounce *prononcer*, 4
pull-over sweater *le pull*, 7
to punch (a ticket) *composter*, 10
purple *violet, violette*, 4
purse *le sac (à main)*, 7
to put on *mettre*, 7
to put away, to tidy *ranger*, 8

Q

quarter *quart*, 4
quiche *la quiche*, 6
Quiet! *Silence!*, 1
quite, rather *assez*, 3

R

racket *la raquette*, 5
radio *la radio*, 2
to rain *pleuvoir*, 5
raincoat *l'imperméable* (m.), 7
to raise *lever*, 4
rare *saignant*, 6
rarely *rarement*, 2
to read *lire*, 2
reception *la réception*, 10; receptionist *le réceptionniste, la réceptionniste*, 10
to recommend *recommander*, 6; What do you recommend? *Qu'est-ce que vous me conseillez?*, 6
recreation center *La Maison des jeunes et de la culture, la MJC*, 2
red *rouge*, 4; red-head *roux* (m.), *rousse* (f.), 3
reduced rate *le tarif réduit*, 10
regularly *régulièrement*, 5

to remarry *remarier*, 3
to remember *rappeler*, 10
to repeat *répéter*, 1; Repeat! *Répétez!*, 1; Could you please repeat that? *Répétez, s'il vous plaît?*, 1
to replace *remplacer*, 4
to reserve *réserver*, 10; reservation *réservation*, 10
restroom *les toilettes*, 8
to return *retourner*, 1
rice *le riz*, 6
right *droite*, 8
right away *tout de suite*, 6
ring *la bague*, 7
room *la pièce*, 8
room *la salle*, 8; bedroom *la chambre*, 8
room with a view *la chambre avec vue*, 10
round-trip *aller-retour*, 10
rug *le tapis*, 8
ruler *la règle*, 4

S

salad *la salade*, 6
salami *le saucisson*, 6
sales *les soldes*, 7; They are on sale for… *Ils/Elles sont soldé(e)s à...*, 7; on sale *en solde*, 7
salt *le sel*, 6
sandals *les sandales*, 7
sandwich *le sandwich*, 6
Saturday *samedi*, 4
to say *dire*, 1
scarf *le foulard*, 7
schedule *l'horaire* (m.), 10
scholastic *scolaire*, 4
school *l'école* (m.), 2; high school *le lycée*, 2; school subject *la matière*, 4; school supplies *les fournitures scolaires*, 4
sea *la mer*, 5
season *la saison*, 5
seat (classroom) *la place*, 1; seat (train) *la place assise*, 10
second *deuxième*, 10; second class *la deuxième classe*, 10; second floor *le premier étage*, 8
to see *voir*, 9; See you later. *À plus tard. À toute à l'heure.*, 1; See you soon. *À bientôt.*, 1; See you tomorrow. *À demain.*, 1
to sell *vendre*, 4
to send *envoyer*, 2; to send e-mails *envoyer des e-mails*, 2
September *septembre*, 5

serious *sérieux, sérieuse*, 3

service *service*, 6; **Is the tip included?** *Le service est compris?*, 6

to set *mettre* 6; **to set the table** *mettre le couvert*, 6; *mettre la table*, 8

seven *sept*, 1

seventeen *dix-sept*, 1

seventy *soixante-dix*, 4; **seventy-one** *soixante et onze*, 4; **seventy-two** *soixante-douze*, 4

Shall we do…? *On fait…?*, 5

she *elle*, 1

sheet (of paper) *la feuille (de papier)*, 4

shirt *la chemise*, 7

shoes *les chaussures*, 7; **shoe size** *la pointure*, 7

shop *le magasin*, 2; *la boutique*, 9

short (length) *court, courte*, 3

shorts *le short*, 4

shy *timide*, 3

silk *soie*, 7; **made of silk** *en soie*, 7

silver *argent*, 7; **made of silver** *en argent*, 7

to sing *chanter*, 2

single bed *le lit simple*, 10

sister *la sœur*, 3; **half sister** *la demi-sœur*, 3; **step sister** *la demi-sœur*, 3

Sit down! *Asseyez-vous!*, 1

six *six*, 1

sixteen *seize*, 1

sixty *soixante*, 4

skateboard *le skate(board)*, 5

skis *les skis* (m.), 5; **skiing** *faire du ski* (m.), 5

skirt *la jupe*, 7

to sleep *dormir*, 2; **sleeping car (in a train)** *la couchette*, 10

small *petit, petite*, 3

sneakers *les baskets*, 4

snorkel *le tuba*, 7

to snow *neiger*, 5; **snow** *la neige*, 5

so (well) *alors*, 7

soccer *le football*, 2

socks *les chaussettes*, 7

soda *le soda*, 6; **Coke** *le coca*, 6

some *des*, 1

something *quelque chose*, 7

son *le fils*, 3; **only son** *le fils unique*, 3

sorry *désolé(e)*, 5; **Sorry, I don't have the time.** *Désolé(e), je n'ai pas le temps.* 5

Spanish *espagnol*, 4

to speak *parler*, 2

to spell *épeler*, 10; **How is… spelled?** *Comment tu épelles…?*, 1; **It is spelled/ written…** *Ça s'écrit…*, 1

spoon *la cuillère*, 6

sports *le sport*, 2

spring *le printemps*, 5

stadium *le stade*, 2

staircase *l'escalier* (m.), 8

stamp *le timbre*, 9

to stand in line *faire la queue*, 10

to start *commencer (à)*, 4

stationery store *la papeterie*, 9

to stay *rester*, 8

steak *le steak*, 6

step father *le beau-père*, 3; **step mother** *la belle-mère*, 3

stereo system *la chaîne-stéréo*, 8

stop *l'arrêt* (m.), 9

to stopover at *faire l'escale à*, 10

store *magasin*, 2

straight ahead *tout droit*, 9

street *la rue*, 9

strong *fort, forte*, 3

student *l'élève* (m. or f.), 1

to study *étudier*, 2

subway *le métro*, 9; **subway station** *la station de métro*, 9; **by subway** *en métro*, 9

suit *le costume*, 7

suitcase *la valise*, 10

summer *l'été* (m.), 5

sun *le soleil*, 5; **sunglasses** *les lunettes de soleil*, 7; **It's sunny.** *Il y a du soleil.*, 5

Sunday *dimanche*, 4

superstore *la grande surface*, 7

supplies *les fournitures*, 4

to surf *surfer*, 2; **to surf the Net** *surfer sur Internet*, 2; **surfboard** *la planche de surf*, 7

sweat shirt *le sweat-shirt*, 4

to sweep *balayer*, 8

sweet *gentil, gentille*, 3

to swim *nager*, 2; **swimming pool** *la piscine*, 2; **swimsuit** *le maillot de bain*, 7

syrup *le sirop*, 6; **syrup (medicine)** *le sirop*, 9

table *la table*, 1; **table cloth** *la nappe*, 6; **table setting** *le couvert*, 6

to take *prendre*, 6; **to take something (with)** *emporter*, 10; **to take a trip** *faire un voyage*, 10; **to take the dog for a walk** *promener/ sortir le chien*, 4; **to take more** *reprendre*, 6; **Do you want more…?** *Tu reprends…?/ Encore…*, 6; **to take out** *sortir*, 8;

to take out the trash *sortir la poubelle*, 8; **Take…** *Prenez…* 9; **I don't know what to take.** *Je ne sais pas quoi prendre.*, 7

to talk (with friends) *discuter (avec des amis)*, 2

taxi *le taxi*, 9; **by taxi** *en taxi*, 9

teacher *le prof(esseur)*, *la professeur*, 1

telephone *le téléphone*, 4; **telephone booth** *la cabine téléphonique*, 9; **telephone card** *la carte téléphonique*, 9

television *la télé(vision)*, 1

tell me *dites-moi*, 9

ten *dix*, 1

tennis *le tennis*, 5

tent *la tente*, 7

terminal *le terminal*, 10

that *ça*, 3

Thank you. *Merci.*, 1

the *l', le, la, les*, 2

theater *le théâtre*, 5

their *leur, leurs*, 3

then *puis, ensuite*, 9

there is, there are *il y a…*, 1; **There are… of them.** *Il y en a…*, 1; **There are… of us.** *Nous sommes…*, 3; **There aren't any.** *Il n'y en a pas.*, 1

these *ces*, 7; **These are…** *Ça, ce sont…*, 3

they *elles, ils*, 1

thin *mince*, 3

thing *la chose*, 6

to think *penser*, 3; **What do you think of…?** *Comment tu trouves…?*, 3; **I think he/she…** *Je le/la trouve*, 3; **I think it's…** *Je trouve ça…*, 4

thirteen *treize*, 1

thirty *trente*, 1; **thirty-one** *trente et un*, 4

this *ce, cet, cette*, 7; *ça*, 3; **This is…** *Ça, c'est…*, 1

three *trois*, 1

throat *la gorge*, 9

to throw *lancer*, 4; *jeter*, 10

Thursday *jeudi*, 4

ticket *le ticket*, **ticket counter** *le guichet*, 9; **ticket collector** *le contrôleur*, 10; **ticket machine** *le distributeur de billets*, 10

tie *la cravate*, 7

tight *étroit, étroite*, 7; *serré, serrée*, 7

time *le temps*, 5; **at what time** *à quelle heure*, 4; **At what time do you have…?** *À quelle heure tu as…?*, 4; **What time is it?** *Quelle heure est-il?*, 4; **time** *fois*, 8; **times per…** *…fois par…*, 8; **on time** *à l'heure*, 10

tip *le pourboire*, 6
tiresome, difficult *pénible*, 3
to, at *à*, 2; **to, at + city** *à*, 10; **to, at + feminine country** *en*, 10; **to, at + masculine country** *au*, 10; **to, at the** *au*, 2; **to, at the** *aux*, 2
toast *le toast*, 6
toasted ham and cheese sandwich *le croque-monsieur*, 6
today *aujourd'hui*, 4; **Today is…** *Nous sommes…*, 4
tomorrow *demain*, 4
too much/many *trop de*, 5
totally *tout à fait*, 7
track *la voie*, 10
track and field *l'athlétisme* (m.), 5
traffic light *le feu*, 9
train *le train*, 10; **train station** *la gare*, 10; **train ticket** *le billet de train*, 10
trash *la poubelle*, 8
to travel *voyager*, 4; **traveler's checks** *le chèque de voyage*, 10; **traveling bag** *le sac de voyage*, 10
trip *le voyage*, 10
to try *essayer*, 7
T-shirt *le tee-shirt*, 4
Tuesday *mardi*, 4
to turn *tourner*, 9; **Turn at the next…** *Tournez au, à la prochain(e)…*, 9
twelve *douze*, 1
twenty *vingt*, 1; **twenty-eight** *vingt-huit*, 1; **twenty-five** *vingt-cinq*, 1; **twenty-four** *vingt-quatre*, 1; **twenty-nine** *vingt-neuf*, 1; **twenty-one** *vingt et un, vingt et une*, 1; **twenty-seven** *vingt-sept*, 1; **twenty-six** *vingt-six*, 1; **twenty-three** *vingt-trois*, 1; **twenty-two** *vingt-deux*, 1
two *deux*, 1; **two hundred** *deux cents*, 4; **two hundred and one** *deux cent un*, 4

umbrella *le parapluie*, 7
uncle *l'oncle* (m.), 3
under *sous*, 8
to understand *comprendre*, 1; **I don't understand.** *Je ne comprends pas.*, 1
Until what time…? *Jusqu'à quelle heure…?*, 10
upstairs *en haut*, 8
usually *d'habitude*, 8

vacation *les vacances*, 2
to vacuum *passer l'aspirateur*, 8
vacuum cleaner *l'aspirateur* (m.), 8
vanity case *la trousse de toilette*, 10
vegetable *le légume*, 6
very *très*, 1; **very badly** *très mal*, 2; **very well** *très bien*, 1, 2
video camera *le caméscope*, 5
video game *le jeu vidéo*, 5
view *la vue*, 10
visa *le visa*, 10
to visit (France) *faire (la France)*, 10
visual arts *les arts* (m.) *plastiques*, 4
volleyball *le volley*, 5

to wait (for) *attendre*, 4
to walk the dog *promener le chien*, 8
walkman *le baladeur*, 2
wallet *le portefeuille*, 7
to want *vouloir/désirer*, 6; **If you want.** *Si vous voulez.* (formal), *Si tu veux.* (informal), 5; **Do you want…?** *Tu veux…?/Vous voulez…?*, 6
wardrobe *l'armoire* (f.), 8
to wash *laver*, 8; **to wash the car** *laver la voiture*, 8
to watch *regarder*, 2; **to watch TV** *regarder la télé*, 2
watch *la montre*, 7
to water *arroser*, 8; **to water the plants** *arroser les plantes*, 8
water *l'eau* (f.), 6; **mineral water** *l'eau minérale* (f.), 6
we *nous*, 1; **We could…** *On pourrait…*, 5; **We have…** *On a…*, 6
to wear *porter*, 7; **I wear a size…** *Je fais du…*, 7
weather *le temps*, 5; **What is the weather like?** *Quel temps fait-il?*, 5
Wednesday *mercredi*, 4
week *la semaine*, 4
weekend *le week-end*, 4
well *bien*, 1; **well-done** *bien cuit*, 6; **Do you…well?** *Tu… bien?*, 2
what *que*, 5
when *quand*, 4

where *où*, 5; **Where?** *Où ça?*, 5; **Where is…?** *Où est…?*, 8; **Where are we meeting?** *Où est-ce qu'on se retrouve…?*, 5
which *quel, quelle, quels, quelles*, 4
white *blanc, blanche*, 3
who *qui*, 3; **Who is that?** *Qui c'est, ça?*, 3
why *pourquoi*, 5; **Why not?** *Pourquoi pas?*, 5
wife *la femme*, 3
wind *le vent*, 5; **It's windy.** *Il y a du vent*, 5
windbreaker *le coupe-vent*, 7
window *la fenêtre*, 1; **teller/ticket window** *le guichet*, 9
winter *hiver*, 5; **winter jacket** *anorak*, 7; **winter scarf** *écharpe*, 7
with *avec*, 2; **with a view** *avec vue*, 10; **With whom…?** *Avec qui…?*, 5
to withdraw *retirer*, 9; **Where do I go to withdraw money?** *Pour prendre de l'argent, s'il vous plaît?*, 9
without *sans*, 10
woman's blouse *le chemisier*, 7
woman's suit *le tailleur*, 7
wool *la laine*, 7; **out of wool** *en laine*, 7
to work *travailler*, 2
Would you like anything else? *Vous désirez autre chose?*, 6
to write *écrire*, 1

yard, garden *le jardin*, 8
yellow *jaune*, 4
yes *oui*, 1; **Yes, fine. Thank you.** *Oui, ça va. Merci.*, 1
yesterday *hier*, 7
yet, again *encore*, 8
you *tu, vous, toi*, 1
young *jeune*, 3
your *ta, ton tes, votre, vos*, 3
You're welcome. *Je vous en prie./ À votre service.*, 4

zero *zéro*, 1
zip code *le code postal*, 9
zoo *le zoo*, 5

Glossaire anglais–français

Index de grammaire

Page numbers in boldface type refer to the first presentation of the topic. Other page numbers refer to the grammar structures presented in *Bien dit!* features, subsequent references to the topic, or review in the **Résumé de grammaire.**

à: combined with **le** to form **au 56,** 334, see also contractions, see also prepositions; combined with **les** to form **aux 56,** 334, see also contractions, see also prepositions; with **commencer 118**; with countries and cities **334,** see also prepositions

acheter: all present tense forms **128**

adjectives **84,** 86, 130, 226, 228; agreement **84,** 86, 130, 132, 226, 228; as nouns **130**; demonstrative adjectives **ce, cet, cette, ces 226**; ending in **-eux** and **-if 84**; feminine forms **84,** 86, 130, 132, 226, 228; interrogative adjectives **quel, quelle, quels, quelles 228**; irregular adjectives **beau, nouveaux, vieux 86**; irregular feminine forms **84,** 86; masculine forms ending in **-s 84**; masculine forms ending in unaccented **-e 84**; placement **84,** 86, 226, 228; plural forms **84,** 86, 226, 228; placed before the noun **84,** 86, 226, 228; possessive adjectives all forms **94**

adverbs: general formation and placement **158**; irregular adverbs **bien** and **mal 158**; **souvent, de temps en temps, rarement, reguliérement 158**; with the **passé composé 242**

aimer: all present tense forms **46**; **aimer + infinitive 46**

aller: all present tense forms **167,** 310; **aller + infinitive (futur proche) 167**; irregular imperative forms **202**; with the **passé composé 274,** 346

amener 128

appeler: all present tense forms **332**

apprendre 200, 310

arriver: past participle **274**; with the **passé composé 274,** 346

articles: definite articles **44**; indefinite articles **24,** 188, 314; partitive articles **188,** 314

attendre: all present tense forms **116,** 310

au: contraction of **à + le 56,** 334, see also contractions, see also prepositions

aux: contraction of **à + les 56,** 334, see also contractions, see also prepositions

avancer 118

avec qui 156, see also information questions, see also question words

avoir: all present tense forms **26,** 238, 310; idiomatic expressions **170**; irregular past participle **240,** 344; **passé composé** with **avoir 238,** 240, 262, 344

balayer 276

beau, nouveau, vieux: irregular adjectives **86,** see also adjectives

bien 158, see also adverbs

boire: all present tense forms **204,** 310; irregular past participle **240,** 344

bon: irregular adverb **bien 158,** see also adverbs; adjectives placed before a noun **84,** see also adjectives

c'est: vs. **il/elle est 98**

ce, cet, cette, ces: demonstrative adjectives **226,** see also adjectives, see also demonstrative adjectives

changer 118

chercher 238, 310

choisir 190, 310

commands **202,** 302, see also imperatives; negative commands **202,** 302, see also imperatives

commencer: all present tense forms **118**; followed by **à + infinitive 118**

comment 156, see also information questions, see also question words

comprendre 200, 310

conjunctions: **et, mais,** and **ou 58**

connaître: all present tense forms **300,** 310; irregular past participle **344**

contractions: with **à 56**; with **de 96,** 188

corriger 118

days of the week: with **dernier** to talk about the past **242**

de: combined with **le** to form **du 96,** 188, 314, see also contractions, see also partitive articles; combined with **les** to form **des 96,** 188, 314, see also contractions, see also partitive articles; replacing **un, une, des** in negative sentences **24,** see also articles; to indicate possession **94**; with cities and countries **334,** see also prepositions

Index de grammaire

la 44, 130, see also definite articles
lancer 118
le 44, 120, 130, see also definite articles; **le** before days of the week to express routine actions **120**
lever 128
les 44, 130, see also definite articles
lire: irregular past participle **240,** 344

maigrir 190, 310
mais 58, see also conjunctions
mal 158, see also adverbs
manger: all present tense forms **118**
mauvais: irregular adverb **mal 158,** see also adverbs
mettre: all present tense forms **230,** 310; irregular past participle **240,** 344
monter: past participle **274;** in the **passé composé 274,** 346
mourir: past participle **274;** in the **passé composé 274,** 346

naître: past participle **274;** in the **passé composé 274,** 346
ne: contraction to **n'** before vowel sound **26,** 202, 238, 264
negation **26,** 238, 264, 344
negative expressions **ne… jamais 264; ne… ni… ni… 264; ne… pas 26,** 202, 238, 264, 302, 344; **ne… pas encore 264; ne… pas** with the **passé composé 238,** 344; **ne… personne 264; ne… plus 264; ne… rien 264;** negatives with commands **202,** 302; negatives with indefinite articles **24,** see also articles
negatives: with the **passé composé 238,** 264, 344
nettoyer: all present tense forms **276,** 310
nouns: as subjects **12,** 312; plural of nouns ending in **-al 48;** plural of nouns ending in **-eau/-eu 48;** irregular plural forms **24,** 48; determining masculine and feminine **44;** proper nouns in inversion questions **312;** plurals **24,** 48; replaced by pronouns **12,** 26, 312
nous 12, 14, see also subject pronouns
numbers: adding **-s** to **quatre-vingts** and multiples of **cent 348;** agreement with feminine nouns **132,** 348; ordinal numbers 348

on 12, **14,** see also subject pronouns; as the subject of an inversion question **312**
ordinal numbers: rules for formation 348
ou 58, see also conjunctions
où 156, see also information questions, see also question words

partir: all present tense forms **272**
partir: past participle **274;** with the **passé composé 274,** 346
partitive articles **188,** 314, see also articles
passé composé: adverbs in the **passé composé 242,** see also adverbs; with **avoir 238,** 240, 242, 262, 298, 344; with **-er** verbs **238,** 262; with **être 274,** 346; with inversion **312;** with irregular verbs **240,** 298, 344
passé récent 168, see also **venir**
past participle: agreement with subject in the **passé composé 274,** 346; past participle of **il y a 240;** past participle of **-ir** verbs **262;** past participle of irregular verbs **240,** 298, 344; past participle of **-re** verbs **262;** past participle of regular **-er** verbs **238;** past participle of verbs conjugated with **être** in the **passé composé 274**
past tense: **passé composé 238,** 240, 242, 262, 274, 298, 344; **passé composé** with **avoir 238,** 240, 242, 262, 298, 344; **passé composé** with **-er** verbs **238,** 262; with **-ir** and **-re** verbs **262; passé composé** with **être 274,** 346; **passé composé** with inversion **312; passé composé** with irregular verbs **240,** 344; **passé récent 168**
payer 276
perdre 116, 310
placer 118
pleuvoir: irregular past participle **240**
plural nouns **24,** 48, 130, see also nouns
possessive adjectives **94,** see also adjectives; before nouns beginning with a vowel **94**
pourquoi 156, see also information questions, see also question words
pouvoir: all present tense forms **260,** 310; irregular past participle **344**
préférer: all present tense forms **128**
prendre: all present tense forms **200;** irregular past participle **240,** 344
prepositions: **à 56,** 334; **de 94,** 334; with cities and countries **334**
promener 128
prononcer 118
pronouns: subject pronouns 12, **14,** 312; replacing nouns **12,** 26, 312

Index de grammaire

Remerciements

ACKNOWLEDGMENTS

For permission to reprint copyrighted material, grateful acknowledgment is made to the following sources:

"L'accent grave" from Paroles by Jacques Prévert. Copyright © 1980 by Editions Gallimard. Reproduced by permission of **Editions Gallimard** and electronic format by permission of **Fatras**.

From Le premier quartier de la lune by Michel Tremblay.

Copyright © 1989 by LEMÉAC. All rights reserved. Reproduced by permission of **Leméac Editeur Inc.**

"Toute la famille" by B. François and Pierre Lozère from Papa Clown Web site, accessed at http://www.papaclown.com. Copyright © 1983 by "Editions MARYPIERRE." Reproduced by permission of **Pierre Lozère.**

PHOTOGRAPHY CREDITS

Abbreviations used: c-center, b-bottom, t-top, l-left, r-right, bkgd-background.
FRONT COVER: (bl) Victoria Smith/HRW; (br) Goodshot; (tl) Jack Sullivan/Alamy; (tr) Getty Images.
AUTHORS: Page iii (DeMado) courtesy John DeMado; (Champeney) Victoria Smith/HRW; (M. Ponterio) courtesy Marie Ponterio; (R. Ponterio) courtesy Robert Ponterio.
TABLE OF CONTENTS: Page vi (t) Royalty-Free/Corbis; vii (tl) PhotoDisc/Getty Images; (tr) Royalty-Free/Corbis; viii (t) Royalty-Free/Corbis; ix (tl) Sam Dudgeon/HRW; (tr) Brand X Pictures; x Medioimages; xi Image Source.
WHY STUDY FRENCH: Page xii (bl) Sam Dudgeon/HRW; (br) Royalty-Free/Corbis; (tl) courtesy of Margot Steinhart; (tr) Victoria Smith/HRW; xiii (bc,br) Sam Dudgeon/HRW; (bl, tr) Victoria Smith/HRW.
FRANCOPHONE WORLD: Page xiv (bl) David Sanger/Alamy; (cl) Louisiana Department of Culture, Recreation and Tourism; (tl) Marty Granger/HRW; (tr) Victoria Smith/HRW; xv (cl) /HRW; (cr) Glen Allison/PhotoDisc/Getty Images; (tl) Ed George/National Geographic/Getty Images; (tr) Gavin Hellier/Robert Harding World Imagery/Getty Images.
ALPHABET: Page xvi (A, B, E, G, H, L, M, U) Royalty-Free/Corbis; (C) Comstock; (D) John White/The Neis Group; (F, I, J, K, O, P, T, V, W, X, Y, Z) PhotoDisc/Getty Images; (N, R, S) Brand X Pictures; (Q) Stockbyte.
COMMON NAMES: Page xvii (t, b) Sam Dudgeon/HRW; (c) Victoria Smith/HRW.
INSTRUCTIONS: Page xviii (b) Sam Dudgeon/HRW; xix (bl) Victoria Smith/HRW; (tl) Sam Dudgeon/HRW; (tr) Stockbyte.
CHAPITRE 1 All photos by Victoria Smith/HRW except: Page xx (b) Owen Franken; (br) Prat Thierry/Corbis Sygma; (c) Jose Fuste Raga/Corbis; (cl) Art Resource/Erich Lessing; (t) Alain Choisnet/Getty Images; 1 (b) Adam Woolfitt/Corbis; (br) Nik Wheeler/Corbis; (tl) Yann Arthus-Bertrand/Corbis; (tr) Royalty-Free/Corbis; 2 (b) Derek Croucher/Corbis; (bl, inset) Alamy Photos; (cr) Francis G. Mayer/Corbis; (tc, tl, tr) Sam Dudgeon/HRW; (tr) Owen Franken/Corbis; 3 (br) Inge Yspeert/Corbis; (br) Bettmann/Corbis; (c) Peter Turnley/Corbis; (c) Jacques Langevin/Corbis Sygma; (tl) Réunion des Musées Nationaux/Art Resource; (tr) Giraudon/Art Resource; 10 (t) Marty Granger/HRW; 13 (cl) 2008 PhotoAlto; (cr) Marty Granger/HRW; (bl) Artville/Getty Images; (br) PhotoDisc/Getty Images; 14 (bc) PhotoDisc/Getty Images; (bc) Royalty-Free/Corbis; (bl) Image Source; (br) Barbara Penoyar/Getty Images; 16 (t) Christian Liewig/Corbis; 17 (b) Royalty-Free/Corbis; (t) Sam Dudgeon/HRW; 30 (br) PhotoDisc/Getty Images; (cr) Sam Dudgeon/HRW; 36 (b) ImageState; (cr) Don Couch/HRW; (tl) Royalty-Free/Corbis; (tr) PhotoDisc/Getty Images; 37 Fine Art Photographic Library, London/Art Resource.
CHAPITRE 2 All photos by Victoria Smith/HRW except: Page 40 (cl) Ingram Publishing; 41 (bc) Sam Dudgeon/HRW; (br) PhotoDisc/Getty Images; (tc) Lucidio Studio/Corbis; (tl) Royalty-Free/Corbis; (tr) Reed Kaestner/Corbis; 42 (tl) PhotoDisc/Getty Images; (cr, tr) Royalty-Free/Corbis; 45 (bc) Index Stock; (br) William Koechling/HRW; (tc) ImageState; (tl) PhotoDisc/Getty Images; 47 (bc) BananaStock; (bl) Dennis Fagen/HRW; (br) Royalty-Free/Corbis; (tc) Peter Van Steen/HRW; (bc, tl) PhotoDisc/Getty Images; 50 (c) EyeWire; (t) Sam Dudgeon/HRW; 51 (b) Jack Kurtz/The Image Works; 53 (bl) Randy Faris/Corbis; (tl) PhotoDisc/Getty Images; (tr) Royalty-Free/Corbis; 55 (1, 2, 3) PhotoDisc/Getty Images; (4) Sam Dudgeon/HRW; 57 (bc) BananaStock; (bl, tc, tr) PhotoDisc/Getty Images; (tl) Royalty-Free/Corbis; 61 (c) Rubberball Productions; (l) Royalty-Free/Corbis; (r) Brand X Pictures; 64 (b, c, t) PhotoDisc/Getty Images; 66 (bc, bl) PhotoDisc/Getty Images; (bl) Peter Van Steen/HRW; 70 (tc) Peter Van Steen/HRW Photo; (tc) image100; (tl) Dennis Fagen/HRW; (tr) Don Couch/HRW; 71 Erich Lessing/Art Resource.
CHAPITRE 3 All photos by Sam Dudgeon/HRW except: Page 72 (c) Altrendo Panoramic/Getty Images; (t) Look BMBH/eStock Photo; 73 (b) Photocanada Digital; (cr) Connie Coleman/Getty Images; (tl) Charles Sleicher/Danita Delimont Stock Photography; (tr) Mike Macri/Masterfile; 74 (br) Staffan Widstran/Corbis; (c) Jean-Pierre Huard/Alamy; (cl) Scott Barrow/SuperStock; (tc, tl) Andy Christiansen/HRW; (tr) Megapress/Alamy; (tr inset) Julie Deshaies; 75 (bc) Hulton Archive/Getty Images; (br) Bettmann/Corbis; (cl) Blaine Harrington; (cr) Tessier/Megapress/Fraser Photos; (t) Dennis McColeman/Getty Images; 78 (all) Victoria Smith/HRW; 79 (blancs) Image Source/Alamy; (bleus) Royalty-Free/Corbis; (chatain) Don Couch/HRW; (courts, longs, marron) PhotoDisc/Getty Images; (noirs) RubberBall/Alamy Photos; (verts) Corbis; 80 (bc, bl, br, tl, tr) PhotoDisc/Getty Images; (tc) Cleo Photography/PhotoEdit; 86 (l) Michel Daunais; 88 (t) Carl & Ann Purcell/Corbis; 89 (t) Rolf Bruderer/Corbis; 90 (bl) Artville/Getty Images; (cl) Royalty-Free/Corbis; 92 (l) Richard Nowitz/Corbis; 93 (b) John Henley/Corbis; (bl) Royalty-Free/Corbis; 97 (bc, bl, c, cr) PhotoDisc/Getty Images; (br) Comstock; (cl) Victoria Smith/HRW; (tr) Royalty-Free/Corbis; 99 (all) "Caillou"™ and all related and associated trademarks are owned by Les Éditions Chouette and used under license from Cookie Jar Entertainment Inc. © 2008 Cookie Jar Entertainment Inc. All Rights Reserved.; 104 (a, b, c) Royalty-Free/Corbis; (d) PhotoDisc/Getty Images; 108 (bl) ImageState; (br) Royalty-Free/Corbis; (tl, tr) Don Couch/HRW; 109 Patrick Altman/Musée National des beaux-arts du Québec.
CHAPITRE 4 All photos by Sam Dudgeon/HRW except: Page 112 (géographie, la physique, les arts) PhotoDisc/Getty Images; (l'allemand) Stephanie Friedman/HRW; (l'espagnol) Jim Zuckerman/Corbis; (l'historie, les mathématiques) Royalty-Free/Corbis; (la biologie) Comstock; 113 (tl) Stephanie Friedman/HRW; 114 (all) Stephanie Friedman/HRW; 117 (1l) John Langford/HRW; (1r, 5) PhotoDisc/Getty Images; (2, 6) Royalty-Free/Corbis; (3) Andy Christiansen/HRW; (4) Stephanie Friedman/HRW; 119 (1, 3, 6) Royalty-Free/Corbis; (2) ImageState; (4) Stewart Cohen/Getty Images; (5) Victoria Smith/HRW; 122 (tl) Snark/Art Resource; 123 (b) Digital Vision/Getty Images; (t) Paul Cooper; 125 (t) Stephanie Friedman/HRW; 126 (c, l, r) Stephanie Friedman/HRW; 127 (c) Victoria Smith/HRW; 128 (l) PhotoDisc/Getty Images; 129 (1) Stephanie Friedman/

HRW; (3) Digital Vision/Getty Images; (4) Brand X Pictures; 131 (l, r) Stephanie Friedman/HRW; (r) Victoria Smith/HRW; 138 (1) PhotoDisc/Getty Images; (2, 3, 4, 6) Stephanie Friedman/HRW; (5) Victoria Smith/HRW; 143 Réunion des Musées Nationaux/Art Resource.

CHAPITRE 5 All photos by Victoria Smith/HRW except: Page 144 (cl) Joe Cornish/Stone; (cr) Image Bank/Getty Images; (t) Ruth Tomlinson/Robert Harding World Imagery/Getty Images; 145 (b) Royalty-Free/Corbis; (br) Jose Fuste Raga/Corbis; (cr) James Hardy/Getty Images; (tl) Eastcott Momatiuk/The Image Bank; (tr) Alain Le Bot/Photononstop; 146 (b) Roger Rozenwajg/Photononstop; (cl) Richard Klune/Corbis; (cr) John Elk III/Lonely Planet Images/Getty Images; (tl) Bridgeman Art Library/Getty Images; (tr) Bettman/Corbis; 147 (bl) V. Michel/Corbis; (br) Eric Travers/Gamma; (tc) Don Couch/HRW; (tl, tr) Sam Dudgeon/HRW; 150 (bcl) Peter Sterling/Getty Images; (bcr) Scott Tysick/Masterfile; (bl) John Terence Turner/Getty Images; (br, tr) Royalty-Free/Corbis; (tcl) A. Inden/zefa/Corbis; (tcr) FogStock/Index Stock Imagery; (tl) Ull Wiesmeier/zefa/Corbis; 151 (1) Royalty-Free/Corbis; (2) Comstock; (3, 4, 6, 7, 8, 9, tl) PhotoDisc/Getty Images; (5) Creatas; 152 (1, 4, 5) PhotoDisc/Getty Images; (2) Sam Dudgeon/HRW; (3) Stephanie Friedman/HRW; (6) Royalty-Free/Corbis; (7) Ingram Publishing; 153 (1, 3, 5) PhotoDisc/Getty Images; (4) Masterfile; (6) Index Stock; 154 (l) Ingram Publishing; 155 (1) iStockphoto; (2) Royalty-Free/Imagestate; (3, 4, t) PhotoDisc/Getty Images; (5) Royalty-Free/Corbis; 158 (1) Stephanie Friedman/HRW; (2, 4) Artville/Getty Images; (3) Comstock; (5) PhotoDisc/Getty Images; 159 (b) Index Stock; (br) PhotoLink/Getty Images; (t) PhotoDisc/Getty Images; (tr) Creatas; 160 (bc, br) Andy Christiansen/HRW; (c) Sam Dudgeon/HRW; (tl) Michael St. Maur Shell/Corbis; 161 (b) George Shelly/Corbis; (t) Creatas; 162 (cl, tl) PhotoDisc/Getty Images; (cr) Richard Bickel/Corbis; (tr) Richard Cummins/Corbis; 164 (1, 4) PhotoDisc/Getty Images; (2, 5, 6) Royalty-Free/Corbis; (3, l) Brand X Pictures/Getty Images; 167 (1, 3) Don Couch/HRW Photo; (2) Gertjan Hooijer; (6) Randy Faris/Corbis; 171 (1) Leah-Anne Thompson; (2) M. Meyer/zefa/Corbis; (3) Peter Van Steen/HRW; (4) Stockbyte; 174 (br, l, tr) PhotoDisc/Getty Images; (cl) Royalty-Free/Corbis; 176 (a, c) Royalty-Free/Corbis; (b) Don Couch/HRW; (d) PhotoDisc/Getty Images; 180 (bot) Jonathan Blair/Corbis; (c) Comstock; (b, d) PhotoDisc/Getty Images; 181 Erich Lessing/Art Resource.

BACKMATTER READINGS: Page 184 (b) Stephanie Friedman/HRW; (cl) Lee Snider/Photo Images/Corbis; (t) clipart.com; 185 (b) Keith Levit/Alamy; (cr) Adam Woolfitt/Corbis; (t) David G. Houser/Corbis; 186 (b, c) Parc Astérix; 187 (bl, t) Parc Astérix; (br) Directphoto/Alamy; 188 (bl, cl, cr) Al Seib/Dominique Lemieux/Cirque du Soleil; 189 (br, cl) Al Seib/Dominique Lemieux/Cirque du Soleil; (cr) Jan Swinkels/Dominique Lemieux/Cirque du Soleil; (r) Masterfile; (tl) Véronique Vial/Dominique Lemieux/Cirque du Soleil; 190 (bl) Joshua Kessler; (br) Ville de Montréal; (tl) Stephanie Friedman/HRW. Book cover (French edition) from Le Premier Quartier de la Lune by Michel Tremblay. Reprinted by permission of Leméac Éditeur. Cover illustration Adagp, Paris; 191 (t) Victoria Smith/HRW.

VOCABULAIRE SUPPLÉMENTAIRE: Page R8 (bl) Victoria Smith/HRW; (cr, tl) PhotoDisc/Getty Images; (cr) Comstock; (tr) Stockbyte; R9 (br, cr) Sam Dudgeon/HRW; (tl) Digital Wisdom; (tr) PhotoDisc/Getty Images; R10 (bl, cr, tl) PhotoDisc/Getty Images; (br) Royalty-Free/Corbis; (cl) Victoria Smith/HRW; (tr) Sam Dudgeon/HRW; R11 (bl, br) Digital Vision/Getty Images; (cl, tl) Ingram Publishing; (cr) Brand X Pictures; (tr) Sam Dudgeon/HRW; R12 (bl) Royalty-Free/Corbis; (br, cl, cr, tr) PhotoDisc/Getty Images; (tl) Brand X Pictures.

TÉLÉ-ROMAN STILL PHOTOS: Edge Media/HRW.

ICONS: All icon photos by Edge Media/HRW except: Page xx Royalty-Free/Corbis; 72 Brand X Pictures; 144 Royalty-Free/Corbis.

Staff Credits

David Alvarado, Jeffrey Atkins, Kimberly Barr, Ed Blake, Marion Bermondy, Priscilla Blanton, Kristina Bigelow, Jeremy Brady, Konstanze Brown, Stacy Cooper, Lynda Cortez, Lana Cox, Nina Degollado, Yamilé Dewailly, Michelle Dike, Lydia Doty, Shawn Farris, James Foster, Rebecca Jordan, Marta Kimball, Kadonna Knape, Cathy Kuhles, Liann Lech, Sean McCormick, Richard Metzger, Mercedes Newman, Amber Nichols, Paul Provence, Mike Rinella, Marleis Roberts, Annette Saunders, Glenna Scott, Kay Selke, Chris Smith, Sara Stavchansky, Jeff Streber, Stephanie Swope, Jeannie Taylor, Géraldine Touzeau-Patrick, Vickie Tripp, Jaishree Venkatesan, Cindy Verheyden